A New
& Ot
fr

In our continuing effort to publish the savviest, most up-to-date, and most appealing travel guides available, we've added some great new features.

Frommer's guides now include a new **star-rating system.** Every hotel, restaurant, and attraction is rated from 0 to 3 stars to help you set priorities and organize your time.

We've also added **seven brand-new features** that point you to the great deals, in-the-know advice, and unique experiences that separate travelers from tourists. Throughout the guide, look for:

Finds	Special finds—those places only insiders know about
Fun Fact	Fun facts—details that make travelers more informed and their trips more fun
Kids	Best bets for kids—advice for the whole family
Moments	Special moments—those experiences that memories are made of
Overrated	Places or experiences not worth your time or money
Tips	Insider tips—some great ways to save time and money
Value	Great values—where to get the best deals

Dedicated to Fran and Arnie

ACKNOWLEDGMENTS

To my mother and father, without whose influence, encouragement, and support I would never have ended up in Miami doing what I'm doing.

To all the publicists and proprietors for putting up with the endless e-mails, inquiries, and spur-of-the-moment visits, I thank you for your cooperation and eagerness to answer pressing questions about hair dryers, irons, hours, and credit cards.

Thanks to Kendra Falkenstein, my fabulous editor, for being on the same page as me and "getting it."

To married Brett, with whom I commiserated and rejoiced over the birth of her baby Daelyn and my baby Frommer's, thanks for an inspiring 9 months and your votes of confidence.

To my best-friend-turned-mapmaker extraordinaire, Tricia—the Patsy to my Edina—for your tireless efforts and for listening intently to my useless knowledge, rough drafts, and incessant complaints, proving that there are no limits to fun and friendship when it comes to life and all its amazing journeys.

Last but not least, thank you, Mrs. Ritchie, for inspiring me to express myself and aspire to greatness.

—Lesley Abravanel

Here's what critics say about Frommer's:

Frommer's®

PORTABLE
Miami

2nd Edition

by Lesley Abravanel

Wiley Publishing, Inc.

Published by:

WILEY PUBLISHING, INC.
909 Third Ave.
New York, NY 10022

ISBN 0-7645-6666-0
ISSN 1531-1511

Editor: Kendra L. Falkenstein
Production Editor: Donna Wright
Photo Editor: Richard Fox
Cartographer: Elizabeth Puhl
Production by Wiley Indianapolis Composition Services

Front cover photo: Miami's Ocean Drive, with cars and hotels, at night.

For information on our other products and services or to obtain technical
support, please contact our Customer Care Department within the U.S. at
800-762-2974, outside the U.S. at 317-572-3993 or fax 317-572-4002.

Wiley also publishes its books in a variety of electronic formats. Some con-
tent that appears in print may not be available in electronic formats.

Manufactured in the United States of America

5 4 3 2 1

Contents

List of Maps

ABOUT THE AUTHOR

Lesley Abravanel is a freelance journalist and a graduate of the University of Miami School of Communication. When she isn't combing South Florida for the latest hotels, restaurants, and attractions, she is on the lookout for vacationing celebrities, about whom she writes in her weekly nightlife and gossip column, "Velvet Underground," for both the *Miami Herald* and its weekly entertainment newspaper, *Street*. She is also a contributor to *Star Magazine*, the Miami correspondent for *Black Book Magazine*, and writes restaurant reviews for America Online's Digital City.

AN INVITATION TO THE READER

In researching this book, we discovered many wonderful places—hotels, restaurants, shops, and more. We're sure you'll find others. Please tell us about them, so we can share the information with your fellow travelers in upcoming editions. If you were disappointed with a recommendation, we'd love to know that, too. Please write to:

Frommer's Portable Miami, 2nd Edition
Wiley Publishing, Inc. • 909 Third Ave. • New York, NY 10022

AN ADDITIONAL NOTE

Please be advised that travel information is subject to change at any time— and this is especially true of prices. We therefore suggest that you write or call ahead for confirmation when making your travel plans. The authors, editors, and publisher cannot be held responsible for the experiences of readers while traveling. Your safety is important to us, however, so we encourage you to stay alert and be aware of your surroundings. Keep a close eye on cameras, purses, and wallets, all favorite targets of thieves and pickpockets.

WHAT THE SYMBOLS MEAN

The following abbreviations are used for credit cards:

AE	American Express	DISC	Discover	V	Visa
DC	Diners Club	MC	MasterCard		

FROMMERS.COM

Now that you have the guidebook to a great trip, visit our website at www.frommers.com for travel information on nearly 2,500 destinations. With features updated regularly, we give you instant access to the most current trip-planning information available. At Frommers.com, you'll also find the best prices on airfares, accommodations, and car rentals—and you can even book travel online through our travel booking partners. At Frommers.com, you'll also find the following:

- Online updates to our most popular guidebooks
- Vacation sweepstakes and contest giveaways
- Newsletter highlighting the hottest travel trends
- Online travel message boards with featured travel discussions

The Best of Miami

Miami has been on both sides of the "in and out" fence for years now, but what always remains consistent is the fact that there's never a dull moment in this magic city. From the fabulous fifties when the Rat Pack ruled the sands to the late nineties when Madonna pranced on South Beach, Miami has always been a magnet for the glitterati.

But the city isn't all glossy tabloid fodder. Miami is a hotbed of political, social, and cultural activity in which Cuban Americans can be seen waving two countries' flags while at the same time, model-stunning drag queens are busy hoisting the rainbow flag in a display of gay pride. This city has witnessed the mass influx and exodus of refugees, supermodels, celebrities, and media, proving that it's not all sun and sand, but considerable substance.

And while *Miami Vice* may have given way to hanging chads and a sanctified toddler named Elián, at the end of the day, the city remains as vibrant and as interesting as ever, not to mention a playground for the curiosity seeker, the culture vulture, the sun worshipper, and, inevitably, the members of the chic elite.

But don't be fooled by the hipper-than-thou celebrity-drenched playground known as South Beach. While the chic elite do, indeed, flock to Miami's coolest enclave, it is surprisingly accessible to the average Joe, Jane, or José. For every Phillippe Starck-designed, bank-account-busting boutique hotel on South Beach, there's a kitschy, candy-coated Art Deco one that's much less taxing on the pockets. For each Pan-MediterAsian haute cuisinerie, there's always the down-home, no-nonsense Cuban *bodega* (a small corner grocery store, usually with a walk-up window for ordering) offering hearty food at ridiculously cheap prices.

There are a ton of greats in Miami; below are some of our favorites.

1 Frommer's Favorite Miami Experiences

- **Lounging Poolside at the Delano:** In addition to tanning, the scene here is about striking a pose and pretending not to notice the others doing so. If you're staying at Miami's Delano, and if you're savvy enough to score one of the luxe lounges, prepare to overhear some interesting conversations between the movers and shakers who bake here. Though the hotel itself is overrated, the pool is worth every bit of its splash and flash. See p. 50.

- **Having a Postbeach Beer at Jimbo's on Key Biscayne:** Who knew that a dive housed in a wooden shack in the mangroves of Virginia Key, serving beer from a cooler, would become one of Miami's best-kept local secrets? That is, until now. See p. 100.

- **Salsa Lessons at Bongo's Cuban Café:** If the only salsa you're familiar with is the kind you put on your tacos, get over to Bongo's, the hottest salsa club north of Havana, where Miami's most talented salsa dancers will teach you how to move your two left feet in the right direction. See p. 162.

- **Midnight Snacking at Versailles:** This iconoclastic, gaudy Cuban diner in the heart of Miami's Little Havana is humming with the buzz of old-timers reminiscing about pre-Castro Cuba, local politicos trying to appease them, and a slew of detached people only there for the fantastically cheap and authentic Cuban fare. See p. 107.

- **Biking, Blading, or Walking Through the Art Deco District on Ocean Drive:** The beauty of South Beach's celebrated Art Deco District culminates on the 15-block beachfront strip known as Ocean Drive. Most of the buildings on this stretch are hotels built in the late 1930s and early 1940s. You'll appreciate the architecture and the colorful characters as you go down this street—by bike, by in-line skates, or on foot. See p. 117.

- **Dancing (and Lounging) Until Dawn:** Choose your soundtrack, from salsa at the Latin clubs and techno and house at cavernous European-style dance clubs to sexy, sultry lounge music at a swanky hotel bar or haute lounge, because in Miami, music truly makes the people come together. See chapter 8.

- **Dining at Big Fish Restaurant on the Miami River:** Some consider dining on the Miami River to be industrial chic; others consider it seedy in a *Miami Vice* sort of way. However you choose to look at it, by all means *do* look at it; the sleepy Miami River is nestled below the sweeping downtown Miami skyline, reminding you that even though you're in a major metropolis, things in this often-frenetic city are capable of slowing down to a more soothing pace. See p. 102.

- **Moonlight Concerts at the Barnacle State Historic Site:** Once a month, on or near the full moon (except during July and Aug), the Barnacle State Historic Site hosts a concert in the backyard of their charming 1908 Coconut Grove bungalow built on 5 acres of waterfront property. Listeners are welcome to picnic and bask in this sublime setting for a mere $5. See p. 126.

- **People-Watching:** Before you roll your eyes insisting that people-watching is a cliché, consider the fact that there is nothing hackneyed about sitting at a cafe and watching the most colorful, motley and eclectic pedestrian parade that, unlike, say, Mardi Gras, has become as much a daily and nightly ritual in Miami as the sunrise and sunset. Even better, this parade can be seen from anywhere in the city, be it downtown, the airport, South Beach, or South Miami.

2 The Best Beaches

- **Best Party Beach:** In Key Biscayne, **Crandon Park Beach,** on Crandon Boulevard, is National Lampoon's *Vacation* on the sand. It's got a diverse crowd consisting of dedicated beach bums and lots of leisure-seeking families, set to a soundtrack of salsa, disco, and reggae music blaring from a number of competing stereos. With 3 miles of oceanfront beach, bathrooms, changing facilities, 493 acres of park, 75 grills, 3 parking lots, several soccer and softball fields, and a public 18-hole championship golf course, Crandon is like a theme park on the sand. Admission is $2 per vehicle. It's open daily from 8am to sunset.
- **Best Beach for People-Watching: Lummus Park Beach** (© 305/673-7714) is world renowned, not necessarily for its pristine sands, but for its more common name of **South Beach.** Here, seeing, being seen, and, at times, the obscene, go hand in hand with the sunscreen and beach towels. It runs along Ocean Drive from about 6th to 14th streets on South Beach.
- **Best Swimming Beach:** The **85th Street Beach,** along Collins Avenue, is the best place to swim away from the maddening crowds. It's one of Miami's only stretches of sand with no condos or hotels looming over sunbathers. Lifeguards patrol the area throughout the day and bathrooms are available, though they are not exactly the benchmark of cleanliness.
- **Best Beaches for Watersports:** Hobie Beach (© 305/361-2833), located on the south side of Key Biscayne's Rickenbacker Causeway, is not really a beach, but an inlet with predictable winds. It's also one of the most popular beaches for watersport enthusiasts, featuring jet ski, sailboat, windsurfing, and sailboard

rentals; shade, if necessary, from the Australian pine; and a sublime view of the picturesque downtown Miami skyline. See p. 135.

- **Best (Ahem) All-Around Tanning Beach:** For that all-over tan, head to **Haulover Beach** (© 305/944-3040), just north of the Bal Harbour border, and join nudists from around the world in a top-to-bottom tanning session. Should you choose to keep your swimsuit on, however, there are changing rooms and bathrooms.

- **Best Surfing Beach: Haulover Beach Park,** just over the causeway from Bal Harbour, seems to get Miami's biggest swells. Go early to avoid getting mauled by the aggressive young locals prepping for Maui.

- **Best Scenic Beach: Matheson Hammock Park Beach,** at 9610 Old Cutler Road in South Miami (© 305/665-5475), is the epitome of tranquility, tucked away off of scenic Old Cutler Road in South Miami. And while it's scenic, it's not too much of a scene. It's a great beach for those seeking "alone time." Bathrooms and changing facilities are available.

- **For Kids:** Miami's **Crandon Beach** (© 305/361-5421) is extremely popular for families with kids because of the shallow water created by a neighboring sandbar. Convenient parking, picnic areas, a winding boardwalk, and a multi-ethnic mix of families grilling, dancing, and relaxing are the benchmarks of this beach. See p. 143.

- **For Seclusion:** The producers of *Survivor* could feasibly shoot their show on the ultra-secluded, picturesque, and deserted **Virginia Key** (© 305/361-2749), on Key Biscayne, where people go purposely not to be found. See p. 117.

- **For Gay Beachgoers:** South Beach's **12th Street Beach** (© 305/673-7714) is the beach of choice for gay residents and travelers who come to show off just how much time they've spent in the gym, and, of course, catch up on the latest gossip and upcoming must-attend parties and events. Oftentimes, this beach is the venue for some of the liveliest parties South Beach has ever seen. See p. 117.

3 Best Hotel Bets

- **Best Historic Hotel:** With a guest registry that reads like a who's who of history crossed with an engrossing whodunit, Miami's **Biltmore Hotel** (© 800/727-1926 or 305/445-1926) opened its doors in 1926. Guests ranging from Al Capone to the duke and duchess of Windsor loved the stately hotel so much that they never left, so say those who claim the hotel is haunted. Ghosts aside, this national landmark boasts the largest hotel pool in the continental United States as well as a 300-foot bell tower modeled after the Cathedral of Seville. See p. 73.

- **Best Celebrity-Saturated Hotel:** The **Delano** (© 800/555-5001 or 305/672-2000) still reigns as Miami's number one celebrity magnet, attracting stars and starlets who you'd find at A-list Hollywood parties. The hotel's star power makes up for its sterile rooms. See p. 50.

- **Best Out-of-Place Bed-and-Breakfast:** Located on the outskirts of gritty, bustling downtown Miami is the historic **Miami River Inn** (© 800/468-3589 or 305/325-0045), housed in five restored clapboard buildings dating back to 1906. By the looks of this place, you could swear you were somewhere in New England—until you take a breath of the balmy air. See p. 72.

- **Best Art Deco Hotel:** The **Raleigh Hotel** (© 800/848-1775 or 305/534-6300) is the reigning diva of Deco, dating back to 1940. It features one of the most photographed palm-lined swimming pools, reminiscent of the days of Esther Williams. See p. 55.

- **Best Beach Hotel:** Miami's **Beach House Bal Harbour** (© 877/782-3557 or 305/865-3551) was inspired by the great beach homes of the Hamptons, Nantucket, and coastal Maine, and when you stay here, you will feel like someone's houseguest rather than an anonymous hotel guest. See p. 63.

- **Best Inexpensive Hotel:** It's hard to find a hotel on South Beach with both good value and excellent service, but the **Crest Hotel Suites** (© 800/531-3880 or 305/531-0321) delivers as one of Miami's best bargains and coolest hotels. See p. 57.

- **Best for Families:** In Miami, the **Sonesta Beach Resort Key Biscayne** (© 800/SONESTA or 305/361-2021) is known for its complimentary children's programs led by trained counselors who supervise kids, grouped by age, in pool and beach activities and on field trips. Fees apply for meals/excursions. See p. 68.

- **Best for Romance:** In Miami, the **Hotel Place St. Michel** (© 800/848-HOTEL or 305/444-1666) is a cozy European-style hotel whose wood-floored dark-paneled rooms are adorned in antiques, transporting you from Florida to Paris. See p. 74.

- **Best Spas:** Taking the concept of immersing oneself in Florida culture to a literal level, the spa at the **Ritz-Carlton Key Biscayne** (© **305/ 648-5900**) will scrub your body down with Key limes and wrap you in towels soaked in Everglades grass. For the tragically hip, the **Agua Spa** at the **Delano** (© **305/ 673-2900**) is a rooftop oasis of milk and honey massages, mineral baths and celebrities indulging in them. See p. 68 and p. 50.

4 Best Dining Bets

- **Best for Celebrating a Big Deal: The Forge Restaurant** on Miami Beach (© **305/538-8533**) is a multichambered, ornately decorated (and priced) monument known for its decadent wines, steak, and fish. See p. 97.
- **Best Waterfront Dining:** It's a tossup between Biscayne Bay and the Atlantic Ocean, but whichever you prefer, there are two restaurants that provide front-row seats to both. The Mandarin Oriental Hotel's global fusion restaurant, **Azul** (© **305/913-8258**), faces the Miami skyline and beautiful, tranquil Biscayne Bay, while the Ritz-Carlton Key Biscayne's **Aria** (© **305/365-4500**) faces the Atlantic, but its Mediterranean cuisine could have you thinking you're floating off the coast of, say, Spain. Tough decisions, but both are winners. See p. 101 and p. 68.
- **Best Restaurant Worth the Wait for a Table:** The legendary South Florida institution known as **Joe's Stone Crab Restaurant,** in Miami Beach (© **305/673-0365**), refuses to take reservations, but that doesn't stop people from clawing their way into the restaurant for a table—despite a wait that's often in excess of 3 hours. See p. 84.
- **Best Cuban Restaurant:** There's always a debate on who has the best, most authentic Cuban cuisine, but for those of you who have never been to Havana, Miami's **Versailles,** in Little Havana (© **305/444-0240**), is *the* quintessential Cuban diner, featuring enormous portions at paltry prices. See p. 107.
- **Sexiest Restaurant: Tantra,** in Miami Beach (© **305/672-4765**), brings a bit of exotic Marrakesh to South Beach with an aphrodisiac-inspired menu, grass-lined floors, and an equally sultry crowd that isn't afraid of getting in touch with its sensual side. See p. 87.
- **Best Scene: Joia Restaurant and Bar,** in Miami Beach (© **305/ 674-8871**), exemplifies South Beach's spin on *La Dolce Vita*

with its fine Italian cuisine, celebrity clientele, and requisite paparazzi hiding nearby in the bushes. See p. 89.

- **Best Comfort Food: Big Pink,** in Miami Beach (© **305/ 532-4700**), serves kitsch in large doses, featuring TV dinners served in trays. Fun and funky, and the food's pretty good, too. See p. 91.

- **Best Seafood: Grillfish,** in South Beach (© **305/538-9908**), is simple, unpretentious, and consistently serves the freshest fish in town—any which way you desire. See p. 92.

- **Best Steakhouse: Kiss,** 301 Lincoln Road (© **305/695- 4445**), may be high on kitsch, with its fire-eating cabaret players, but the real meat is sublime and it's right on your plate. See p. 84. For less fanfare and a really delicious prime cut at a prime price, try **The Forge Restaurant** (p. 97). **Christy's,** in Coral Gables (© **305/446-1400**), is another Miami carnivore's choice, with superb steaks and famous Caesar salads. See p. 108.

- **Best Sunday Brunch: Nemo,** on Miami Beach (© **305/532- 4550**), turns its open kitchen into a help-yourself-to-anything, calorie-busting Sunday brunch of gourmet fare and insanely good desserts. See p. 85. For a bargain a la carte brunch, **Front Porch Café,** 1418 Ocean Drive, Miami Beach, (© **305/531-8300**) is a no frills outdoor cafe, a locals' favorite for French toast and down home, delicious American brunch fare. See p. 85 and p. 94.

- **Best View: Big Fish,** in Miami (© **305/373-1770**), is all about gritty-chic, located on the Miami River, where tugboats and cargo ships slink by as you indulge in fresh fish and sip good Italian wine under the glow of the brilliant downtown skyline hovering above. See p. 102.

- **Best Mexican:** The fresh, authentic Mexican fare at **El Rancho Grande,** in Miami Beach (© **305/673-0480**), will have you swearing off Taco Bell forever. See p. 91.

- **Best Sushi: Nobu,** at the Shore Club Hotel in Miami Beach (© **305/695-3100**), is known for its star sushi chef and owner, the legendary Nobu Matsuhisa, but the raw facts about this restaurant are as simple as its stellar clientele (which includes Madonna, among others): It's unquestionably the best sushi in town. For fabulous sushi minus the Hollywood vibe, Miami Beach's **Shoji Sushi** (© **305/532-4245**) is at the top of the A-list. See p. 86 and p. 90.

- **Best People-Watching:** The **News Café,** in South Beach (© **305/538-6397**), practically invented the sport of people-watching, encouraging its customers to sit at an outdoor table all day if they want, lingering over the passing parades of people while sipping a cappuccino. The Delano Hotel's pricey **Blue Door** restaurant (© **305/674-6400**), in Miami Beach, provides a front-row seat to the hordes of hipsters who flock there. See p. 95 and p. 82.

- **Kitschiest Dining: Wolfie Cohen's Rascal House** (© **305/ 947-4581**) is a must for those looking for a retro-fabulous North Miami Beach experience, with a wait staff as old as the vinyl booths and the best corned beef on rye south of the Lower East Side. See p. 98.

- **Best Fast Food: Pizza Rustica** (863 Washington Ave., Miami Beach; © **305/674-8244** and 1447 Washington Ave., Miami Beach; © **305/538-6009**) serves up gimmick free, phenomenal pizza with gourmet ingredients. See p. 95.

5 The Rest of the Best

- **Best Museum:** A collector's dream come true, Miami's **Wolfsonian** is a treasure trove of miscellany (a matchbook that once belonged to the King of Egypt) and artifacts hailing from the propaganda age of World War II. See p. 123.

- **Best Cultural Experience:** A walk through **Little Havana** is a fascinating study in the juxtaposition and fusion of two very vibrant cultures in which pre-Castro Cuba is as alive and well as the McDonald's right next door. See p. 35.

- **Best Public Golf Course:** Miami's **Biltmore Golf Course,** Biltmore Hotel, is an excellent course with a picture-postcard setting. If it's good enough for former President Clinton, it's good enough for those of you who don't travel with a bevy of Secret Service agents. But the real question is: Are *you* good enough for the course? See p. 137.

- **Best Place to Satisfy Your Morbid Curiosity: The Mystery, Murder, and Mayhem Bus Tour.** Not that we're implying anything here, but Miami is a haven for people like O.J. Simpson and, at one time, Al Capone. It's a place where shady characters come to reinvent themselves. However, at times, they also tend to reincriminate themselves. See the spots where some of these criminals fell off the wagon—it's morbidly delicious. See p. 133.

- **Best Latin Club:** Although the predominant language spoken at **La Covacha** is Spanish, the only word you need to know here is *agua,* because you will certainly need it after working up a sweat on the dance floor. Music—the best Latin music in town—is, in fact, the common language at this rustic, open-aired Latin dance club that features salsa, merengue, and Latin rock. See p. 169.
- **Best Dance Club: Club Space.** South Beach devotees said that downtown Miami would never make it as a club hub, but they were wrong. A 24-hour liquor license, stellar DJs, and a dance room the size of four converted warehouses make Club Space Miami's best dance club. Sorry, South Beach. See p. 162.

2

Planning Your Trip to Miami

Peak season in Miami runs from October to March. And while peak season is the most popular time to visit, pre- and postseason offer you a less congested, less expensive travel experience. Regardless of when you choose to travel, a little advanced planning will help you make the most of your trip.

1 Visitor Information

The **Greater Miami Convention and Visitor's Bureau,** 701 Brickell Ave., Miami, FL 33131 (*©* **800/933-8448;** www.miamiand beaches.com), is the best source for specialized information about the city and its beaches. Even if you don't have a specific question, you should request a free copy of *Tropicool,* the bureau's vacation planner for greater Miami and the beaches. And remember that just because information on a particular establishment you're inquiring about is not available, that doesn't mean the place doesn't exist: The GMCVB only endorses member businesses.

2 Money

ATMS

For as many palm trees as there are in Miami, there are just as many, if not more, **automated teller machines (ATMs)** linked to a major national and international network that will likely include your bank at home. In Miami, there are ATMs in malls, grocery stores, convenience stores, bars, nightclubs, and in every major, highly trafficked neighborhood. Be sure you know your four-digit PIN before you leave home, and be sure to find out your daily withdrawal limit before you depart. Keep in mind that many banks impose a fee every time a card is used at an ATM in a different city or bank. Additionally, the bank from which you withdraw cash may charge its own fee.

CREDIT CARDS

Credit cards are invaluable when traveling. They are a safe way to carry money and provide a convenient record of all your expenses. You can also withdraw cash advances from your credit cards at any bank (though you'll start paying hefty interest on the advance the moment you receive the cash). At most banks, you don't even need to go to a teller; you can get a cash advance at the ATM if you know your PIN.

WHAT TO DO IF YOUR WALLET GETS STOLEN

Be sure to block charges against your account the minute you discover a card has been lost or stolen. Then be sure to file a police report. Almost every credit card company has an emergency toll-free number to call if your card is stolen. It may be able to wire you a cash advance off your credit card immediately, and in many places, it can deliver an emergency credit card in a day or two. Call the toll-free number directory at ✆ **800/555-1212** to get the number you need.

Odds are that if your wallet is gone, the police won't be able to recover it. However, it's still worth informing the authorities. Your credit card company or insurer may require a police report number or record of the theft.

If you choose to carry traveler's checks, be sure to keep a record of their serial numbers separate from your checks. You'll get a refund faster if you know the numbers.

If you need emergency cash over the weekend when all banks and American Express offices are closed, you can have money wired to you from **Western Union** (✆ **800/325-6000;** www.westernunion.com). You must present valid ID to pick up the cash at the Western Union office. However, you can pick up a money transfer even if you don't have valid identification, as long as you can answer a test question provided by the sender. If you need to use a test question instead of ID, the sender must take cash to his or her local Western Union office, rather than transferring the money over the phone or online.

3 When to Go

Contrary to popular belief, the notion of sunny Florida isn't always 100% correct. While the term is hardly an oxymoron, when it comes to weather, sunny Florida undergoes major mood swings. While it may be pouring on the ocean side of Miami Beach, on the bay side, the only thing pouring down may be UV rays.

For many people, the worst time to come to Miami is during the summer, when temperatures are usually scorching, humidity is oppressive, and rain at 4pm is a daily occurrence. Wintertime in Miami is spectacular—not too hot, not too cool. Temperatures can, however, dip down into the low 50s during a cold front.

Weather aside, peak season in Miami means more tourists, snow-birds, and models—and the influx of celebrities, who also call Miami their winter home. In the summer, Miami practically comes to a standstill as far as special events, cultural activities, and overall pace is concerned. Locals love it; it is their time to reclaim their cities. If you can brave the temperature, you will not have to face the long lines in restaurants and at attractions that you will encounter during peak season. For some people, however, the lines and the waiting are all part of the allure of Miami, as they provide an opportunity to see and be seen.

Miami's Average Monthly High/Low Temperatures & Rainfall

	Jan	Feb	Mar	Apr	May	June	July	Aug	Sept	Oct	Nov	Dec
Avg. High (°F)	76	77	80	83	86	88	89	90	88	85	80	77
Avg. Low (°F)	60	61	64	68	72	75	76	76	76	72	66	61
Avg. High (°C)	24.4	25	26.7	28.3	30	31.1	31.7	32.2	31.1	29.4	26.7	25
Avg. Low (°C)	15.6	16.1	17.8	20	22.2	23.9	24.4	24.4	24.4	22.2	18.9	16.1
Avg. Rain (in.)	2.0	2.1	2.4	3.0	5.9	8.8	6.0	7.8	8.5	7.0	3.1	1.8

MIAMI CALENDAR OF EVENTS
January

FedEx Orange Bowl Classic, Miami. Football fanatics flock down to the big Orange Bowl game (oddly taking place not at the Orange Bowl in seedy downtown, but at the much more savory Pro Player Stadium) on New Year's Day, featuring two of the year's best college football teams. Tickets are available at ☎ **305/ 371-4600,** but call early as they sell out quickly.

Three Kings Parade, Miami. Miami's Cuban community makes up for the fact that Castro banned this religious celebration over 25 years ago by throwing a no-holds-barred parade throughout the streets of Little Havana's *Calle Ocho* neighborhood, usually the first Sunday of January. Call ☎ **305/447-1140.**

Art Deco Weekend, South Beach. Gain a newfound appreciation for the Necco-wafered Art Deco buildings, Deco furniture, history, and fashion at this weekend-long festival of street fairs, films, lectures, and other events. Call ☎ **305/672-2014.** Mid- to late January.

Taste of the Grove Food and Music Festival, Coconut Grove. Brave massive crowds of hungry folk at this fund-raising festival featuring booths from various neighborhood eateries hawking their goods for the price of a few prepurchased tickets. Call

© **305/444-7270.** Dates vary from mid-November to mid-January.

Royal Caribbean Golf Classic, Key Biscayne. Watch as pro golfers tee off for over $1 million at this tournament played on the scenic Crandon Park Golf Course. Call © **305/374-6180.** Late January.

February

Miami Film Festival. Though not exactly Cannes, the Miami Film Festival is an impressive 10-day celluloid celebration, featuring world premiers of Latin American, domestic, and other foreign and independent films. Call © **305/377-FILM.** Early to mid-February.

Coconut Grove Arts Festival, Coconut Grove. Florida's largest art festival features over 300 artists who are selected from thousands of entries. Possibly one of the most crowded street fairs in South Florida, the festival attracts art lovers, artists, and lots of college students who seem to think this event is the Mardi Gras of art fairs. Call © **305/447-0401** for information. Presidents' Day weekend.

Miami International Boat Show, Miami Beach. Agoraphobics beware, as this show draws a quarter of a million boat enthusiasts to the Miami Beach Convention Center. Some of the world's priciest megayachts, speedboats, sailboats, and schooners are displayed for purchase or for gawking. Call © **305/531-8410.** Mid-February.

Doral Ryder Golf Open, West Miami. This prestigious annual golf tournament swings into Miami at the legendary courses at the Doral Resort and Club. Call © **305/477-GOLF.** Late February.

March

Winter Party, Miami Beach. Gays and lesbians from around the world book trips to Miami as far as a year in advance to attend this weekend-long series of parties and events benefiting the Dade Human Rights Foundation. Travel arrangements can be made through Different Roads Travel, the event's official travel company, by calling © **888/ROADS-55,** ext. 510. For information on the specific events and prices, call © **305/538-5908** or visit www.winterparty.com. Early March.

Italian Renaissance Festival, Miami. Villa Vizcaya gets in touch with its Renaissance roots at this festival, which features strolling musicians, stage plays, and a cast of period-costumed characters who do their best to convince you that you're in a time warp. Call © **305/250-9133.** Mid-March.

Calle Ocho Festival, Little Havana. What Carnavale is to Rio, the Calle Ocho Festival is to Miami. This 10-day extravaganza, also called Carnival Miami, features a lengthy block party spanning 23 blocks, live salsa music, parades, and, of course, tons of savory Cuban delicacies. Those afraid of mob scenes should avoid this party at all costs. Call ℂ **305/644-8888.** Mid-March.

Grand Prix of Miami, Homestead. A little bit of Daytona in Miami, the Grand Prix is a premier racing event, attracting celebrities, Indy car drivers, and curious spectators who get a buzz off the smell of gasoline. Get tickets early, as this event sells out quickly. Call ℂ **305/250-5200.** Late March.

NASDAQ 100 Open, Key Biscayne. Sampras, Agassi, Kournikova, and the Williams sisters are only a few of the Grand Slammers who appear at this, one of the world's foremost tennis tournaments. Tickets for the semifinals and finals are hard to come by, so order early. Call ℂ **305/446-2200.** End of the month.

April

Little Acorns International Kite Festival, South Beach. This free kite festival is a true spectacular in the sky, attracting thousands of expert flyers and their flying works of art from 5th to 15th streets. Kids can build their own kites and scrounge for candy, which is dropped piñata style along the beach. Call ℂ **888/298-9815.** Third weekend in April.

June

Coconut Grove Goombay Festival, Coconut Grove. They may say it's better in the Bahamas, but that's questionable after you've attended Miami's own Bahamian bash, featuring lots of dancing in the streets, marching bands, scorching Caribbean temperatures, and the ever buzz-worthy and refreshing Goombay punch. For information, call ℂ **305/372-9966.** Early June.

July

Independence Day, Miami. Watch the masterful display of professional fireworks throughout the entire city. Best views are from Key Biscayne and Bayfront Park. For specific information on July 4 events, check the local newspapers.

September

Festival Miami, Miami. The University of Miami School of Music presents a 4-week program of performing arts, classical, jazz, and world music. For a schedule of performances, call ℂ **305/ 284-4940.** Mid-September.

October

Caribbean Carnival, Miami. If you've never been to the Caribbean, then this can be your introduction to the colorful, multicultural island nations of Trinidad, Jamaica, Haiti, St.

Vincent, Barbados, and St. Croix, as natives from the islands participate in a masquerade parade in their traditional costumes. Call ℂ **305/653-1877.** Early October.

Columbus Day Regatta, Miami. On the day that Columbus discovered America, the party-hearty of today's Florida discover their fellow Americans' birthday suits—this bacchanalia in the middle of Biscayne Bay encourages participants in this so-called regatta (there is a boat race at some point during the day, but most people are too preoccupied to notice) to strip down to their bare necessities and party at the sandbar in the middle of the bay. You may not need a bathing suit, but you will need a boat to get out to where all the action is. Consider renting one on Key Biscayne, which is the closest to the sandbar.

November

South Florida International Auto Show, Miami Beach. Cars are everywhere—literally—at this massive auto show, displaying the latest and most futuristic modes of transportation on the market. Try to take public transportation or call a cab to get to this gridlocked event. Call ℂ **305/947-5950.** Early November.

Jiffy Lube Miami 300 Weekend of NASCAR, Homestead. World-class racing takes place at Miami's outstanding 344-acre motor sports complex. Rev your engines early for tickets to this event. Call ℂ **305/230-5200.** Mid-November.

Miami Book Fair International, downtown Miami. Bibliophiles, literati, and some of the world's most prestigious and prolific authors descend upon downtown Miami for a week-long homage to the written word, which also happens to be the largest book fair in the United States. The weekend street fair is the best attended of the entire event, in which regular folk mix with wordsmiths such as Tom Wolfe and Jane Smiley while indulging in snacks, antiquarian books, and literary gossip. All lectures are free, but they fill up quickly, so get there early. Call ℂ **305/237-3258** for lecture schedules. Mid-November.

White Party Week, Miami. This week-long series of parties to benefit AIDS research is built around the main event, the White Party, which takes place at Villa Vizcaya and sells out as early as a year in advance. Philanthropists and celebrities such as Calvin Klein and David Geffen join thousands of white-clad, mostly gay men (and some women) in what has become one of the world's hottest and hardest-to-score party tickets. Call ℂ **305/667-9296** or visit www.whitepartyweek.com for a schedule of parties and events. Thanksgiving week.

Santa's Enchanted Forest, Miami. Billing itself as the world's largest Christmas theme park, Santa's Enchanted Forest is an assault on the eyes, with thousands of lights lining Tropical Park plus rides, games, and lots of food. This is a great place to bring kids. Call ✆ **305/893-0090.** Early November to mid-January.

4 Health

STAYING HEALTHY

Paramount to staying well in Miami (and maintaining a sunny disposition) is sunscreen. Even on the cloudiest of days, you *will* feel the effects of the powerful UV rays, so it's best to take precautions at all times. Limit your exposure to the sun, especially during the first few days of your trip and thereafter from 11am to 2pm. Use a sunscreen with a high sun protection factor (SPF) and apply it liberally. Remember that children need more protection than do adults.

WHAT TO DO IF YOU GET SICK AWAY FROM HOME

If you worry about getting sick away from home, consider purchasing **medical travel insurance** and carry your ID card in your purse or wallet. In most cases, your existing health plan will provide the coverage you need.

If you suffer from a chronic illness, consult your doctor before your departure. For conditions like epilepsy, diabetes, or heart problems, wear a **Medic Alert Identification Tag** (✆ **800/825-3785;** www.medicalert.org), which will immediately alert doctors to your condition and give them access to your records through Medic Alert's 24-hour hot line.

Pack **prescription medications** in your carry-on luggage, and carry them in their original containers. Also bring along copies of your prescriptions in case you lose your pills or run out.

If you get sick, consider asking your hotel concierge to recommend a local doctor—even his or her own. You can also try the emergency room at a local hospital; many have walk-in clinics for emergency cases that are not life threatening. You may not get immediate attention, but you won't pay the high price of an emergency room visit (usually a minimum of $300 just for signing your name). For any medical concerns or emergencies, Doctor's Hospital, 5000 University Dr., Coral Gables (✆ **305/666-2111**), has a 24-hour physician-staffed emergency department.

5 Tips for Travelers with Special Needs

TRAVELERS WITH DISABILITIES

Most disabilities shouldn't stop anyone from traveling. There are more options and resources out there than ever before.

AGENCIES/OPERATORS

- **Access Adventures** (© 716/889-9096), a Rochester, N.Y.–based agency, offers customized itineraries for a variety of travelers with disabilities.
- **Accessible Journeys** (© 800/TINGLES or 610/521-0339; www.disabilitytravel.com) caters specifically to slow walkers and wheelchair travelers and their families and friends.

ORGANIZATIONS

- **The Moss Rehab Hospital** (© 215/456-9603; www.moss resourcenet.org) provides friendly, helpful phone assistance through its **Travel Information Service.**
- **The Society for Accessible Travel and Hospitality** (© 212/447-7284; fax 212/725-8253; www.sath.org) offers a wealth of travel resources for all types of disabilities and informed recommendations on destinations, access guides, travel agents, tour operators, vehicle rentals, and companion services. Annual membership costs $45 for adults; $30 for seniors and students.

PUBLICATIONS

- **Twin Peaks Press** (© 360/694-2462) publishes travel-related books for travelers with special needs.
- *Open World for Disability and Mature Travel* magazine, published by the Society for Accessible Travel and Hospitality (see above), is full of good resources and information. A year's subscription is $13 ($21 outside the U.S.).

GAY & LESBIAN TRAVELERS

Miami, particularly South Beach, has a thriving gay community, supported by a wide range of services and establishments. There are several local gay-oriented publications full of information on gay and gay-friendly events, businesses, and services. *TWN, Wire, Hot Spots,* and *Miamigo* are among the free publications available in boxes on street corners, in stores, and on newsstands.

For a map and directory of gay businesses or a copy or the gay and lesbian community calendar sponsored by the **Dade Human Rights Foundation,** call © 305/572-1841. For a copy of the calendar and other information, you can also visit www.dhrf.com. One organization that is extremely helpful for gay and lesbian travelers is the **Miami Dade and South Beach Business Guild** (better known as the Gay Chamber of Commerce; ℂ **305/751-8855**).

PUBLICATIONS

- *Out and About* (ℂ **800/929-2268** or 415/644-8044; www.outandabout.com) offers guidebooks and a newsletter 10 times a year packed with solid information on the global gay and lesbian scene.
- *Spartacus International Gay Guide* and *Odysseus* are good, annual English-language guidebooks focused on gay men, with some information for lesbians. You can get them from most gay and lesbian bookstores, or order them from **Giovanni's Room** bookstore, 1145 Pine St., Philadelphia, PA 19107 (ℂ **215/923-2960;** www.giovannisroom.com).
- *Gay Travel A to Z: The World of Gay & Lesbian Travel Options at Your Fingertips,* by Marianne Ferrari (Ferrari Publications; www.ferrariguides.com), is a very good gay and lesbian guidebook series.

SENIOR TRAVEL

Mention the fact that you're a senior citizen when you first make your travel reservations. All major airlines and many hotels offer discounts for seniors. In most cities, people over the age of 60 qualify for reduced admission to theaters, museums, and other attractions, as well as discounted fares on public transportation.

Members of **AARP** (formerly known as the American Association of Retired Persons), 601 E St. NW, Washington, DC 20049 (ℂ **800/424-3410** or 202/434-2277; www.aarp.org), get discounts on hotels, airfares, and car rentals. **The Alliance for Retired Americans,** 8403 Colesville Rd., Suite 1200, Silver Spring, MD 20910 (ℂ **301/578-8422;** www.retiredamericans.org), offers a newsletter six times a year and discounts on hotel and auto rentals; annual dues are $13 per person or couple.

PUBLICATIONS

- *The Book of Deals* is a collection of more than 1,000 senior discounts on airlines, lodging, tours, and attractions around the country; it's available for $9.95 by calling ℂ **800/460-6676.**
- *The 50+ Traveler's Guidebook* (St. Martin's Press).
- *Unbelievably Good Deals and Great Adventures That You Absolutely Can't Get Unless You're Over 50* (Contemporary Publishing Co.).

6 Getting There

BY PLANE

Miami is one of **American Airlines**' (© 800/433-7300; www.aa.com) biggest hubs, and most major domestic airlines fly to and from many Florida cities, including **Continental** (© 800/525-0280; www.continental.com), **Delta** (© 800/221-1212; www.delta.com), **Northwest/KLM** (© 800/241-6522; www.nwa.com), **TWA** (© 800/221-2000; www.twa.com), **United** (© 800/241-6522; www.united.com), and **US Airways** (© 800/428-4322; www.usairways.com).

Several budget airlines also fly to South Florida, including **Southwest Airlines** (© 800/435-9792; www.southwest.com), **Air Tran** (© 800/AIR-TRAN; www.airtran.com), **Spirit** (© 800/772-7117; www.spiritair.com), and **Jet Blue** (© 800/538-2583; www.jetblue.com).

Several international carriers also make the trip to Miami, including **British Airways** (© **081/897-4000** from within the UK), **Virgin Atlantic** (© **012/937-47747** from within the UK), **Air Canada** (© **800/776-3000**), and many others.

NEW AIR TRAVEL SECURITY MEASURES

In the wake of the terrorist attacks of September 11, 2001, the airline industry began implementing sweeping security measures in airports. Expect a lengthy check-in process and extensive delays. Although regulations vary from airline to airline, you can expedite the process by taking the following steps: arrive early (at least 2 hr. before your flight); be sure to carry plenty of identifying documentation (a government-issued ID is required); and prepare to be searched. For the most up-to-date information on what you can and can not carry onto a plane, check out the Transportation Security Administration's (TSA—the government agency that now handles all aspects of airport security) website at www.tsa.gov.

FLYING FOR LESS: TIPS FOR GETTING THE BEST AIRFARE

Passengers within the same airplane cabin are rarely paying the same fare. Business travelers who need to purchase tickets at the last minute, change their itinerary at a moment's notice, or get home for the weekend pay the premium rate. Passengers who can book their ticket long in advance, who can stay over Saturday night, or who are willing to travel on a Tuesday, Wednesday, or Thursday after 7pm will pay a fraction of the full fare. Here are a few other easy ways to save:

- Airlines periodically lower prices on their most popular routes. Check the travel section of your Sunday newspaper for advertised discounts or call the airlines directly and ask if any **promotional rates** or special fares are available. If your schedule is flexible, say so, and ask if you can secure a cheaper fare by staying an extra day, by flying midweek, or by flying at less trafficked hours. If you already hold a ticket when a sale breaks, it may even pay to exchange your ticket, which usually incurs a charge.

- **Council Travel** (℀ **800/226-8624**; www.counciltravel.com) and **STA Travel** (℀ **800/781-4040**; www.statravel.com) cater especially to young travelers, but their bargain-basement prices are available to people of all ages. **The TravelHub** (℀ **888/AIR-FARE;** www.travelhub.com) represents nearly 1,000 travel agencies, many of whom offer consolidator and discount fares. Other reliable consolidators include **1-800-FLY-CHEAP** (www.1800 flycheap.com); **TFI Tours International** (℀ **800-745-8000** or 212/736-1140; www.lowestprice.com), which serves as a clearinghouse for unused seats; or "rebators" such as **Travel Avenue** (℀ **800/333-3335;** www.travelavenue.com) and the **Smart Traveller** (℀ **800/448-3338** in the U.S. or 305/448-3338), which rebate part of their commissions to you.

- Search **the Internet** for cheap fares. Great last-minute deals are available through free weekly e-mail services provided directly by the airlines. See "Planning Your Trip Online," below, for more information.

- Join a travel club such as **Moment's Notice** (℀ **718/234-6295;** www.moments-notice.com) or **Sears Discount Travel Club** (℀ **800/433-9383,** or 800/255-1487 to join; www.travelers advantage.com), which supply unsold tickets at discounted prices. You pay an annual membership fee to get the club's hotline number. Of course, you're limited to what's available, so you have to be flexible.

⟮Tips⟯ Fly for Less

When booking airfare to Miami, consider flying into the Fort Lauderdale Hollywood International Airport for considerably cheaper fares. The airport is only a half hour from downtown Miami.

BY CAR

Although four major roads run to and through Miami—I-95, S.R. 826, S.R. 836, and U.S. 1—chances are you'll reach Miami by way of I-95. This north–south interstate is South Florida's lifeline and an integral part of the region. The highway connects all of Miami's different neighborhoods, the airport, the beaches, and all of South Florida to the rest of the country. Miami's road signs are notoriously confusing and notably absent when you most need them. Think twice before you exit from the highway if you aren't sure where you're going: Some exits lead to unsavory neighborhoods.

Florida law allows drivers to make a right turn on a red light after a complete stop, unless otherwise indicated. In addition, all passengers are required to wear seat belts, and children under 3 must be securely fastened in government-approved car seats.

For information on car-rental companies with offices in South Florida, see "Getting Around" in chapter 3 "Getting to Know Miami."

Saving Money on a Rental Car   Car-rental rates vary even more than airline fares. The price you pay will depend on the size of the car, where and when you pick it up and drop it off, the length of the rental period, where and how far you drive it, whether you purchase insurance, and a host of other factors. A few key questions could save you hundreds of dollars:

- Are weekend rates lower than weekday rates? Ask if the rate is the same for pickup Friday morning, for instance, as it is for Thursday night.
- Is a weekly rate cheaper than the daily rate? Even if you only need the car for 4 days, it may be cheaper to keep it for 5.
- Are special promotional rates available? If you see an advertised price in your local newspaper, be sure to ask for that specific rate; otherwise you may be charged the standard cost.
- Are discounts available for members of AARP, AAA, frequent-flier programs, or trade unions?
- How much tax will be added to the rental bill? Local tax? State tax?
- What is the cost of adding an additional driver's name to the contract?
- How many free miles are included in the price? Free mileage is often negotiable, depending on the length of your rental.

- How much does the rental company charge to refill your gas tank if you return with the tank less than full? Fuel is almost always cheaper in town; try to allow enough time to refuel the car yourself before returning it.

Many packages are available that include airfare, accommodations, and a rental car with unlimited mileage. Compare these prices with the cost of booking airline tickets and renting a car separately to see if these offers are good deals.

7 Planning Your Trip Online

Researching and booking your trip online can save time and money. Then again, it may not. It is simply not true that you always get the best deal online. Most booking engines do not include schedules and prices for budget airlines, and from time to time you'll get a better last-minute price by calling the airline directly, so it's best to call the airline to see if you can do better before booking online.

On the plus side, Internet users today can tap into the same travel-planning databases that were once accessible only to travel agents—and do it at the same speed. Sites such as **Frommers.com, Travelocity, Expedia.com,** and **Orbitz** allow consumers to comparison shop for airfares, access special bargains, book flights, and reserve hotel rooms and rental cars.

Although online booking sites offer tips and hard data to help you bargain shop, they cannot endow you with the hard-earned experience that makes a seasoned, reliable travel agent an invaluable resource, even in the Internet age. And for consumers with a complex itinerary, a trusty travel agent is still the best way to arrange the most direct flights to and from the best airports.

Still, there's no denying the Internet's emergence as a powerful tool in researching and plotting travel time. The benefits of researching your trip online can be well worth the effort.

Last-minute specials, such as weekend deals or Internet-only fares, are offered by airlines to fill empty seats. Most of these are announced on Tuesday or Wednesday and must be purchased online. They are only valid for travel that weekend, but some can be booked weeks or months in advance. Sign up for weekly e-mail alerts at airline websites or check megasites that compile comprehensive lists of last-minute specials, such as **Smarter Living** (smarterliving.com) or **WebFlyer** (www.webflyer.com).

Some sites, such as Expedia.com, will send you **e-mail notification** when a cheap fare becomes available to your favorite destination. Some will also tell you when fares to a particular destination are lowest.

SMART E-SHOPPING

The savvy traveler is armed with insider information. Here are a few tips to help you navigate the Internet successfully and safely.

- **Know when sales start.** Last-minute deals may vanish in minutes. If you have a favorite booking site or airline, find out when last-minute deals are released to the public.
- **Shop around.** If you're looking for bargains, compare prices on different sites and airlines—and against a travel agent's best fare. Try a range of times and alternative airports before you make a purchase.
- **Avoid online auctions.** Sites that auction airline tickets and frequent-flier miles are the number one perpetrators of Internet fraud, according to the National Consumers League.
- **Maintain a paper trail.** If you book an E-ticket, print out a confirmation, or write down your confirmation number, and keep it safe and accessible—or your trip could be a virtual one!

8 Tips on Accommodations

TIPS FOR SAVING ON YOUR HOTEL ROOM

The **rack rate** is the maximum rate that a hotel charges for a room. It's the rate you'd get if you walked in off the street and asked for a room for the night. Hardly anybody pays these prices, however, and there are many ways around them.

- **Don't be afraid to bargain.** Most rack rates include commissions of 10% to 25% for travel agents, which some hotels may be willing to reduce if you make your own reservations and haggle a bit. Always ask whether a room less expensive than the first one quoted is available, or whether any special rates apply to you. You may qualify for corporate, student, military, senior, or other discounts. Be sure to mention membership in AAA, AARP, frequent-flier programs, or trade unions, which may entitle you to special deals as well. Find out the hotel policy on children—do kids stay free in the room, or is there a special rate?
- **Rely on a qualified professional.** Certain hotels give travel agents discounts in exchange for steering business their way, so if you're shy about bargaining, an agent may be better equipped to negotiate discounts for you.

- **Dial direct.** When booking a room in a chain hotel, compare the rates offered by the hotel's local line with that of the toll-free number. Also check with an agent and online. A hotel makes nothing on a room that stays empty, so the local hotel reservation desk may be willing to offer a special rate unavailable elsewhere.

- **Remember the law of supply and demand.** Resort hotels are most crowded and therefore most expensive on weekends, so discounts are usually available for midweek stays. Business hotels in downtown locations are busiest during the week, so you can expect big discounts over the weekend. Avoid high-season stays whenever you can: Planning your vacation just a week before or after official peak season can mean big savings.

- **Avoid excess charges.** When you book a room, ask whether the hotel charges for parking. Find out whether your hotel imposes a surcharge on local and long-distance calls. Ask about local taxes and service charges, which could increase the cost of a room by 25% or more. Always ask what's included in the price of a room—a so-called moderate hotel that charges for beach towels and chairs may cost a lot more than a so-called expensive hotel that includes extras in the price. Also be sure to ask if your hotel gives free transfers from the airport and if kids stay free.

- **Watch for coupons and advertised discounts.** Scan ads in your local Sunday newspaper travel section, an excellent source for up-to-the-minute hotel deals.

- Join hotel **frequent-visitor clubs,** even if you don't use them much. You'll be more likely to get upgrades and other perks.

9 For International Visitors

Whether it's your first visit or your tenth, a trip to the United States may require an additional degree of planning. This chapter will provide you with essential information, helpful tips, and advice for the more common problems that some visitors encounter.

PREPARING FOR YOUR TRIP
ENTRY REQUIREMENTS

Immigration laws are a hot political issue in the United States these days, and the following requirements may have changed somewhat by the time you plan your trip. Check at any U.S. embassy or consulate for current information and requirements. You can also plug into the **U.S. State Department's** Internet site at **http://state.gov**.

VISAS   The U.S. State Department has a **Visa Waiver Program** allowing citizens of certain countries to enter the United States without a visa for stays of up to 90 days. At press time these included Andorra, Australia, Austria, Belgium, Brunei, Denmark, Finland, France, Germany, Iceland, Ireland, Italy, Japan, Liechtenstein, Luxembourg, Monaco, the Netherlands, New Zealand, Norway, Portugal, San Marino, Singapore, Slovenia, Spain, Sweden, Switzerland, the United Kingdom, and Uruguay. Citizens of these countries need only a valid passport and a round-trip air or cruise ticket in their possession upon arrival. Canadian citizens may enter the United States without visas; they need only proof of residence.

Citizens of all other countries must have (1) a valid passport that expires at least 6 months later than the scheduled end of their visit to the United States, and (2) a tourist visa, which may be obtained from any U.S. consulate.

MEDICAL REQUIREMENTS   Unless you're arriving from an area known to be suffering from an **epidemic** (particularly cholera or yellow fever), inoculations or vaccinations are not required for entry into the United States. If you have a medical condition that requires **syringe-administered medications,** carry a valid signed prescription from your physician—the Federal Aviation Administration (FAA) no longer allows airline passengers to pack syringes in their carry-on baggage without documented proof of medical need. If you have a disease that requires treatment with **narcotics,** you should also carry documented proof with you—smuggling narcotics aboard a plane is a serious offense that carries severe penalties in the U.S.

DRIVER'S LICENSES   Foreign driver's licenses are mostly recognized in the U.S., although you may want to get an international driver's license if your home license is not written in English.

PASSPORT INFORMATION

Safeguard your passport in an inconspicuous, inaccessible place like a money belt. Make a copy of the critical pages, including the passport number, and store it in a safe place, separate from the passport itself. If you lose your passport, visit the nearest consulate of your native country as soon as possible for a replacement.

CUSTOMS
What You Can Bring In

For information on customs regulations for those entering or leaving the United States, call the **U.S. Customs** office at ℂ **202/927-1770** or visit their website at www.customs.ustreas.gov/travel/travel.htm.

What You Can Take Home

U.K. citizens should contact HM Customs & Excise, Passenger Enquiry Point, 2nd Floor Wayfarer House, Great South West Road, Feltham, Middlesex, TW14 8NP (℘ **0181/910-3744**) or see www. open.gov.uk.

Canadian citizens should write for the booklet *I Declare,* issued by Revenue Canada, 2265 St. Laurent Blvd., Ottawa, ON K1G 4K3 (℘ **506/636-5064**).

Australian citizens can get the helpful brochure, available from Australian consulates or Customs offices, *Know Before You Go.* For more information, contact Australian Customs Services, GPO Box 8, Sydney NSW 2001 (℘ **02/9213-2000**).

New Zealand citizens can get the free pamphlet available at New Zealand consulates and Customs offices: *New Zealand Customs Guide for Travellers, Notice no. 4.* For more information, contact New Zealand Customs, 50 Anzac Ave., P.O. Box 29, Auckland (℘ **09/ 359-6655**).

HEALTH INSURANCE

Although it's not required of travelers, health insurance is highly recommended. Unlike many European countries, the United States does not usually offer free or low-cost medical care to its citizens or visitors. Doctors and hospitals are expensive, and in most cases will require advance payment or proof of coverage before they render their services. Policies can cover everything from the loss or theft of your baggage and trip cancellation to the guarantee of bail in case you're arrested. Good policies will also cover the costs of an accident, repatriation, or death. Packages such as **Europ Assistance's "Worldwide Healthcare Plan"** are sold by European automobile clubs and travel agencies at attractive rates. **Worldwide Assistance Services, Inc.** (℘ **800/821-2828;** www.worldwideassistance.com) is the agent for Europ Assistance in the United States.

Though lack of health insurance may prevent you from being admitted to a hospital in nonemergencies, don't worry about being left on a street corner to die; the American way is to fix you now and bill the living daylights out of you later.

MONEY

CURRENCY   The U.S. monetary system is very simple: The most common **bills** are the $1 (colloquially, a "buck"), $5, $10, and $20 denominations. There are also $2 bills (seldom encountered), $50 bills, and $100 bills (the last two are usually not welcome as payment for small purchases). All the paper money was recently redesigned, making the famous faces adorning them disproportionately large. The old-style bills are still legal tender.

There are seven denominations of **coins:** 1¢ (1 cent, or a penny); 5¢ (5 cents, or a nickel); 10¢ (10 cents, or a dime); 25¢ (25 cents, or a quarter); 50¢ (50 cents, or a half dollar); the new gold "Sacagawea" coin worth $1; and, prized by collectors, the rare, older silver dollar.

Note: The "foreign-exchange bureaus" so common in Europe are rare even at airports in the United States, and nonexistent outside major cities. It's best not to change foreign money (or traveler's checks denominated in a currency other than U.S. dollars) at a small-town bank, or even a branch in a big city; in fact, leave any currency other than U.S. dollars at home—it may prove a greater nuisance to you than it's worth.

CREDIT CARDS & ATMS Credit cards are the most widely used form of payment in the United States: **Visa** (Barclaycard in Britain), **MasterCard** (EuroCard in Europe, Access in Britain, Chargex in Canada), **American Express, Diners Club,** and **Discover.** There are, however, a handful of stores and restaurants that do not take credit cards, so be sure to ask in advance. Most businesses display a sticker near their entrance to let you know which cards they accept. (*Note:* Businesses may require a minimum purchase, usually around $10, to use a credit card.)

It is strongly recommended that you bring at least one major credit card. You must have a credit or charge card to rent a car. Hotels and airlines usually require a credit-card imprint as a deposit against expenses, and in an emergency a credit card can be priceless.

For information about **automated teller machines (ATMs),** see section 2, "Money" earlier in this chapter.

3

Getting to Know Miami

Apropos jokes about bad drivers, Grandma forgetting to shut off her turn signal, and traffic nightmares aside, Miami is a fascinating city to explore, be it by foot, bike, scooter, boat, or car. Because of its larger-than-life persona, Miami may seem a lot bigger than it really is, but although the city comprises many different neighborhoods, it's really not that difficult to learn the lay of the land. Much like the bodies beautiful on Ocean Drive, the Magic City is a tidy package that's a little less than 2,000 square miles.

1 Orientation

ARRIVING

Originally carved out of scrubland in 1928 by Pan American Airlines, **Miami International Airport (MIA)** has become second in the United States for international passenger traffic and 10th in the world for total passengers. Despite the heavy traffic, the airport is quite user-friendly and not as much of a hassle as you'd think. Visitor information is available 24 hours a day at the **Miami International Airport Main Visitor Counter,** Concourse E, second level (© 305/876-7000). Information is also available at **www.miami-airport.com**. Because MIA is the busiest airport in South Florida, travelers may want to consider flying into the less crowded, but expanding, **Fort Lauderdale Hollywood International Airport (FLL)** (© 954/359-1200), which is closer to north Miami than MIA, or the **Palm Beach International Airport (PBI)** (© 561/471-7420), about 90 minutes away.

GETTING INTO TOWN

Miami International Airport is located about 6 miles west of downtown and about 10 miles from the beaches, so it's likely you can get from the plane to your hotel room in less than half an hour. Of course, if you're arriving from an international destination, it will take more time to go through Customs and Immigration.

BY CAR All the major car-rental firms operate off-site branches reached via shuttles from the terminals. See "Getting Around," later

Miami at a Glance

in this chapter, for a list of major rental companies. Signs at the airport's exit clearly point the way to various parts of the city, but the car-rental firm should also give you directions to your destination. If you're arriving late at night, you might want to take a taxi to your hotel and have the car delivered to you the next day.

BY TAXI   Taxis line up in front of a dispatcher's desk outside the airport's arrivals terminals. Most cabs are metered, though some have flat rates to popular destinations. The fare should be about $20 to Coral Gables, $18 to downtown, and $24 to South Beach, plus tip, which should be at least 10% (add more for each bag the driver handles). Depending on traffic, the ride to Coral Gables or downtown takes about 15 to 20 minutes and 20 to 25 minutes to South Beach.

BY LIMO OR VAN   Group limousines (multipassenger vans) circle the arrivals area looking for fares. Destinations are posted on the front of each van, and a flat rate is charged for door-to-door service to the area marked.

SuperShuttle (© 305/871-2000; www.supershuttle.com) is one of the largest airport operators, charging between $10 and $20 per person for a ride within the county. Its vans operate 24 hours a day and accept American Express, MasterCard, and Visa. This is a cheaper alternative to a cab (if you are traveling alone or with one other person), but be prepared to be in the van for quite a while, as you may have to make several stops to drop passengers off before you reach your own destination.

BY PUBLIC TRANSPORTATION   Public transportation in Miami is a major hassle bordering on a nightmare. Painfully slow and unreliable, buses heading downtown leave the airport only once per hour (from the arrivals level), and connections are spotty at best. It could take about an hour and a half to get to South Beach. Journeys to downtown and Coral Gables are more direct. The fare is $1.25, plus an additional 25¢ for a transfer.

VISITOR INFORMATION

The most up-to-date information is provided by the **Greater Miami Convention and Visitor's Bureau,** 701 Brickell Ave., Suite 700, Miami, FL 33131 (© **800/933-8448** or 305/539-3000; fax 305/530-3113; www.miamiandbeaches.com).

If you arrive at the Miami International Airport, you can pick up visitor information at the airport's main visitor counter on the second floor of Concourse E. It's open 24 hours a day.

Always check local newspapers for special events during your visit. The city's only daily, the *Miami Herald,* is a good source for current events listings, particularly the "Weekend" section in Friday's edition and the paper's entertainment weekly offshoot, *The Street,* available free every Friday in freestanding boxes anchored to city streets. Even better is the free weekly alternative paper, the *Miami New Times,* found in bright red boxes throughout the city. Information on everything from dining to entertainment in Miami is available on the Internet at www.miami.citysearch.com.

CITY LAYOUT

Miami may seem confusing at first, but it quickly becomes easy to negotiate. The small cluster of buildings that make up the downtown area is at the geographical heart of the city. In relation to downtown, the airport is northwest, the beaches are east, Coconut Grove is south, Coral Gables is west, and the rest of the city is north.

FINDING AN ADDRESS   Miami is divided into dozens of areas with official and unofficial boundaries. Street numbering in the city of Miami is fairly straightforward, but you must first be familiar with the numbering system. The mainland is divided into four sections (NE, NW, SE, and SW) by the intersection of Flagler Street and Miami Avenue. Flagler divides Miami from north to south and Miami Avenue divides the city from east to west. It's helpful to remember that avenues generally run north–south, while streets go east–west. Street numbers (First St., Second St., and so forth) start from here and increase as you go further out from this intersection, as do numbers of avenues, places, courts, terraces, and lanes. Streets in Hialeah are the exceptions to this pattern; they are listed separately in map indexes.

Getting around the barrier islands that make up Miami Beach is somewhat easier than moving around the mainland. Street numbering starts with First Street, near Miami Beach's southern tip, and increases to 192nd Street, in the northern part of Sunny Isles. Collins Avenue makes the entire journey, from head to toe of the island. As in the city of Miami, some streets in Miami Beach have numbers as well as names. When they are part of listings in this book, both name and number are given.

The numbered streets in Miami Beach are not the geographical equivalents of those on the mainland, but they are close. For example, the 79th Street Causeway runs into 71st Street on Miami Beach.

STREET MAPS   It's easy to get lost in sprawling Miami, so a reliable map is essential. The Trakker Map of Miami is a four-color accordion map that encompasses all of Dade County. The map is available at newsstands and shops throughout Miami or online at www.trakkermaps.com.

Some maps of Miami list streets according to area, so you'll have to know which part of the city you are looking for before the street can be found. All the listings in this book include area information for this reason.

THE NEIGHBORHOODS IN BRIEF
SOUTH BEACH—THE ART DECO DISTRICT   Though there are many monikers used to describe Miami's publicity darling— Glitter Beach, SoBe, America's Riviera, Hollywood South, Manhattan

South—South Beach is a uniquely surreal, Dalí-esque cocktail of cosmopolitan influences with a splash of saltwater thrown in to remind you that you're not in a concrete jungle anymore. South Beach's 10 miles of beach are alive with a frenetic, circus-like atmosphere and are center stage for a motley crew of characters, from eccentric locals, seniors, snowbirds, and college students to gender-benders, celebrities, club kids, and curiosity seekers: individuality is as widely accepted on South Beach as Visa and MasterCard.

Bolstered by a Caribbean-chic cafe society and a sexually charged, tragically hip nightlife, people-watching on South Beach (from 1st to 23rd sts.) is almost as good as a front-row seat at a Milan fashion show. Sure, the beautiful people do flock here, but the models aren't the only sights worth drooling over. The thriving Art Deco District within South Beach contains the largest concentration of Art Deco architecture in the world. In 1979, much of South Beach was listed in the National Register of Historic Places. The pastel-hued structures are supermodels in their own right—only these models improve with age.

MIAMI BEACH In the fabulous '40s and '50s, Miami Beach was America's true Riviera. The stomping ground of choice for the Rat Pack and notorious mobsters such as Al Capone, its huge self-contained resort hotels were vacations unto themselves, providing a full day's worth of meals, activities, and entertainment. Then, in the 1960s and 1970s, people who fell in love with Miami began to buy apartments rather than rent hotel rooms. Tourism declined, Capone disappeared, the Rat Pack fled to Vegas, and many area hotels fell into disrepair.

However, since the late 1980s and South Beach's renaissance, Miami Beach (24th St. and up) has experienced a tide of revitalization. Huge beach hotels are finding their niche with new international tourist markets and are attracting large convention crowds. New generations of Americans are discovering the qualities that originally made Miami Beach so popular, and they are finding out that the sand and surf now come with a thriving international city.

Surfside, Bal Harbour, and **Sunny Isles** make up the north part of the beach (island). Hotels, motels, restaurants, and beaches line Collins Avenue and, with some outstanding exceptions, the farther north one goes, the cheaper lodging becomes. All told, excellent prices, location, and facilities make Surfside and Sunny Isles attractive places to stay, although they are still a little rough around the edges. However, a revitalization is in the works for these areas, and, while it's highly unlikely they will ever become as chic as South

Beach, there is potential, especially as South Beach falls prey to the inevitable spoiler: commercialism. Keep in mind that beachfront properties are at a premium, so many of the area's moderately priced hotels have been converted to condominiums, leaving fewer and fewer affordable places to stay.

In exclusive and ritzy Bal Harbour, where well-paid police officers are instructed to ticket drivers who go above the 30 mph speed limit, few hotels remain amid the many beachfront condominium towers. Instead, fancy homes, tucked away on the bay, hide behind gated communities, and the Rodeo Drive of Miami (known as the Bal Harbour Shops) attracts shoppers who don't flinch at four-, five-, and six-figure price tags.

Note that **North Miami Beach,** a residential area near the Dade–Broward County line (north of 163rd Street; part of North Dade County), is a misnomer. It is actually northwest of Miami Beach, on the mainland, and has no beaches, though it does have some of Miami's better restaurants and shops. Located within North Miami Beach is the posh residential community of **Aventura,** best known for its high-priced condos, the Turnberry Isle Resort, and the Aventura Mall.

Note: South Beach, the historic Art Deco District, is treated as a separate neighborhood from Miami Beach.

KEY BISCAYNE   Miami's forested and secluded Key Biscayne is technically one of the first islands in the Florida Keys. However, this island is nothing like its southern neighbors. Located south of Miami Beach, off the shores of Coconut Grove, Key Biscayne is protected from the troubles of the mainland by the long Rickenbacker Causeway and its $1 toll.

Largely an exclusive residential community, with million-dollar homes and sweeping water views, Key Biscayne also offers visitors great public beaches, some top (read: pricey) resort hotels, and several good restaurants. Hobie Beach, adjacent to the causeway, is the city's premier spot for sailboarding and jet-skiing (see "Watersports," in chapter 6, "What to See & Do in Miami"). On the island's southern tip, Bill Baggs State Park has great beaches, bike paths, and dense forests for picnicking and partying.

DOWNTOWN   Miami's downtown boasts one of the world's most beautiful cityscapes. Unfortunately, that's about all it offers. During the day, a vibrant community of students, businesspeople, and merchants make their way through the bustling streets. Vendors sell fresh-cut pineapples and mangos while young consumers on shopping

Impressions

The wonderful thing about Miami is that you don't have to make anything up. You don't have to have an imagination at all. All you have to do is read the newspaper here.

—Dave Barry

sprees lug bags and boxes. However, at night, downtown is desolate (except for NE 11th St, where there is a burgeoning nightlife scene) and not a place in which you'd want to get lost. The downtown area does have a mall (Bayside Marketplace, where many cruise passengers come to browse), some culture (Miami–Dade Cultural Center), and a few decent restaurants (see chapter 5, "Where to Dine"), as well as the new American Airlines Arena. Additionally, a downtown revitalization project is in the works, in which a cultural arts center, among other things, is expected to bring downtown back to life.

DESIGN DISTRICT   With restaurants springing up between galleries and furniture stores galore, the Design District is, as locals say, the new South Beach, adding a touch of New York's SoHo to an area formerly known as downtown Miami's "Don't Go." The district, which is a hotbed for furniture import companies, interior designers, architects, and more, has also become a player in Miami's ever-changing nightlife, with a cavernous nightclub/restaurant/production studio/recording studio/live music venue that has become hipster central for South Beach expatriates and artsy bohemian types. In anticipation of its growing popularity, the district has also banded together to create an up-to-date website, www.designmiami.com, which includes a calendar of events and is chock-full of information. The district is loosely defined as the area bounded by NE 2nd Avenue, NE 5th Avenue east and west, and NW 36th Street to the south.

BISCAYNE CORRIDOR   From downtown near Bayside to the 70s, where trendy curio shops and upscale restaurants are slowly opening, Biscayne Boulevard is aspiring to reclaim itself as a safe thoroughfare where tourists can wine, dine, and shop. Previously known for sketchy, dilapidated 1950s- and '60s-era hotels that had fallen on hard times, residents fleeing the high prices of the beaches in search of affordable housing are renovating Biscayne block by block, trying to make this once-again famous boulevard worthy of a Sunday drive. With the trendy Design District immediately west of 36th and Biscayne by two blocks, there is hope for the area.

LITTLE HAVANA If you've never been to Cuba, just visit this small section of Miami and you'll come pretty close. The sounds, tastes, and rhythms are very reminiscent of Cuba's capital city. Some even jokingly say you don't have to speak a word of English to live an independent life here—even street signs are in Spanish and English.

Cuban coffee shops, tailor and furniture stores, and inexpensive restaurants line *Calle Ocho* (pronounced *Ka*-yey *O*-choh), SW 8th Street, the region's main thoroughfare. Salsa and merengue beats ring loudly from old record stores while old men in *guayaberas* (loose fitting cotton or gauzy shirts, short sleeved, used to keep cool in Cuba and now a fashion statement in Miami) smoke cigars over their daily game of dominoes. The spotlight focused on the neighborhood during the Elián González situation in 2000, but the area was previously noted for the groups of artists and nocturnal types who have moved their galleries and performance spaces here, sparking a culturally charged neo-bohemian nightlife.

CORAL GABLES "The City Beautiful," created by George Merrick in the early 1920s, is one of Miami's first planned developments. This is not Levittown: The houses here were built in a Mediterranean style along lush tree-lined streets that open onto beautifully carved plazas, many with centerpiece fountains. The best architectural examples of the era have Spanish-style tiled roofs and are built from Miami oolite, native limestone commonly called "coral rock."

The Gables' European-flaired shopping and commerce center is home to many thriving corporations. Coral Gables also has landmark hotels, great golfing, upscale shopping, and some of the city's best restaurants, headed by world-renowned chefs.

COCONUT GROVE An arty, hippie hangout in the psychedelic '60s, Coconut Grove has given way from swirls of tie-dyes to the uniform color schemes of the Gap. Chain stores, theme restaurants, a megaplex, and bars galore make Coconut Grove a commercial success, but this gentrification has pushed most alternative types out.

The intersection of Grand Avenue, Main Highway, and McFarlane Road pierces the area's heart. Right in the center of it all is CocoWalk and the Shops at Mayfair, filled with boutiques, eateries, and bars. Sidewalks here are often crowded, especially at night, when University of Miami students who frequent this adopted college town come out to play.

SOUTHERN MIAMI–DADE COUNTY To locals, South Miami is both a specific area, southwest of Coral Gables, and a general region that encompasses all of southern Dade County and includes Kendall, Perrine, Cutler Ridge, and Homestead. For the purposes of clarity, this book has grouped all these southern suburbs under the rubric "Southern Miami–Dade County." Similar attributes unite the communities: They are heavily residential and packed with strip malls amidst a few remaining plots of farmland. Tourists don't usually stay in these parts, unless they are on their way to the Everglades or the Keys. However, Southern Miami–Dade County contains many of the city's top attractions (see chapter 6), meaning that you're likely to spend some time here.

2 Getting Around

Officially, Dade County has opted for a "unified, multimodal transportation network," which basically means you can get around the city by train, bus, and taxi. However, in practice, the network doesn't work very well. Things may improve when the city completes its transportation center in 2005, but until then, unless you are going from downtown Miami to a not-too-distant spot, you are better off in a rental car or taxi.

With the exception of downtown Coconut Grove and South Beach, Miami is not a walker's city. Because it is so spread out, most attractions are too far apart to make walking between them feasible. In fact, most Miamians are so used to driving that they do so even when going just a few blocks.

BY PUBLIC TRANSPORTATION

BY RAIL   Two rail lines, operated by the **Metro-Dade Transit Agency** (© **305/770-3131;** www.co.miami-dade.fl.us/mdta/), run in concert with each other:

Metrorail, the city's modern high-speed commuter train, is a 21-mile elevated line that travels north–south, between downtown Miami and the southern suburbs. Locals like to refer to this semi-useless rail system as Metro*fail.* If you are staying in Coral Gables or Coconut Grove, you can park your car at a nearby station and ride the rails downtown. However, that's about it. There are plans to extend the system to service Miami International Airport, but until those tracks are built, these trains don't go most places tourists go, with the exception of the Vizcaya Museum in Coconut Grove. Metrorail operates daily from about 6am to midnight. The fare is $1.25.

Metromover, a 4½-mile elevated line, circles the downtown area and connects with Metrorail at the Government Center stop. This is a good way to get to Bayside (a waterfront marketplace, see p. 153) if you don't have a car. Riding on rubber tires, the single-car train winds past many of the area's most important attractions and shopping and business districts. You may not go very far, but you will get a beautiful perspective from the towering height of the suspended rails. System hours are daily from about 6am to midnight. The fare is 25¢.

BY BUS Miami's suburban layout is not conducive to getting around by bus. Lines operate and maps are available, but instead of getting to know the city, you'll find that relying on bus transportation will acquaint you only with how it feels to wait at bus stops. In short, a bus ride in Miami is grueling. You can get a bus map by mail, either from the Greater Miami Convention and Visitor's Bureau (see "Visitor Information," earlier in this chapter) or by writing the Metro-Dade Transit System, 3300 NW 32nd Ave., Miami, FL 33142. In Miami, call © **305/770-3131** for public-transit information. The fare is $1.25.

BY CAR

Tales circulate about vacationers who have visited Miami without a car, but they are very few indeed. If you are counting on exploring the city, even to a modest degree, a car is essential. Miami's restaurants, hotels, and attractions are far from one another, so any other form of transportation is relatively impractical. You won't need a car, however, if you are spending your entire vacation at a resort, are traveling directly to the Port of Miami for a cruise, or are here for a short stay centered in one area of the city, such as South Beach, where everything is within walking distance and parking is a costly nightmare.

When driving across a causeway or through downtown, allow extra time to reach your destination because of frequent drawbridge openings and slow boat crossings. Some bridges open about every half hour for large sailing vessels to make their way through the wide bays and canals that crisscross the city, stalling traffic for several minutes.

RENTALS It seems as though every car-rental company, big and small, has at least one office in Miami. Consequently, the city is one

---

Words to Live By

I figure marriage is kind of like Miami; it's hot and stormy, and occasionally a little dangerous . . . but if it's really so awful, why is there still so much traffic?
                    —Sarah Jessica Parker's character, Gwen Marcus,
                                        in *Miami Rhapsody*

of the cheapest places in the world to rent a car. Many firms regularly advertise prices in the neighborhood of $140 per week for their economy cars. You should also check with the airline you have chosen to get to Miami; there are often special discounts when you book a flight and reserve your rental car simultaneously. A minimum age, generally 25, is usually required of renters, while some rental agencies have also set maximum ages. A national car-rental broker, **Car Rental Referral Service** (✆ **800/404-4482**), can often find companies willing to rent to drivers between the ages of 21 and 24 and can also get discounts from major companies as well as some regional ones.

National car-rental companies with toll-free numbers include **Alamo** (✆ 800/327-9633), **Avis** (✆ 800/331-1212), **Budget** (✆ 800/527-0700), **Dollar** (✆ 800/800-4000 or 800/327-7607), **Hertz** (✆ 800/654-3131), **National** (✆ 800/328-4567), and **Thrifty** (✆ 800/367-2277). One excellent company that has offices in every conceivable part of town and offers extremely competitive rates is **Enterprise** (✆ 800/325-8007). Call around and comparison shop—car-rental prices can fluctuate more than airfares.

Many car-rental companies also offer cellular phones or electronic map rentals. It might be wise to opt for these additional safety features (the phone will definitely come in handy if you get lost), although the cost can be exorbitant.

Finally, think about splurging on a convertible (at most companies, the price for convertibles is approximately 20% more). Not only are convertibles one of the best ways to see the beautiful surroundings, but they're also an ideal way to perfect a tan!

PARKING   Always keep plenty of quarters on hand to feed hungry meters. Or, on Miami Beach, stop by the Chamber of Commerce at 1920 Meridian Ave. or any Publix grocery store to buy a magnetic **parking card** in denominations of $10, $20, or $25. Parking is usually plentiful (except on South Beach and Coconut Grove), but when it's not, be careful: Fines for illegal parking can be stiff, starting at a hefty $18.

In addition to parking garages, valet services are commonplace and often used. Expect to pay from $5 to $15 for parking in Coconut Grove and on South Beach's busy weekend nights.

LOCAL DRIVING RULES   Florida law allows drivers to make a right turn on a red light after a complete stop, unless otherwise indicated. In addition, all passengers are required to wear seat belts, and children under 3 must be securely fastened in government-approved car seats.

BY TAXI

If you're not planning on traveling much within the city, an occasional taxi is a good alternative to renting a car. If you plan on spending your vacation within the confines of South Beach's Art Deco District, you might also want to avoid the parking hassles that come with renting your own car. Taxi meters start at $1.50 for the first quarter-mile and 25¢ for each additional one-eighth mile. There are standard flat-rate charges for frequently traveled routes—for example, Miami Beach's Convention Center to Coconut Grove will cost about $16.

Major cab companies include **Metro** (© 305/888-8888), **Yellow** (© 305/444-4444), and, on Miami Beach, **Central** (© 305/532-5555).

BY BIKE

Miami is a biker's paradise, especially on Miami Beach, where the hard-packed sand and boardwalks make it an easy and scenic route. However, unless you are a former New York City bike messenger, you won't want to use a bicycle as your main means of transportation.

For more information on bicycles, including where to rent the best ones, see "More Ways to Play, Indoors & Out" in chapter 6.

 FAST FACTS: Miami

Airport See "Orientation," earlier in this chapter.

American Express You'll find American Express offices in downtown Miami at 100 North Biscayne Blvd. (© 305/358-7350); 9700 Collins Ave., Bal Harbour (© 305/865-5959); and 32 Miracle Mile, Coral Gables (© 305/446-3381). Offices are open weekdays from 9am to 5:30pm and Saturday from 9am to 5pm. To report lost or stolen traveler's checks, call © 800/221-7282.

Area Code The original area code for Miami and all of Dade County was 305. That is still the code for older phone numbers, but all phone numbers assigned since July 1998 have the area code 786 (SUN). For all local calls, even if you're just calling across the street, you must dial the area code (305 or 786) first. Even though the Keys still share the Dade County area code of 305, calls to there from Miami are considered long distance and must be preceded by 1-305.

(Within the Keys, simply dial the seven-digit number.) The area code for Fort Lauderdale is 954; for Palm Beach, Boca Raton, Vero Beach, and Port St. Lucie, it's 561.

Business Hours Offices are usually open weekdays from 9am to 5pm. Banks are open weekdays from 9am to 3pm or later, and sometimes Saturday mornings. Stores, especially those in shopping complexes on South Beach and Coconut Grove, tend to stay open late: until about 9pm on weekdays and as late as 11pm on weekends.

Car Rentals See "Getting Around," earlier in this chapter.

Climate See "When to Go," in chapter 2.

Curfew Although not strictly enforced, there is an alleged curfew in effect for minors after 11pm on weeknights and midnight on weekends in all of Miami–Dade County. After those hours, children under 17 cannot be out on the streets or driving unless accompanied by a parent or on their way to work. Somehow, however, they still manage to sneak out and congregate in popular areas such as Coconut Grove and South Beach.

Dentists A&E Dental, 11400 N. Kendall Dr., Mega Bank Building (© 305/271-7777), offers round-the-clock care and accepts MasterCard and Visa.

Doctors In an emergency, call an ambulance by dialing © 911 from any phone. The Dade County Medical Association sponsors a **Physician Referral Service** (© 305/324-8717), weekdays from 9am to 5pm. **Health South Doctors' Hospital,** 5000 University Dr., Coral Gables (© 305/666-2111), is a 285-bed acute-care hospital with a 24-hour physician-staffed emergency department.

Drinking Laws The legal age for purchase and consumption of alcoholic beverages is 21; proof of age is required and often requested at bars, nightclubs, and restaurants, so it's always a good idea to bring ID when you go out. On South Beach, in particular, the clubs and bars are strict. Beer and wine can often be purchased in supermarkets, but liquor laws vary throughout the state.

Do not carry open containers of alcohol in your car or any public area that isn't zoned for alcohol consumption. The police can, and probably will, fine you on the spot. And nothing will ruin your trip faster than getting a citation for DUI ("driving under the influence"), so don't even think about driving while intoxicated.

Driving Rules See "Getting Around," earlier in this chapter.

Drugstores See "Pharmacies," later in this section.

Emergencies To reach the police, ambulance, or fire department, dial ✆ **911** from any phone. No coins are needed. Emergency hotlines include **Crisis Intervention** (✆ **305-358-HELP** or 305/358-4357) and the **Poison Information Center** (✆ **800/282-3171**).

Eyeglasses **Pearle Vision Center,** 7901 Biscayne Blvd. (✆ **305/754-5144**) can usually fill prescriptions in about an hour.

Hospitals See "Doctors," earlier in this section.

Information See "Visitor Information," earlier in this chapter.

Laundry/Dry Cleaning For dry cleaning, self-service machines, and a wash-and-fold service by the pound, call **All Laundry Service,** 5701 NW 7th St. (✆ **305/261-8175**); it's open daily from 7am to 10pm. **Clean Machine Laundry,** 226 12th St., South Beach (✆ **305/534-9429**), is convenient to South Beach's Art Deco hotels and is open 24 hours a day. **Coral Gables Laundry & Dry Cleaning,** 250 Minorca Ave., Coral Gables (✆ **305/446-6458**), has been dry cleaning, altering, and laundering since 1930. It offers a lifesaving same-day service and is open weekdays from 7am to 7pm and Saturday from 8am to 3pm.

Liquor Laws Only adults 21 or older may legally purchase or consume alcohol in the state of Florida. Minors are usually permitted in bars, as long as they also serve food. Liquor laws are strictly enforced; if you look young, carry identification. Beer and wine are sold in most supermarkets and convenience stores. The city of Miami's liquor stores are closed on Sundays. Liquor stores in the city of Miami Beach are open all week.

Lost Property If you lost something at the airport, call the **Airport Lost and Found** office (✆ **305/876-7377**). If you lost something on the bus, Metrorail, or Metromover, call **Metro-Dade Transit Agency** (✆ **305/770-3131**). If you lost something anywhere else, phone the **Dade County Police Lost and Found** (✆ **305/375-3366**). You may also want to fill out a police report for insurance purposes.

Luggage Storage/Lockers In addition to the baggage check at Miami International Airport, most hotels offer luggage storage facilities. If you are taking a cruise from the Port of Miami, bags can be stored in your ship's departure terminal.

Newspapers/Magazines The *Miami Herald* is the city's only English-language daily. It is especially known for its extensive Latin American coverage and has a decent Friday "Weekend" entertainment guide. The most respected alternative weekly is the give-away tabloid called *New Times,* which contains up-to-date listings and reviews of food, films, theater, music, and whatever else is happening in town. Also free, if you can find it, is *Ocean Drive,* an oversize glossy magazine that's limited on text (no literary value) and heavy on ads and society photos. It's what you should read if you want to know who's who and where to go for fun; it's available at a number of chic South Beach boutiques and restaurants. It is also available on newsstands.

For a large selection of foreign-language newspapers and magazines, check with any of the large bookstores (see chapter 7, "Shopping") or try **News Café** at 800 Ocean Dr., South Beach (© **305/538-6397**), or in Coconut Grove at 2901 Florida Ave. (© **305/774-6397**). Adjacent to the **Van Dyke Cafe,** 846 Lincoln Rd., South Beach (© **305/534-3600**) is a fantastic newsstand with magazines and newspapers from all over the world. Also check out **Eddie's Normandy,** 1096 Normandy Dr., Miami Beach (© **305/866-2026**), and **Worldwide News,** 1629 NE 163rd St., North Miami Beach (© **305/940-4090**).

Pharmacies **Walgreens Pharmacy** has dozens of locations all over town, including 8550 Coral Way (© **305/221-9271**) in Coral Gables; 1845 Alton Rd. (© **305/531-8868**) in South Beach; and 6700 Collins Ave. (© **305/861-6742**) in Miami Beach. The branch at 5731 Bird Rd. at SW 40th St. (© **305/666-0757**) is open 24 hours, as is **Eckerd Drugs,** 1825 Miami Gardens Dr. NE, at 185th Street, North Miami Beach (© **305/932-5740**).

Police For emergencies, dial © **911** from any phone. No coins are needed. For other matters, call © **305/595-6263**.

Post Office The **Main Post Office,** 2200 Milam Dairy Rd., Miami, FL 33152 (© **305/639-4280**), is located west of Miami International Airport. Conveniently located post offices include 1300 Washington Ave. in South Beach and 3191 Grand Ave. in Coconut Grove. There is one central number for all post offices: © **800/275-8777**.

Radio On the AM dial, 610 (WIOD), 790 (WNWS), 1230 (WJNO), and 1340 (WPBR) are all talk. There is no all-news station in town, although 940 (WINZ) gives traffic updates and headline news in between its talk shows. WDBF (1420) is a good big-band station and WPBG (1290) features golden oldies. Switching to the FM dial, the two most popular R&B stations are WEDR/99 Jams (99.1) and Hot 105 (105.1). The best rock stations on the FM dial are WZTA (94.9), WBGG/Big 106 (105.9), and the progressive college station WVUM (90.5). WKIS (99.9) is the top country station. Top-40 music can be heard on WHYI (100.3) and classic disco on Mega 103 (103.5). WGTR (97.3) plays easy listening, WDNA (88.9) has the best Latin jazz and multiethnic sounds, and public radio can be heard either on WXEL (90.7) or WLRN (91.3).

Religious Services Miami houses of worship are as varied as the city's population and include St. Patrick Catholic Church, 3716 Garden Ave., Miami Beach (② 305/531-1124); Coral Gables Baptist Church, 5501 Granada Blvd. (② 305/665-4072); Temple Judea, 5500 Granada Blvd., Coral Gables (② 305/667-5657); Coconut Grove United Methodist, 2850 SW 27th Ave. (② 305/443-0880); Christ Episcopal Church, 3481 Hibiscus St. (② 305/442-8542); Plymouth Congregational Church, 3400 Devon Rd., at Main Highway (② 305/444-6521); Hindu Temple of South Florida, 12511 SW 112th Ave. (② 305/792-2494); Masjid Al-Ansar (Muslim), 5245 NW 7th Ave. (② 305/757-8741); and Buddhist Temple of Miami, 15200 SW 240th St. (② 305/245-2702).

Restrooms Stores rarely let customers use their rest rooms, and many restaurants offer their facilities only for their patrons. However, most malls have bathrooms, as do many fast-food restaurants. Public beaches and large parks often provide toilets, though in some places you have to pay or tip an attendant. Most large hotels have clean rest rooms in their lobbies.

Safety As always, use your common sense and be aware of your surroundings at all times. Don't walk alone at night, and be extra wary when walking or driving though downtown Miami and surrounding areas.

Reacting to several highly publicized crimes against tourists several years ago, both local and state governments have taken steps to help protect visitors. These measures include special highly visible police units patrolling the airport and surrounding neighborhoods and better signs on the state's most tourist-traveled routes.

Spas & Massage There are a number of great spa packages at some of the ritzier hotels, but those without spas often have relationships with on-call massage therapists, which can be arranged by asking the concierge to make an appointment for an in-room session. Popular day spas include the **Russian Turkish Baths**, 5445 Collins Ave. at the Castle Hotel (© 305/867-8316), otherwise known as "The Schvitz," where the old guard meets the new in eucalyptus-scented Turkish steam rooms and aroma baths bolstered by marble columns. **Some Like It Hot,** 841 Lincoln Rd., Miami Beach (© 305/532-8703), has expanded from a small second-floor salon into a full-service, 5,250-square-foot spa, offering massages, waxing, manicures, and a sublime signature hot-rock massage. **Le Spa Miami**, 150 8th St., Miami Beach (© 305/674-6744), is the newest day spa to hit the shores, exclusively using Lancôme products and featuring a laundry list of facials, body treatments, make-up applications, waxing, manicure, pedicures, and even photo shoots.

Taxes A 6% state sales tax (plus 0.5% local tax, for a total of 6.5% in Miami–Dade County [from Homestead to North Miami Beach]) is added on at the register for all goods and services purchased in Florida. In addition, most municipalities levy special taxes on restaurants and hotels. In Surfside, hotel taxes total 10.5%; in Bal Harbour, 9.5%; in Miami Beach (including South Beach), 11.5%; and in the rest of Dade County, a whopping 12.5%. In Miami Beach, Surfside, and Bal Harbour, the resort (hotel) tax also applies to hotel restaurants and restaurants with liquor licenses.

Taxis See "Getting Around," earlier in this chapter.

Television The local stations are Channel 6, WTVJ (NBC); Channel 4, WCIX (CBS); Channel 7, WSVN (Fox); Channel 10, WPLG (ABC); Channel 17, WLRN (PBS); Channel 23, WLTV (independent); and Channel 33, WBFS (independent). Channel 39 is the WB (WBZL) and channel 33 is UPN (WBFS).

Time Zone Miami, like New York, is in the Eastern Standard Time zone. Between April and October, daylight saving time is adopted, and clocks are set 1 hour ahead. America's eastern seaboard is 5 hours behind Greenwich Mean Time. To find out what time it is, call © 305/324-8811.

Transit Information For Metrorail or Metromover schedule information, phone © 305/770-3131 or surf over to **www.co. miami-dade.fl.us/mdta/**.

Weather Hurricane season runs from August through November. For an up-to-date recording of current weather conditions and forecast reports, call © 305/229-4522. Also see the "When to Go" section in chapter 2.

4

Where to Stay

As much a part of the landscape as the palm trees, many of Miami's hotels are on display as if they were contestants in a beauty pageant. The city's long-lasting status on the destination A-list has given rise to an ever-increasing number of upscale hotels, and no place in Miami has seen a greater increase in construction than Miami Beach. Since the area's renaissance, which began in the late 1980s, the beach has turned what used to be a beachfront retirement home into a sand-swept hot spot for the Gucci and Prada set. Contrary to popular belief, however, the beach does not discriminate, and it's the juxtaposition of the chic elite and the hoi polloi that contributes to its allure.

While the increasing demand for rooms on South Beach means increasing costs, you can still find a decent room at a fair price. In fact, most hotels in the Art Deco District are less Ritz-Carlton than they are Holiday Inn, unless, of course, they've been renovated (many hotels in this area were built in the 1930s for the middle class). Unless you plan to center your vacation entirely in and around your hotel, most of the cheaper Deco hotels are adequate and a wise choice for those who plan to use the room only to sleep. Smart vacationers can almost name their price if they're willing to live without a few luxuries, such as an oceanfront view.

Many of the old hotels from the 1930s, 1940s, and 1950s have been totally renovated, giving way to dozens of "boutique" (small, swanky, and independently owned) hotels. Keep in mind that when a hotel claims that it was just renovated, it can mean that they've completely gutted the building—or just applied a coat of fresh paint. Always ask what specific changes were made during a renovation, and be sure to ask if a hotel will be undergoing construction while you're there. You should also find out how near your room will be to the center of the nightlife crowd; trying to sleep directly on Ocean Drive or Collins and Washington avenues, especially during the weekend, is next to impossible, unless your lullaby of choice happens to include throbbing salsa and bass beats.

The best hotel options in each price category and those that have been fully upgraded recently are listed below. You should also know that along South Beach's Collins Avenue, there are dozens of hotels and motels—in all price categories—so there's bound to be a vacancy somewhere. If you do try the walk-in routine, don't forget to ask to see a room first. A few dollars extra could mean all the difference between flea and fabu.

While South Beach may be the nucleus of all things hyped and hip, it's not the only place with hotels. The advantage to staying on South Beach as opposed to, say, Coral Gables or Coconut Grove, is that the beaches are within walking distance, the nightlife and restaurant options are aplenty, and, basically, everything you would need is right there. However, staying there is definitely not for everyone. If you're wary, don't worry: South Beach is centrally located and only about a 15- to 30-minute drive from most other parts of Miami.

For a less expensive stay that's only a 10-minute cab ride from South Beach, Miami Beach proper (the area north of 23rd St. and Collins Ave. all the way up to 163rd St. and Collins Ave.) offers a slew of reasonable stays, right on the beach, that won't cost you your kids' college education fund.

For a less frenetic, more relaxed, and more tropical experience, the resorts on Key Biscayne exude an island feel, even though, if you look across the water, a cosmopolitan vibe beckons, thanks to the shimmering, spectacular Miami skyline.

Those who'd rather bag the beach in favor of shopping bags will enjoy North Miami Beach's proximity to the Aventura Mall as much as tan-o-holics are drawn to the sand on South Beach. And for Miami with an Old World European flair, Coral Gables and its charming hotels and exquisite restaurants provide a more prim and proper, well-heeled perspective of Miami than the trendy boutique hotels on South Beach.

SEASONS & RATES Miami's tourist season is well defined, beginning in mid-November and lasting until Easter. Hotel prices escalate until about March, after which they begin to decline. During the off-season, hotel rates are typically 30% to 50% lower than their winter highs.

But timing isn't everything. In many cases, rates also depend on your hotel's proximity to the beach and how much ocean you can see from your window. Small motels a block or two from the water can be up to 40% cheaper than similar properties right on the sand.

Rates below have been broken down into two broad categories: winter (generally, Thanksgiving through Easter) and off-season (about mid-May–Aug). The months in between, the shoulder season, should fall somewhere in between the highs and lows, while rates always go up on holidays. Remember, too, that state and city taxes can add as much as 12.5% to your bill in some parts of Miami. Some hotels, especially those in South Beach, also tack on additional service charges, and don't forget that parking is a pricey endeavor.

PRICE CATEGORIES   The hotels below are divided first by area and then by price (**very expensive, expensive, moderate,** or **inexpensive**). Prices are based on published rates (or rack rates) for a standard double room during the high season. You should also check with the reservations agent, since many rooms are available above and below the category ranges listed below, and ask about packages, since it's often possible to get a better deal than these "official" rates. Most importantly, always call the hotel to confirm rates, which may be subject to change without notice because of special events, holidays, or blackout dates.

1 South Beach

Choosing a hotel on South Beach is similar to deciding whether you'd rather pay $1.50 for french fries at Denny's or $8.50 for the same fries—but let's call them *pomme frites*—in a pricey haute cuisinerie. It's all about atmosphere. The rooms of some hotels may *look* ultrachic, but they can be as comfortable as sleeping on a concrete slab. Once you decide how much atmosphere you want, the choice will be easier. Fortunately, for every chichi hotel in South Beach—and there are many—there are just as many moderately priced, more casual options.

Prices mentioned here are rack rates—that is, the price you would be quoted if you walked up to the front desk and inquired about rates. The actual price you will end up paying will usually be less than this—especially if a travel agent makes the reservations for you. Many hotels on South Beach have stopped quoting seasonal and off-season rates and have, instead, chosen to go with a low-to-high rate representing the hotel's complete pricing range. It pays to try to negotiate the price of a room. In some of the trendier hotels, however, negotiating is highly unfashionable and not well regarded. In other words, your attempt at negotiation will either be met with a blank stare or a snippy refusal. It never hurts to try, though.

If status is important to you, as it is to many South Beach visitors, then you will be quite pleased with the number of haute hotels in the area, which are as popular as nightclubs and restaurants are on South Beach. Art Deco hotels, while pleasing to the eye, may be

South Beach Accommodations

Abbey Hotel **2**
Albion Hotel **8**
Aqua **10**
Banana Bungalow **1**
Chesterfield **21**
Clay Hotel &
    International Hostel **12**
Crest Hotel Suites **7**
The Delano **6**
The Hotel **24**
Hotel Astor **17**
Hotel Chelsea **18**
Hotel Impala **13**
Hotel Leon **22**
The Kent **16**
Loews Hotel **9**
The Loft Hotel **19**
Marlin **14**
Mercury **27**
Mermaid Guest House **20**
Pelican Hotel **23**
Raleigh Hotel **5**
Royal Hotel **26**
Royal Palm Crown Plaza
    Resort **11**
The Shore Club **3**
The Tides **15**
Townhouse **4**
Whitelaw Hotel **25**

a bit run-down inside. Par for the course on South Beach, appearances are at times deceiving.

VERY EXPENSIVE

The Delano ⊕ *(Overrated)*   Unless your name's Madonna or the equivalent, you will definitely feel like you are paying for the privilege of staying here. The Delano may not be the friendliest place, but it certainly is amusing to look at. The rooms are done up sanitarium style: sterile, yet toxically trendy, in pure white save for a perfectly crisp green Granny Smith apple in each room—the only freebie you're going to get here. A bathroom renovation recently took place in all of the rooms—but they remain small and Spartan.

An attractive, white-clad staff looks as if they were handpicked from last month's *Vogue*. While they may sigh if you ask for something, eventually they'll get it for you. The gym here is great, but is costs $15 a day, even if you are a guest. The fantastic wading pool, thankfully, is free, but get out early to snag a chair. The lobby's Rose Bar is command central for the chic elite who don't flinch at paying in excess of $10 for a martini. The hotel's major saving grace is Agua, the rooftop spa, where, if you can afford it, an hour massage while overlooking the ocean is blissful.

1685 Collins Ave., South Beach, FL 33139. ℂ **800/555-5001** or 305/672-2000. Fax 305/532-0099. 209 units, 1 penthouse. Winter $325–$810 standard; $750–$2,000 suite; $2,000–$3,000 bungalow or 2-bedroom; $2,800–$3,000 penthouse. Off-season $245–$660 standard; $600–$2,000 suite; $940–$3,000 bungalow or 2-bedroom; $2,400–$3,000 penthouse. Additional person $35. AE, DC, DISC, MC, V. Valet parking $20. **Amenities:** 3 restaurants; bar; large outdoor pool; 24-hr. state-of-the-art David Barton gym; extensive watersports equipment; children's programs; concierge; business center; room service; in-room massage; same-day dry-cleaning and laundry services. *In room:* A/C, TV/VCR, CD player, minibar, hair dryer.

Loews Hotel ⊕   The Loews Hotel is one of the largest beach hotels to arrive in South Beach in almost 30 years, consuming an unprecedented 900 feet of oceanfront. This 800-room behemoth is considered an eyesore by many, an architectural triumph by others. Rooms are a bit boxy and bland: nothing to rave about, but are clean and have new carpets and bedspreads to erase signs of early wear and tear from the hotel's heavy traffic.

The best rooms are those that do not face the very congested Collins Avenue, since those tend to be quite noisy. Though Loews attempts to maintain the intimacy of an Art Deco hotel while trying to accommodate business travelers, it is so large that it tends to feel like a convention hall. You're not going to get personal doting service here, but the staff does try, even if it takes them awhile. If you can steer your way through all the name-tagged business people in the lobby, you can escape to the pool (with an undisputedly gorgeous, landscaped entrance that's more Maui than Miami), which is large enough to accommodate families and conventioneers alike. The hotel's Argentine steak house, Gaucho Room, is superb.

1601 Collins Ave., South Beach, FL 33139. *C* **800/23-LOEWS** or 305/604-1601. www.loewshotels.com. 800 units. Winter from $229 double. Off-season from $189 double. AE, DC, DISC, MC, V. Valet parking $19. Pets accepted. **Amenities:** 3 restaurants; 3 bars; coffee bar; sprawling outdoor pool; health club; Jacuzzi; sauna; watersports rentals; concierge; business center; 24-hr. room service; babysitting; dry cleaning. *In room:* A/C, TV, dataport, minibar, coffeemaker, hair dryer.

The Shore Club *G*   Despite the fact that this newly opened, hyper-hip hotel is little more than a concrete canyon, a mod version of the eerily deserted house in *The Shining*, it has been slowly making waves within the jet set and fabulatti thanks to one thing in particular: Florida's first-ever Nobu sushi restaurant and cocktail lounge (a major hit in New York, Las Vegas, Paris, and London). The hotel's other restaurant, Sirena, also makes up for the hotel's somewhat trying-too-hard-to-be-hip lackluster vibe.

The Shore Club also boasts that 80% of its 325 rooms have an ocean view. Contrary to the cold, cavernous lobby, exquisite gardens draw guests toward the beach through courtyards and reflecting pools. Rooms are loaded with state-of-the-art amenities, not to mention 400-thread linen bedding, Mexican sandstone flooring in the bathroom with custom-designed glass, and an enclosed "wet area" with bathtub, shower, and teak bench. (Molton Brown bathroom amenities are worth bringing an extra bag for.) If you can't afford the penthouse or a poolside cabana, consider an Ocean View room, which is stellar in its own right, with its massive, two-nozzled shower-tub combo that's almost better than a day at the beach. If you are wondering whether to choose the always-hip mainstay, the Delano, over this hotel, consider that the Shore Club is hardly as crowded, has little or no scene, and its rooms boast a bit more personality than the Delano's.

1901 Collins Ave., Miami Beach, FL 33139. *C* **877/640-9500** or 305/695-3100. Fax 305/695-3299. www.shoreclubsouthbeach.com. 325 units; 8 cabanas. Winter $525–$775 double; $1,125 suite; $2,500 cabana. Off-season $425–$675 double; $1,025 suite; $1,500 cabana. AE, DC, DISC, V. Valet parking $20. **Amenities:** 3 restaurants; 4 bars; outdoor reflecting pools with poolside dataports; health club with steam room and outdoor equipment; spa; concierge; 24-hr. room service. *In room:* A/C, TV, Intrigue System with digitally downloaded movies and high-speed Internet access, CD player, stereo, fax, minibar.

The Tides ⚘⚘⚘   This 12-story Art Deco masterpiece is reminiscent of a gleaming ocean liner, with porthole windows and lots of stainless steel and frosted glass. Rooms are starkly white but much more luxurious and comfortable than those at the Delano. Also, all rooms are at least twice the size of a typical South Beach hotel room and have a view of the ocean. They feature king beds, spacious closets, large bathrooms, and even a telescope from which to view the vast ocean. The penthouses on the 9th and 10th floors are situated at the highest point on Ocean Drive, allowing for a priceless panoramic view of the ocean, the skyline, and the beach. Although small, the freshwater pool is a welcome plus for those who aren't in the mood to feel the sand between their toes; but it really doesn't fit with the rest of the hotel, lacking in ambience and view (it overlooks an alley). The hotel's restaurant, Twelve Twenty, is an elegant, excellent, and pricey eatery with seating in the lobby. The Terrace is a less expensive outdoor cafe. The Tides is a place where celebrities like Ben Affleck, Jennifer Lopez, and Bono come to stay for some R&R, but you won't find gawkers or paparazzi lurking in the lobby, just an elegant clientele and staff who are respectful of people's privacy and desire for peace and quiet.

1220 Ocean Dr., South Beach, FL 33139. ℭ **800/OUTPOST** or 305/604-5000. Fax 305/672-6288. www.islandoutpost.com. 45 units. Winter $525 suite; $3,000 penthouse. Off-season $375 suite; $2,000 penthouse. Additional person $15. AE, DC, DISC, MC, V. Valet parking $18. **Amenities:** 2 restaurants; lounge; bar; outdoor heated pool; small health club and discount at large nearby health club or yoga studio; concierge; secretarial services; 24-hr. room service; beach lounge service; in-room massage; babysitting; laundry and dry-cleaning service. *In room:* A/C, TV/VCR, stereo/CD player with selection of music, video rentals, minibar, hair dryer, iron, safe.

EXPENSIVE

Albion Hotel ⚘⚘   An architectural masterpiece, originally designed in 1939 by internationally acclaimed architect Igor Polevitzky (of Havana's legendary Hotel Nacional fame), this sleek, modern, nautical-style hotel was once the local headquarters for Abbie Hoffman and the Students for a Democratic Society during the 1972 Democratic National Convention in Miami. Though it was totally renovated under the guidance of the hip hotel family, the Rubells, the hotel still maintains a neo-hippie democratic feeling of peace, love, togetherness—albeit with a hipster twist. Despite its location 2 blocks from the beach, a large portholed pool and artificial beach are enough to keep you at the property and off the real beach. Rooms are industrial chic, and, for some people, not very warm; recent renovations have taken a little of the edge off. The staff is wonderful. Kiss, a pricey, sceney steakhouse/cabaret opened in the hotel in October 2001; for lighter fare, the mezzanine-level Pantry provides snacks and continental breakfast items.

1650 James Ave. (at Lincoln Rd.), South Beach, FL 33139. (✆) **877/RUBELLS** or 305/913-1000. Fax 305/674-0507. www.rubellhotels.com. 94 units. Winter $255–$375 double. Off-season $165–$265 double. AE, DC, DISC, MC, V. Valet parking $17. Pets accepted. **Amenities:** Restaurant; bar; large outdoor heated pool with adjacent artificial sand beach; small exercise room; concierge; airport limo service; business and secretarial services; 24-hr. room service; in-room massage; babysitting; dry cleaning. *In room:* A/C, TV/VCR, stereo with CD and cassette player, dataport, minibar, hair dryer, iron.

The Hotel 🐾🐾🐾 Kitschy fashion designer Todd Oldham whimsically restored this 1939 gem (formerly the Tiffany Hotel) as he would have a vintage piece of couture. He laced it with lush, cool colors, hand-cut mirrors, and glass mosaics from his ready-to-wear factory, then added artisan detailing, terrazzo floors, and porthole windows. The small, soundproof rooms are very comfortable and incredibly stylish, though the bathrooms are a bit cramped. There's no need to pay more for an oceanfront view—go up to the rooftop, where the pool is, to get an amazing view of the Atlantic. The hotel's restaurant, Wish (see p. 89), is one of South Beach's best.

801 Collins Ave., South Beach, FL 33139. (✆) **877/843-4683** or 305/531-2222. Fax 305/531-2222. www.thehotelofsouthbeach.com. 52 units. Winter $275–$405 double. Off-season $215–$355 double. AE, DC, DISC, MC, V. Valet parking $18. **Amenities:** Restaurant; bar; pool bar; small pool; health club; concierge; business center; room service. *In room:* A/C, TV/VCR, stereo system with CD and cassette players, Kiehl's products, video library, dataport, minibar, coffeemaker, hair dryer.

Hotel Astor 🐾🐾🐾 Cozy-chic best describes this diminutive Deco hotel built in 1936. There is a small lap pool and a beautiful waterfall outside the bar area, but if you're looking to catch some sun, you may want to consider walking the 2 blocks to the beach, because there are very few lounge chairs at the pool. The rooms are small but soothing, featuring plush and luxurious details—Belgian linens and towels, funky custom mood lighting with dimmer switches, and incredibly plush mattresses that are difficult to leave. I especially recommend the rooms overlooking the courtyard, for their views and for a bit more serenity than that which is afforded in rooms overlooking the street. Views are probably the worst thing about this hotel, as most rooms face the street or a neighboring seedy hotel.

956 Washington Ave., South Beach, FL 33139. (✆) **800/270-4981** or 305/531-8081. www.hotelastor.com. 40 units. Winter $155–$420 double. Off-season $110–$250 double. Additional person $30. AE, DC, MC, V. Valet parking $20. **Amenities:** Restaurant; 2 bars; small outdoor pool; access to nearby health club; 24-hr. concierge

service; secretarial services; limited room service; in-room massage; babysitting; laundry and dry-cleaning service. *In room:* A/C, TV, dataport, minibar, fridge, hair dryer.

Hotel Impala ✿✿✿ *(Finds)*   This renovated Mediterranean inn is one of the area's best, and it's just beautiful, from the Greco-Roman frescos and friezes to an intimate garden that is perfumed with the scents from carefully hanging lilies and gardenias. Rooms are extremely comfortable, with super-cushy sleigh beds, sisal floors, wrought-iron fixtures, imported Belgian cotton linens, wood furniture, and fabulous roomy bathrooms done up in stainless steel and coral rock. Adjacent to the hotel is Spiga, an intimate, excellent Italian restaurant that is reasonably priced. Enclaves like this one are rare on South Beach.

1228 Collins Ave., South Beach, FL 33139. ✆ **800/646-7252** or 305/673-2021. Fax 305/673-5984. hotelimpala1@aol.com. 17 units. Winter $200–$400 double. Off-season $169–$279 double. AE, DC, MC, V. Valet parking $18. No children under 16 permitted. **Amenities:** Restaurant; concierge; room service. *In room:* A/C, TV/VCR, stereo, CD player, complimentary videos, dataport, hair dryer.

Marlin ✿✿   Don't be surprised if you hear guitar riffs upon entering the Marlin. This rock-and-roll hotel, owned by Chris Blackwell, founder of Island Records, also houses South Beach Studios, a recording and mixing facility, which has been put to use by Aerosmith and U2 among others. And don't be taken aback if you see beautiful models strolling by—the Elite Modeling Agency also calls the Marlin home.

The rooms here sport a sleek, industrial Caribbean decor, with soft earth tones, custom furniture, and hardwood floors; each suite feels like a private bungalow. No two rooms are alike, and each one is distinctive enough that even Martha Stewart approved by staying here. The very hip and whimsical but relaxed Marlin Bar and restaurant attracts a sleek crowd trying to escape the overblown South Beach bar scene and features what only music industry people could describe as Hi Fidelity cuisine. The major drawbacks of this hotel are its location on a busy, highly trafficked corner of Collins Avenue and its lack of a pool. However, the rooftop garden/bar area provides a fantastic view of the beach and the city.

1200 Collins Ave., Miami Beach, FL 33139. ✆ **800/OUTPOST** or 305/672-5254. Fax 305/672-6288. www.islandoutpost.com. 11 units. Winter $325–$395 double. Off-season $195–$275 double. AE, DC, DISC, MC, V. Valet parking $16. **Amenities:** Restaurant; bar; reduced rates at Crunch Fitness and VIP access to local clubs; concierge; secretarial services; room service provided by the Tides (see above); babysitting; laundry service. *In room:* A/C, TV/VCR, CD player, dataport, kitchenette, minibar, fridge, microwave, coffeemaker, hair dryer.

Mercury *(R) (Finds)* This small boutique hotel is located in the fast-rising area known as SoFi, or South of Fifth Street, South Beach's latest recipient of a hipster takeover. The Mercury is an upscale, modern all-suite resort that combines Mediterranean charm with trendy South Beach flair. A member of Design Hotels, a worldwide collection of notable boutique hotels, the Mercury is actually a well-kept secret that's attached to two of the beach's best restaurants, Nemo and Shoji Sushi, both of which also provide the hotel's room service. A small outdoor heated pool and Jacuzzi are located in a courtyard that's shared with both restaurants (yes, diners can see you swim). Accommodations are ultrastylish, with sleek light-wood furnishings, Belgian cotton bedding, European kitchens, and spacious bathrooms with spa tubs. If you're looking to stay in style without the hassle of the South Beach hustle and bustle, this is the place.

100 Collins Ave., Miami Beach, FL 33139. ℂ **877/786-2732** or 305/398-3000. www.mercuryresort.com. 44 units. Seasonal rates $165–$995. AE, DC, DISC, MC, V. Valet parking $18. **Amenities:** 2 restaurants (Pan-Asian and Sushi); heated pool; access to local fitness center (Crunch); full-service spa; Jacuzzi; concierge; room service; in-room massage; laundry service; free airport pickup. *In room:* TV/VCR, entertainment center with CD player and stereo, video and music library, fax, dataport, kitchen, minibar, coffeemaker, hair dryer.

Raleigh Hotel *(R)(R)* Upon entering the lobby of this oceanfront Art Deco hotel, you will feel like you've stepped back into the 1940s. Polished wood, original terrazzo floors, and an intimate martini bar add to the fabulous atmosphere that's favored by fashion photographers and production crews, for whom the hotel's fleur-de-lis pool is the favorite subject. In fact, one look at the pool and you'll expect Esther Williams to dramatically splash up. Should you glance quickly inside the dimly lit lobby restaurant, the constantly changing Tiger Oak Room (last we checked, it was Mediterranean), you could swear Dorothy Parker and her fellow round-tablers took a detour from New York's Algonquin Hotel and landed here. Rooms are tidy and efficient (those overlooking the resplendent pool and ocean are the most peaceful)—nothing too elaborate, but that's not why people stay here. It's the Raleigh's romantic Deco lure that has people skipping over from the chilly, antiseptic Delano a few blocks up for much-needed warmth.

1775 Collins Ave., Miami Beach, FL 33139. ℂ **800/848-1775** or 305/534-6300. Fax 305/538-8140. www.raleighhotel.com. 111 units. Winter $339–$769 double. Off-season $209–$609 double. Rates are cheaper if booked on the hotel's website. AE, DC, DISC, MV, V. Valet parking $20. **Amenities:** Restaurant; bar; coffee bar; large outdoor pool; small open-air fitness center; concierge; business services; room service (24 hr. in winter; limited off-season), massage; overnight laundry service. *In room:* A/C, TV/VCR, CD player, dataport, minibar, fridge, safe.

Royal Palm Crowne Plaza Resort 🦀   This conveniently located 422-room resort stands apart from other area resorts in that it's the nation's first and largest African-American owned and developed beachfront resort. The hotel is massive, too, composed of five buildings located adjacent to Ocean Drive. Three of the five buildings are restored, the two towers are brand new, and, despite the fact that this resort is a small city, it miraculously maintains a sense of intimacy not typical with many large resorts. While the rooms aren't as appealing as the building itself, they are comfortable and modern. The outdoor areas of the hotel are spectacular, with one pool on a mezzanine level and the other beachside. As is to be expected, the hotel is decidedly Deco, albeit with a modern twist.

1545 Collins Ave., Miami Beach, FL 33139. 🕜 **800/2-CROWNE** or 305/604-5700. Fax 305/604-2059. www.sixcontinentshotels.com. 422 units. Winter $189–$599 double. Off-season $159–$559 double. AE, DC, DISC, MC, V. Valet parking $20. Pets under 20 lb. welcome with $50 deposit. **Amenities:** 2 restaurants; lounge; 2 large outdoor pools; state-of-the-art fitness center; concierge; babysitting; business services; room service; overnight laundry service; watersports rental. *In room:* A/C, TV, dataport, minibar, hair dryer, iron, safe.

MODERATE

Abbey Hotel 🦀🦀 *(Finds*   This charming, off-the-beaten-path, '40s-revival boutique hotel is possibly the best deal on the entire beach. A haven for artists looking for quiet inspiration, the Abbey has recently undergone a $2.5 million renovation that restored its original Deco glory. Soft, white-covered chairs and candles grace the lobby, which doubles as a chic Mediterranean-style restaurant, the Abbey Dining Room. Rooms are furnished with oversized earth-toned chairs and chrome beds that are surprisingly comfortable. It's extremely quiet at this hotel, as it is located in the midst of a sleepy residential neighborhood, but it's only 1 block from the beach and within walking distance of the Jackie Gleason Theater, the Convention Center, the Bass Museum of Art, and the Miami City Ballet.

300 21st St., Miami Beach, FL 33139. 🕜 **305/531-0031.** Fax 305/672-1663. www. abbeyhotel.com. 50 units. Winter $165–$210 double; $225 studio. Off-season $80–$165 double; $195 studio. AE, DC, DISC, MC, V. Off-site parking $17. Pets accepted with $500 deposit. **Amenities:** Restaurant; bar; exercise room; concierge; business services; room service; laundry and dry-cleaning service. *In room:* A/C, TV/VCR, dataport, hair dryer, iron. Studios also have stereo with CD player and a safe.

Aqua 🦀 *(Value*   It's been described as the Jetsons meets Jaws, but the Aqua isn't all Hollywood. Animated, yes, but with little emphasis on special effects and more on a friendly staff, Aqua is a good catch for those looking to stay in style without compromising their budget. Rooms are ultra-modern in an Ikea sort of way; in other words, cheap chic. There are apartment-like junior suites, suites, and a really fabulous penthouse, but the standard deluxe rooms aren't too shabby either, with decent-sized bathrooms and high-tech amenities. This '50s-style motel has definitely been spruced up and its sundeck, courtyard garden, and small pool are popular hangouts for those who prefer to stay off the nearby sand. A small yet sleek lounge inside is a good place for a quick cocktail, breakfast, or a snack.

1530 Collins Ave., Miami Beach, FL 33139. ✆ 305/538-4361. www.aqua miami.com. 50 units. Winter $125–$395. Off-season $95–$295. Rates include European-style breakfast buffet. AE, DC, DISC, MC, V. Valet parking $18. **Amenities:** Cafe; bar; small pool; sundeck. *In room:* A/C, TV, CD player, minibar, Web TV.

Chesterfield Hotel 🕸🕸   The Chesterfield Hotel is an oft-over-looked kitschy place, located in the heart of South Beach's Deco District, just a skip away from all the restaurants on Ocean Drive or the nightclubs on Washington Avenue. A recent renovation to the 50 rooms added a luxe touch, with Frette linens and robes, down feather pillows, Judith Jackson spa amenities, and wood, chrome, and glass accents. Bathrooms are industrial, with free-floating show-ers with rainmaker showerheads, concrete sinks on aluminum stands, and mirrored walls. A new full-service spa features yoga and Pilates. The hotel's Safari Bar/Café is now a full-service restaurant and caters to both a European and an alternative crowd and turns into a spot for a quaint Euro continental breakfast in the morning. There's also a happy hour each evening from 4 to 8pm, with two-for-one cocktails. The hotel's proximity to area clubs and modeling agencies, and its ability to create its own eclectic nightlife, make the Chesterfield an award-worthy locale for people-watching.

855 Collins Ave., South Beach, FL 33139. ✆ 800/244-6023 or 305/531-5831. Fax 305/672-4900. www.southbeachgroup.com. Winter $175–$250 double. Off-season $135–$175 double. Rates include complimentary continental breakfast and compli-mentary cocktails from 8–9pm nightly. AE, MC, DC, V. Valet parking $18. **Amenities:** Restaurant; bar; full-service spa; in-room massage; rooftop sundeck; concierge; access to VIP lists at area clubs; free airport transportation; dry-cleaning services; free Internet connection. *In room:* A/C, TV, CD player, fax, minibar, coffeemaker, hair dryer, iron, safe.

Crest Hotel Suites 🕸🕸 *(Finds*   One of South Beach's best-kept secrets, the Crest Hotel is located next to the pricier, trendier Albion Hotel, in the heart of the Art Deco Historic District near all the major attractions, and features a quietly fashionable, contemporary, relaxed atmosphere with fantastic service. Built in 1939, the Crest was restored to preserve its Art Deco architecture, but the interior of the hotel is thoroughly modern, with rooms resembling cosmopolitan apartments. All suites have a living room/dining room area, kitchenette, and executive workspace. An indoor/outdoor cafe with terrace and poolside dining isn't besieged with trendy locals, but does attract a younger crowd.

1670 James Ave., Miami Beach, FL 33139. ✆ **800/531-3880** or 305/531-0321. Fax 305/531-8180. www.cresthotel.com. Winter $155–$235 double. Off-season $115–$175 double. Packages available and 10% discount offered if booked on website. AE, MC, V. **Amenities:** Restaurant; cafe; pool; laundry and dry-cleaning service. *In room:* A/C, TV, dataport, kitchenette, fridge, coffeemaker.

Hotel Chelsea ★★   This recently restored Art Deco property is a boutique hotel with a bit of a twist, with accents and decor based on the Chinese art of Feng Shui. Soft amber lighting, bamboo floors, full-slate bathrooms, and Japanese-style furniture arranged in a way that's meant to refresh and relax you are what separate the Chelsea from just about any other so-called boutique hotel on South Beach. Complimentary breakfast, beach yoga classes, free sake at happy hour, and, in case you've had enough relaxation, free passes to South Beach's hottest nightclubs are added bonuses.

944 Washington Ave. (at 9th St.), Miami Beach, FL 33139. ✆ **305/534-4069.** Fax 305/672-6712. www.thehotelchelsea.com. 42 units. $95–$225 double. Rates include complimentary continental breakfast and complimentary cocktails 8–9pm daily. AE, MC, DC, V. Valet parking $18. **Amenities:** Bar; concierge; access to local gym; full-service spa; beach yoga; in-room massage; laundry services; free pickup from the airport. *In room:* A/C, TV, CD player, dataport, hair dryer, iron, minibar, safe.

Hotel Leon ★★ *Finds*   A fabulous hotel without the fabulous attitude, the Hotel Leon is like a reasonably priced high-fashion garment found hidden on a rack full of overpriced threads. This charismatic sliver of a property has won the loyalty of fashion industrialists and romantics alike. Built in 1929 and restored in 1996, the hotel still retains many original details such as facades, woodwork, and even fireplaces (every room has one, not that you'll need to use it). The very central location 1 block from the ocean is a plus, especially since the Leon lacks a pool. Most of the spacious and stylish rooms are immaculate and reminiscent of a loft apartment; spacious bathrooms with large, deep tubs are especially enticing.

Wood floors and simple pale furnishings are appreciated in a neighborhood where many others overdo the Art Deco motif. However, some rooms are dark and have not seen such upgrades (we have gotten complaints) and are to be avoided; do not hesitate to ask to change rooms. Service is warm, friendly, and accommodating. The lobby has an informal bar and restaurant, not to mention a large communal table at which guests tend to mix and mingle. Because its entrance is not directly on pedestrian-heavy Collins Avenue, the Hotel Leon remains one of South Beach's best-kept secrets.

841 Collins Ave., South Beach, FL 33139. ℃ **305/673-3767**. www.hotelleon.com. 18 units. Winter $145–$245 suite; $395 penthouse. Off-season $100–$195 suite; $335 penthouse. Additional person $10. AE, DC, MC, V. Valet parking $18. "Well-behaved" pets accepted for $20 per night. **Amenities:** Restaurant; lobby bar; reduced rates at local gym; concierge; business services; room service (breakfast); massage; babysitting; laundry and dry-cleaning service. *In room:* A/C, TV, CD player, hair dryer.

The Kent 🟠🟠 *Value*   This is an excellent value, right in South Beach's active center. All rooms were recently made over and feature wood floors and ultra modern steel furnishings and accessories, which surprisingly aren't cold, but rather inviting and whimsical. The staff is eager to please. Frequent photo shoots are coordinated in the lobby and conference room, where full office services are available. Thanks to a vacant lot in the backyard (for now), some rooms in the rear offer nice views of the ocean. The decor is high on the kitsch factor, heavy on multicolored Lucite with toys and other assorted articles of whimsy, and even if you can't afford to stay in it, the very James Bond-esque Lucite Suite is a must-see. There's no pool or sundeck, but you're only 1 block from the beach.

1131 Collins Ave., South Beach, FL 33139. ℃ **800/OUTPOST** or 305/604-5000. Fax 305/531-0720. www.islandlife.com. 54 units. Winter $145–$250 suite. Off-season $125–$250 suite. Additional person $15. Rates include continental breakfast bar. AE, DC, DISC, MC, V. Valet parking $16; self-parking $6. **Amenities:** Access to concierge at the Tides and massage service at the Marlin (see listings earlier in this chapter). *In room:* A/C, TV/VCR, CD player, minibar, hairdryer, iron, safe.

Mermaid Guesthouse 🟠🟠   There's something magical about this little hideaway tucked behind tropical gardens in the very heart of South Beach and less than 2 blocks from the ocean. You won't find the amenities of the larger hotels here, but the charm and hospitality at this one-story guesthouse keep people coming back. The owners did a thorough cleanup, adding new brightly colored fretwork around the doors and windows and installing phones in each room. Also, the wood floors have been stripped or covered in straw matting, one of the many Caribbean touches that make this place so cheery. Rooms have four-poster beds with mosquito nets. There are no TVs, so guests tend to congregate in the lush garden in the evenings. The owners sometimes host free impromptu dinners for their guests and friends. Ask if they've scheduled any live Latin music during your stay; you won't want to miss it. What you also don't want to miss is a preview of your room before you put down a deposit, as some rooms tend not to be as tidy as the quaint garden.

909 Collins Ave., Miami Beach, FL 33140. ✆ **305/538-5324.** Fax 305/538-2822. 8 units. Winter $115–$280 single or double. Off-season $95–$215 single or double. Additional person $10. Discounts available for longer stays. AE, MC, V. **Amenities:** Bar. *In room:* A/C, TV upon request, radio.

Pelican Hotel 🐦🐦   Owned by the same creative folks behind the Diesel Jeans company, the Pelican is South Beach's only self-professed "toy-hotel," in which each of its 30 rooms and suites is decorated as outrageously as some of the area's more colorful drag queens. Each room has been designed daringly and rather wittily by Swedish interior decorator Magnus Ehrland, whose countless trips to antiques markets, combined with his wild imagination, have turned Room 309, for instance, into the "Psychedelic(ate) Girl," Room 201 into the "Executive Fifties" suite, and Room 313 into the "Jesus Christ Megastar" room. But the most popular room is the tough-to-score Room 215, or the "Best Whorehouse." As South Beach is known for poseurs of all types, this hotel fits right in.

826 Ocean Dr., Miami Beach, FL 33139. ✆ **800/7-PELICAN** or 305/673-3373. Fax 305/673-3255. www.pelicanhotel.com. Winter $170–$220 double; $240 oceanfront suite. Off-season $135–$155 double; $225 oceanfront suite. AE, DC, MC, V. Valet parking $16. **Amenities:** Restaurant; bar; access to area gyms; concierge; business services; same-day laundry and dry cleaning. *In room:* A/C, TV/VCR, stereo/CD player, dataport, fridge, hair dryer, iron, safe.

Royal Hotel 🐦🐦 *(Finds)*   There are several words to describe this mod, hipster hotel located in the heart of South Beach. Jetsonian, funkadelic, and, as the hotel proudly and aptly declares, "Barbarella at bedtime." What it really is, however, is truly different, in that the rooms' curvy, white plastic beds (less comfortable than chic) have headboards that double as bars. Designer Jordan Mozer of Barneys New York fame has managed to transform this historic Art Deco hotel into a trippy, 21st-century, state-of-the-art facility. Chaise longues have attached computer and television. Italian marble, pastel colors, and large, newly tiled bathrooms manage to successfully thwart a sterility that's all too common with many chic boutique hotels.

758 Washington Ave., Miami Beach, FL 33139. ✆ **888/394-6835** or 305/673-9009. Fax 305/673-9244. www.royalhotelsouthbeach.com. Winter $130–$240 double. Off-season $120–$230 double. AE, DC, MC, V. Valet parking $20. **Amenities:** Bar; small swimming pool; rooftop sundeck; concierge. *In room:* A/C, TV/VCR, stereo/CD player, dataport, fridge, hair dryer, iron, safe.

Townhouse ★★ New York hipster Jonathan Morr felt that Miami Beach had lost touch with the bon vivants who gave the city its original cache, so he decided to take matters into his own hands. His solution: this 67-room, five-story, not-exorbitantly-priced hotel. The charm of this hotel is found in its clean and simple yet chic design with quirky details: exercise equipment that stands alone in the hallways, free laundry machines in the lobby, a water-bed-lined rooftop. Comfortable, shabby-chic rooms boast L-shaped couches for extra guests (for whom you aren't charged). Though the rooms are all pretty much the same, consider the ones with the partial ocean view. The hotel's basement features the hot New York import, Bond St. Lounge.

150 20th St., South Beach, FL 33139. ✆ **877/534-3800** or 305/534-3800. Fax 305/534-3811. www.townhousehotel.com. Winter $195–$225 double; $395 penthouse. Off-season $125–$155 double; $395 penthouse. Rates include Parisian-style breakfast. AE, MC, V. Valet parking $18. **Amenities:** Restaurant; bar; workout stations; bike rental; free laundry; rooftop terrace with water beds. *In room:* A/C, TV/VCR, CD player, dataport, fridge, hair dryer, safe.

Whitelaw Hotel ★★ With a slogan that reads "clean sheets, hot water, and stiff drinks," the Whitelaw Hotel stands apart from the other boutique hotels with a fierce sense of humor, but never compromises on its fabulous amenities. Only half a block from Ocean Drive, this hotel, like its clientele, is full of distinct personalities, pairing such disparate elements as luxurious Belgian sheets with shag carpeting to create a completely innovative setting. All-white rooms manage to be homey and plush and not at all antiseptic. Bathrooms are large and well stocked with just about everything. Complimentary cocktails in the lobby every night from 8 to 10pm contribute to a very social atmosphere.

808 Collins Ave., Miami Beach, FL 33139. ✆ **305/398-7000.** www.whitelawhotel.com. Winter $175 double; $195 suite. Off-season $125 double; $145 suite. Rates include complimentary continental breakfast and free cocktails in the lobby 8–10pm every night. AE, MC, DC, V. Parking $18. **Amenities:** Lounge; concierge; business services; laundry service; free airport pickup; complimentary passes to area nightclubs. *In room:* A/C, TV, CD player, dataport, minibar, hair dryer, safe.

INEXPENSIVE

Banana Bungalow This hostel-like hotel is cheap, campy, and quintessentially Miami Beach. Popular with the MTV set, this is a redone 1950s two-story motel where it's always Spring Break. The hotel surrounds a pool and deck complete with shuffleboard, a small alfresco cafe serving cheap meals, and a tiki bar where young European travelers hang out. The best rooms face a narrow canal where motorboats and kayaks are available for a small charge. In general, rooms are clean and well kept, despite a few rusty faucets and chipped Formica furnishings. Guests in shared rooms need to bring their own towels. This is one of the only hotels in this price range with a private pool.

2360 Collins Ave., Miami Beach, FL 33139. © **800/746-7835** or 305/538-1951. Fax 305/531-3217. www.bananabungalow.com. 90 units. Winter $18–$20 per person in shared units; $95–$104 double. Off-season $16–$18 per person in shared units; $50–$60 double. MC, V. Free parking. **Amenities:** Cafe; bar; large pool; access to nearby health club; game room; theater; coin-op laundry. *In room:* A/C, TV, fridge.

Clay Hotel & International Hostel

A member of the International Youth Hostel Federation (IYHF), the Clay occupies a beautiful 1920s-style Spanish Mediterranean building at the corner of historic Española Way. Like other IYHF members, this hostel is open to all ages and is a great place to meet people. The usual smattering of Australians, Europeans, and other budget travelers makes it Miami's best clearinghouse of "insider" travel information. Even if you don't stay here, you might want to check out the ride board or mingle with fellow travelers over a beer at the sidewalk cafe.

Although a thorough renovation in 1996 made this hostel an incredible value and a step above any others in town, don't expect nightly turndown service or chocolates. But, for a hostel, it's full of extras. Ninety rooms have private bathrooms and 12 VIP rooms have balconies overlooking quaint Española Way. You will find occasional movie nights, an outdoor weekend market, and a tour desk with car rental available. Reservations for private rooms are essential in season and recommended year-round.

1438 Washington Ave. (at Española Way), South Beach, FL 33139. © **800/379-2529** or 305/534-2988. Fax 305/673-0346. www.theclayhotel.com. 350 units. $45–75 double; $15–$17 dorm beds. During the off-season, pay for 6 nights in advance and get 7th night free. MC, V. Parking $10. **Amenities:** Cafe; access to nearby health club; bike rental; concierge; computer center; coin-op washers and dryers; lockers; kitchen. *In room:* A/C, TV, dataport, fridge, hair dryer.

The Loft Hotel

A boutique hotel along the lines of the Aqua Hotel (though less whimsical, enticing, and airy-feeling), this renovated apartment building (which really gives you the feeling of staying in an apartment rather than a hotel) offers 20 suites, all surrounding a tidy, tropically landscaped garden. Rooms are especially spacious, with queen-size beds, breakfast room, conversation area, and hardwood or tile floors. Bathrooms are brand new and, for an old Art Deco building, pretty spacious. This hotel is popular with young, hip European types, just as the Aqua Hotel is, but there isn't that much difference between the two hotels other than the fact that the Loft's rooms have fully equipped kitchens while Aqua's rooms don't, and Aqua has a bar/restaurant while the Loft does not. Prices at the Loft are very reasonable and the owners are extremely accommodating.

952 Collins Ave., Miami Beach, FL 33139. ℂ 305/534-2244. Fax 305/538-1509. 57 units. Winter $149–$179 double. Off-season $89–$129 double. AE, DC, MC, V. Valet parking $20. **Amenities:** On-site laundry; VIP passes to local nightclubs. *In room:* A/C, TV/VCR, kitchen, hair dryer.

2 Miami Beach: Surfside, Bal Harbour & Sunny Isles

The area just north of South Beach, known as Miami Beach, encompasses Surfside, Bal Harbour, and Sunny Isles. Unrestricted by zoning codes throughout the 1950s, 1960s, and especially the 1970s, area developers went crazy, building ever-bigger and more brazen structures, especially north of 41st Street, which is now known as Condo Canyon. Consequently, there's now a glut of medium-quality condos, with a few scattered holdouts of older hotels and motels casting shadows over the beach by afternoon.

The western section of the neighborhood used to be inundated with Brooklyn's elderly Jewish population during the season. Though the area still maintains a religious preference, visiting tourists from Argentina to Germany, replete with Speedos and thong bikinis, are clearly taking over.

Miami Beach, as described here, runs from 24th Street to 192nd Street, a long strip that varies slightly from end to end. Staying in the southern section, from 24th to 42nd streets, can be a good deal—it's still close to the South Beach scene, but the rates are more affordable. The North Beach area begins at 63rd Street and extends north to the city limit at 87th Terrace and west to Biscayne Bay (at Bay Drive West). Bal Harbour and Bay Harbor are at the center of Miami Beach and retain their exclusivity and character. The neighborhoods north and south of here, like Surfside and Sunny Isles, have nice beaches and some shops, but are a little worn around the edges.

VERY EXPENSIVE

Beach House Bal Harbour 🌟🌟🌟 *(Finds*   The Beach House Bal Harbour is the closest thing the city has to a summer beach home— comfortable, unpretentious, and luxurious, yet decidedly low-key. In place of an elaborate hotel lobby, the public spaces of the Rubell-owned Beach House are divided into a series of intimate homey environments, from the wicker-furnished screened-in porch to the Asian-inspired Bamboo Room.

The ultraspacious rooms (those ending in 04 are the most spacious) are literally brimming with the comforts of home. The Atlantic Restaurant offers a little of Nantucket in Miami from Sheila Lukins, author of the best-selling Silver Palate cookbooks, who creates some delicious feasts (such as buttermilk fried chicken with Austin baked beans and homemade cornbread). The 200-foot private beach, hammock grove, and topiary garden are so lush, they're said to have caused several New York hipsters to renege on their summer shares in the Hamptons in favor of the Beach House.

9449 Collins Ave., Surfside, FL 33154. ⓒ **877/RUBELLS** or 305/535-8606. Fax 305/535-8602. www.rubellhotels.com. 170 units. Winter $215–$315 double; $245–$305 junior suite. Off-season $180–$210 double; $230–$270 junior suite. Year-round $800 1-bedroom suite. AE, DC, DISC, MC, V. Valet parking $15. **Amenities:** Restaurant; 24-hr. pantry bar; heated pool; health club and spa; watersports equipment; children's playground; business center. *In room:* A/C, TV, stereo/CD player, dataport, fridge, hair dryer, iron, wireless TV Web access.

Eden Roc Renaissance Resort and Spa ⓕⓕ   Just next door to the mammoth Fontainebleau Hilton, this large Morris Lapidus–designed flamboyant hotel, which opened in 1956, seems almost intimate by comparison. The hotel completed a top-to-bottom $24 million renovation in late 1999 and an $11 million renovation of the beachfront in 2001. The nautical Deco decor is a bit gaudy, but nonetheless reminiscent of Miami Beach's Rat-Packed glory days of the '50s. The 55,000-square-foot modern Spa of Eden has excellent facilities and exercise classes, including yoga. The big, open, and airy lobby is often full of name-tagged conventioneers and tourists looking for a taste of Miami Beach kitsch. The rooms, uniformly outfitted with purple- and aquatic-colored interiors and retouched 1930s furnishings, are unusually spacious, and the bathrooms boast Italian marble baths. Because of the hotel's size, you should be able to negotiate a good rate unless there's a big event going on. Harry's Grille specializes in seafood and steaks. From Jimmy Johnson's, the poolside sports bar, patrons can watch swimmers through an underwater "porthole" window.

4525 Collins Ave., Miami Beach, FL 33140. ⓒ **800/327-8337** or 305/531-0000. Fax 305/674-5568. www.edenrocresort.com. 349 units. Winter $299–$359 double; $369 suite; $2,500 penthouse. Off-season $159–$224 double; $310 suite; $1,500 penthouse. Additional person $15. Packages available. AE, DC, DISC, MC, V. Valet parking $20–$25. Pets under 20 lb. accepted for a $75 fee. **Amenities:** 2 restaurants; lounge; bar; 2 outdoor pools; squash courts; racquetball courts; basketball courts; rock-climbing arena; health club and spa; watersports equipment; concierge; tour desk; car-rental desk; business center; salon; limited room service; in-room massage; babysitting; laundry and dry-cleaning service. *In room:* A/C, TV, VCRs for rent, dataport, kitchenettes in suites and penthouse, minibar, hair dryer.

Miami Beach, Surfside, Bal Harbour & Sunny Isles
Accommodations & Dining

ACCOMMODATIONS ■

Baymar Ocean Resort **3**
Beach House Bal Harbour **3**
Eden Roc Renaissance
　Resort and Spa **8**
Fontainebleau Hilton **9**
Indian Creek Hotel **12**
The Palms South Beach **11**

DINING ◆

Atlantic Restaurant **3**
Cafe Prima Pasta **6**
Curry's **5**
The Forge Restaurant **10**
Lemon Twist **4**
Sheldon's Drugs **2**
Shula's Steak House **7**
Wolfie Cohen's Rascal House **1**

Fontainebleau Hilton 🐸🐸 *Overrated* *Kids*   In many ways, this is the quintessential Miami Beach hotel. Also designed by Morris Lapidus, who oversaw an expansion in 2000, this grand monolith symbolizes Miami decadence. Since its opening in 1954, the Fontainebleau has hosted presidents, pageants, and movie productions, including the James Bond thriller *Goldfinger.* This is where all the greats, including Sinatra and his pals, performed in their prime. Club Tropigala is reminiscent of Ricky Ricardo's Tropicana and features a Las Vegas–style floor show with dozens of performers and two orchestras. Rooms are luxurious and decorated in various styles from 1950s to ultramodern; bathrooms are done up in Italian marble. In 2001, the hotel underwent a $10 million food and beverage renovation, introducing the massive, cruise-ship-esque 150-seat Bleu View Mediterranean restaurant and cocktail lounge. Adding to the Fontainebleau's opulence is the 7,000-square-foot Cookie's World water park; the water slide and river-raft ride bring a bit of Disney to Deco-land, which, along with supervised children's activities, is catered toward (though not reserved for) the little ones.

4441 Collins Ave., Miami Beach, FL 33140. ⓒ **800/HILTONS** or 305/538-2000. Fax 305/674-4607. www.fontainebleau.hilton.com. 1,206 units. Winter $289–$459 double. Off-season $209–$329 double. Year-round $525–$1300 suite. Additional person $30. Packages available. AE, DC, DISC, MC, V. Overnight valet parking $13. Pets accepted at no extra cost. **Amenities:** 7 restaurants (including 2 by the pool); 5 cocktail lounges; 2 large outdoor pools; 7 lighted tennis courts; state-of-the-art health club; 3 whirlpool baths; watersports rentals; children's programs; game rooms; concierge; tour desk; car-rental desk; business center; shopping arcade; salon; room service; in-room massage; babysitting; laundry and dry-cleaning service. *In room:* A/C, TV, fax, dataport, minibar, coffeemaker, hair dryer, iron, safe.

EXPENSIVE

The Palms South Beach 🐸   A $5 million renovation has transformed this formerly shabby, uninspired oceanfront tourist trap into an antebellum tropical oasis in which Art Deco meets *Gone With the Wind.* Lush tropical landscaping, both indoors and out, is a welcome respite from the hustle and bustle on congested Collins Avenue. Rooms have been spruced up beautifully, bordering on boutiquey, with high-tech amenities. A huge outdoor area is landscaped with palms and hibiscus and has a large freshwater pool as its centerpiece. It faces a popular boardwalk for runners and strollers as well as a large beach where watersports equipment is available. To sway you from leaving the premises, the Palms has an excellent beach service, in which umbrellas, towels, lounges, and, of course, that tropical drink with a paper umbrella are just a short order away. *Note:* This hotel is not in South Beach, as the name would have you believe. However, it is in the heart of Miami Beach and only a short ride to South Beach.

3025 Collins Ave., Miami Beach, FL 33140. ✆ **800/550-0505** or 305/534-0505. www.thepalmshotel.com. 243 units. Winter $245–$295 double; $365–$700 suite. Off-season $220–$265 double; $325–$650 suite. AE, DC, MC, V. Valet parking $8. **Amenities:** Restaurant; garden cafe; poolside bar; lounge; outdoor freshwater pool; bike rental; game room; concierge; tour desk; car-rental desk; salon; room service; babysitting; coin-op washers and dryers; laundry and dry-cleaning services. *In room:* A/C, TV, CD player, dataport, minibar, coffeemaker, hair dryer, iron, safe.

MODERATE

Baymar Ocean Resort *(Value)*   Depending on what you're looking for, this could be one of the beach's best buys. It's just south of Bal Harbour, in sleepy Surfside, right on the ocean, with a low-key beach that attracts few other tourists. In 2001, efficiencies were transformed into junior suites and all carpets were removed and replaced with terra-cotta tile. The location is close enough to walk to tennis courts and some shopping and dining; it's just a few minutes' drive to larger attractions. It may not be worth it to pay for the oceanfront rooms, since they tend to be smaller than the others. Rooms overlooking the large pool and sundeck area can get loud on busy days. The first-floor oceanview rooms have a nice shared balcony space.

9401 Collins Ave., Miami Beach, FL 33154. ✆ **800/8-BAYMAR** or 305/866-5446. 96 units. Winter $115–$125 double; $125–$235 suite. Off-season $75–$95 double; $95–$185 suite. Additional person $10. AE, DC, DISC, MC, V. Parking $5. **Amenities:** Restaurant; lounge; Tiki bar; Olympic-size pool. *In room:* A/C, TV, kitchen.

Indian Creek Hotel *(★★ Finds)*   Located off the beaten path, this is a meticulously restored 1936 building featuring one of the beach's first operating elevators. It's also the most charming hotel in the area, with impeccable service, too. Because of its location facing the Indian Creek waterway and its lush landscaping, this place feels more like an old-fashioned Key West bed-and-breakfast than your typical Miami Beach Art Deco hotel. The rooms are outfitted in Art Deco furnishings, such as an antique writing desk, pretty tropical prints, and small but spotless bathrooms. All the rooms have been completely renovated. Just 1 short block from a good stretch of sand, the hotel is also within walking distance of shops and restaurants and has a landscaped pool area that is a great place to lounge in the sun. If you're looking for charm, friendly service, and peace and quiet, stay away from the South Beach hype and come here instead.

2727 Indian Creek Dr. (1 block west of Collins Ave. and the Ocean), Miami Beach, FL 33140. ✆ **800/491-2772** or 305/531-2727. Fax 305/531-5651. www.indian creekhotel.com. 61 units. Winter $140–$240 double. Off-season $90–$150 double.

Additional person $10. Group packages and summer specials available. AE, DC, DISC, MC, V. **Amenities:** Restaurant; bar; pool; concierge; car-rental desk; limited room service; laundry and dry-cleaning service. *In room:* A/C, TV/VCR, CD player, dataport, fridge in suites, hair dryer.

3 Key Biscayne

Locals call it the Key, and, technically, Key Biscayne is the northernmost island in the Florida Keys even though it is located in Miami. A relatively unknown area until an impeached Richard Nixon bought a home here in the '70s, Key Biscayne, at 1.25 square miles, is an affluent but hardly lively residential and recreational island known for its pricey homes, excellent beaches, and actor Andy Garcia, who makes his home here. The island is far enough from the mainland to make it feel semiprivate, yet close enough to downtown for guests to take advantage of everything Miami has to offer.

VERY EXPENSIVE

Ritz-Carlton Key Biscayne ★★★ *Kids*   Described by some as an oceanfront mansion, the Ritz-Carlton takes Key Biscayne to the height of luxury with 44 acres of tropical gardens, a 20,000-square-foot European-style spa, and a world-class tennis center under the direction of tennis pro Cliff Drysdale. Decorated in British-colonial style, the Ritz-Carlton looks as if it came straight out of Bermuda, with its impressive flower-laden landscaping. The Ritz Kids programs provide children ages 5 to 12 with fantastic activities, and the 1,200-foot beachfront offers everything from pure relaxation to fishing, boating, or windsurfing. Spacious and luxuriously appointed rooms are elegantly Floridian, featuring large balconies overlooking the ocean or the lush gardens. Unlike many behemoth hotels, the Ritz-Carlton is as much a part of the aesthetic value of the island as is its natural beauty, and its oceanfront Mediterranean-style restaurant, Aria, is exquisite. The best spa in Miami is also here, with 20,000 square feet of space that overlook the Atlantic Ocean and unheard-of-elsewhere treatments.

415 Grand Bay Dr., Key Biscayne, FL 33149. ⓒ **800/241-3333** or 305/365-4500. Fax 305/365-4509. www.ritzcarlton.com. 402 units. Winter $440–$690 suite. Off-season $215–$405 suite. AE, DC, DISC, MC, V. Valet parking $23.43 per day. **Amenities:** Restaurant; pool grill; spa cafe; 3 bars; 2 outdoor heated pools; tennis center w/lessons available; health club and spa; watersports equipment; children's programs; 24-hr. room service; overnight laundry service. *In room:* A/C, TV, dataport, minibar, hair dryer, safe.

Sonesta Beach Resort Key Biscayne ★★ *Kids*   The Sonesta is an idyllic, secluded resort on Key Biscayne—like a souped-up summer

Key Biscayne, Downtown, Little Havana, Coral Gables, Coconut Grove & West Miami/Airport Area

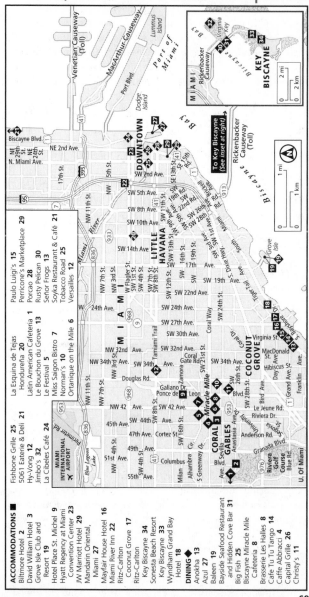

ACCOMMODATIONS ■

Biltmore Hotel **2**
David William Hotel **3**
Grove Isle Club and Resort **19**
Hotel Place St. Michel **9**
Hyatt Regency at Miami Convention Center **23**
JW Marriott Hotel **29**
Mandarin Oriental, Miami **27**
Mayfair House Hotel **16**
Miami River Inn **22**
Ritz-Carlton Coconut Grove **17**
Ritz-Carlton Key Biscayne **34**
Sonesta Beach Resort Key Biscayne **33**
Wyndham Grand Bay Hotel **18**

DINING ◆

Anokha **13**
Azul **27**
Baleen **19**
Bayside Seafood Restaurant and Hidden Cove Bar **31**
Big Fish **25**
Biscayne Miracle Mile Cafeteria **8**
Brasserie Les Halles **8**
Cafe Tu Tu Tango **14**
Caffe Abbracci **4**
Capital Grille **26**
Christy's **11**

Fishbone Grille **25**
5061 Eaterie & Deli **21**
Hy-Vong **12**
Jimbo's **32**
La Cibeles Café **24**

La Esquina de Tejas **15**
Hondureña **20**
Latin American Cafeteria **1**
Le Bouchon du Grove **13**
Le Festival **5**
Miss Saigon Bistro **7**
Norman's **10**
Ortanique on the Mile **6**

Paulo Luigi's **15**
Perricone's Marketplace **29**
Porcao **28**
Rusty Pelican **30**
Señor Frogs **13**
Soyka Restaurant & Café **21**
Tobacco Road **25**
Versailles **12**

camp. Families and couples alike love this place for its oceanfront location and its many high-caliber amenities, which make it unlikely you'll want to venture off the property. Each of the plush 292 rooms, recently upgraded, has a private balcony or terrace. Room 828 is particularly appealing, with its sweeping views of the ocean, comfortable (to say the least) king-size bed, and top-floor location.

Known for having the best piña coladas in the entire city, the pool and beach bars are popular with locals and vacationers alike. The hotel's Two Dragons restaurant is good, featuring Chinese, Thai, and Japanese food. A fantastic, free, and fully supervised kids' program (ages 3–12) will actually allow parents to have a vacation of their own. Although you may not want to leave the lush grounds, Bill Baggs State Recreation Area and the area's best beaches are nearby and worth the trip. Travelers here are only about 15 minutes from Miami Beach and even closer to the mainland and Coconut Grove.

350 Ocean Dr., Key Biscayne, FL 33149. ⓒ **800/SONESTA** or 305/361-2021. Fax 305/361-3096. www.sonesta.com. 292 units. Winter $295–$465 double; $875–$1,475 suite. Off-season $195–$285 double; $650–$1,000 suite. 15% gratuity added to food and beverage bills. Special packages available. AE, DC, DISC, MC, V. Valet parking $12. **Amenities:** 4 restaurants; 2 bars; lounge; outdoor heated Olympic-size pool; access to nearby golf; 7 tennis courts; fitness center; full-service spa; 2 waterfront Jacuzzis; extensive watersports equipment rental; bike and moped rental; children's programs; sports court; sailing lessons; shuttle service to shopping and entertainment; business center; salon; limited room service; laundry and dry-cleaning service. *In room:* A/C, TV, dataport, minibar, coffeemaker, hair dryer.

4 Downtown

If you've ever read Tom Wolfe's *Bonfire of the Vanities,* you may understand what downtown Miami is all about. If not, it's this simple: Take a wrong turn and you could find yourself in some serious trouble. Desolate and dangerous at night, downtown is trying to change its image, but it's a long, tedious process. Recently, however, part of the area has experienced a renaissance in terms of nightlife, with several popular dance clubs and bars opening up in the environs of NE 11th Street off Biscayne Boulevard. Most downtown hotels cater primarily to business travelers and pre- and postcruise passengers. Although business hotels are expensive, quality and service are of a high standard. Look for discounts and packages for the weekend, when offices are closed and rooms often go empty. If you're the kind of person who digs an urban setting, you may enjoy downtown, but if you're looking for shiny, happy Miami, you're in the wrong place (for now). As of press time, the developer of the Ritz-Carlton on South Beach was about to close a deal with downtown's shoddy

DuPont Plaza, located on the sketchier side of the Miami River, in which millions of dollars would be invested to revamp the decrepit property, upgrading it into a classy lower-end hotel. Keep your eyes on this area.

VERY EXPENSIVE

Mandarin Oriental, Miami ⚶⚶⚶ Corporate big shots finally have a high-end luxury hotel to stay in while wheeling and dealing their way through Miami. Catering to business travelers, conventioneers, and the occasional leisure traveler who doesn't mind spending in excess of $500 a night for a room, the swank Mandarin Oriental features a waterfront location, residential-style rooms with Asian touches (most with balconies), and several upscale dining and bar facilities. The waterfront view of the city is the hotel's best asset, both priceless and absolutely stunning. Much of the hotel's staff was flown in from Bangkok and Hong Kong to demonstrate the hotel's unique brand of superattentive Asian-inspired service. The hotel's two restaurants, the high-end Azul and the more casual Café Sambal, are up to Mandarin standards and are both wonderful, as is the 15,000-square-foot spa in which traditional Thai massages and Ayurvedic treatments are your tickets to nirvana.

500 Brickell Key Dr., Miami, FL 33131. ⓒ **305/913-8288.** Fax 305/913-8300. www.mandarinoriental.com. 329 units. $550–$575 double; $1,200–$4,000 suite. AE, DC, DISC, MC, V. Valet parking $24. **Amenities:** 2 restaurants; bar; outdoor pool; state-of-the-art health club; full-service spa; outdoor Jacuzzi; concierge; 24-hr. business center. *In room:* A/C, TV, dataport, minibar, hair dryer, iron, safe.

EXPENSIVE

Hyatt Regency at Miami Convention Center ⚶⚶ The Hyatt Regency is located just off the Miami River in the heart of downtown Miami. It shares space with the Miami Convention Center, the James L. Knight Convention Center Theater, an exhibition hall, and an auditorium and concert hall. This hotel is perfect for large groups, business travelers, or basketball fanatics in town to see the Miami Heat play at the nearby American Airlines Arena. The People Mover and Metrorail are just blocks away, and water taxis are available at the front steps. Most of the spacious guest rooms have a balcony with a view of either the city or the bay.

400 SE Second Ave., Miami, FL 33131. ⓒ **800/233-1234** or 305/358-1234. Fax 305/374-1728. www.miami.hyatt.com. 612 units. Winter $205–$250 double. Off-season $120–$205 double. AE, DC, DISC, MC, V. Valet parking $18. **Amenities:** Restaurant; outdoor pool; health club; extensive business center. *In room:* A/C, TV, dataport, coffeemaker, hair dryer, safe.

MODERATE

JW Marriott Hotel *★★*   Located smack in the middle of the business-oriented Brickell Avenue near downtown Miami, the JW Marriott is a *really* nice Marriott catering mostly to business travelers, but located conveniently enough between Coconut Grove and South Beach that it isn't a bad choice for vacationers, either. A small but elegant lobby features the classy, appropriately named Drake's Power Bar. The buzz of business deals being sealed amidst clouds of cigar smoke contributes to the smoky, but not staid, atmosphere here. Rooms are equipped with every amenity you might need. A lovely outdoor pool, fitness center, sauna, and hot tub should become everybody's business at this hotel. Next door is the area's bustling brewery, Gordon Biersch, which attracts well-heeled, young professional types who gather for postwork revelry.

1111 Brickell Ave., Miami, FL 33131. (€) 800/228-9290 or 305/374-1224. Fax 305/374-4211. www.marriott.com. Winter $219 deluxe room; $319 concierge room; $450 junior suite. Off-season $149 deluxe room; $189 concierge room; $350 junior suite. AE, DC, DISC, MC, V. Valet parking $18; self-parking $16. **Amenities:** 2 restaurants; bar; outdoor pool; health club; spa; sauna; concierge; tour desk; business center; laundry service. *In room:* A/C, TV, dataport (with free Internet access), minibar, coffeemaker, hair dryer, iron, safe.

Miami River Inn *★★★* *(Finds)*   The Miami River Inn, listed on the National Register of Historic Places, is a quaint country-style hideaway (Miami's *only* bed-and-breakfast!) consisting of four cottages smack in the middle of downtown Miami. In fact, it's so hidden that most locals don't even know it exists, which only adds to its panache. Every room has hardwood floors and is uniquely furnished with antiques dating from 1908. In one room, you might find a hand-painted bathtub, a Singer sewing machine, and an armoire from the turn of the 20th century, restored to perfection. Thirty-eight rooms have private bathrooms—4 have a shower only, 6 have a tub only, and 28 have a splendid shower-and-tub combo. One- and two-bedroom apartments are available as well. In the foyer, you can peruse a library filled with books about old Miami. It's close to public transportation, restaurants, and museums, and only 5 minutes from the business district.

118 SW South River Dr., Miami, FL 33130. (€) 800/468-3589 or 305/325-0045. Fax 305/325-9227. www.miamiriverinn.com. 40 units. Winter $99–$229 double. Off-season $69–$109 double. Rates include continental breakfast. Additional person $15. AE, DC, DISC, MC, V. Free parking. Pets accepted for $25 per night. **Amenities:** Small, lushly landscaped swimming pool; access to nearby YMCA facilities; Jacuzzi; babysitting; coin-op washers and dryers; laundry and dry-cleaning service. *In room:* A/C, TV, hair dryer, iron.

5 Coral Gables

Translated appropriately as "City Beautiful," the Gables, as it's affectionately known, was one of Miami's original planned communities and is still among the city's prettiest, pedestrian-friendly (albeit preservation-obsessed) neighborhoods. Pristine with a European flair, Coral Gables is best known for its wide array of excellent upscale restaurants of various ethnicities, as well as a hotly contested megashopping complex featuring upscale stores such as Nordstrom (the quiet city didn't want to welcome new traffic).

If you're looking for luxury, Coral Gables has a number of wonderful hotels, but if you're on a tight budget, you may be better off elsewhere. Two popular and well-priced chain hotels in the area are a **Holiday Inn** (© **800/327-5476** or 305/667-5611) at 1350 S. Dixie Hwy., with rates between $75 and $125, and a **Howard Johnson** (© **800/446-4656** or 305/665-7501) at 1430 S. Dixie Hwy., with rates ranging from $65 to $95. Both are located directly across the street from the University of Miami and are popular with families and friends of students.

VERY EXPENSIVE

Biltmore Hotel 🏰🏰🏰   A romantic sense of Old World glamour combined with a rich history permeate the Biltmore as much as the pricey perfume of the guests who stay here. Built in 1926, it's the oldest Coral Gables hotel and a National Historical Landmark—one of only two operating hotels in Florida to receive that designation. Over the years, the Biltmore has passed through many incarnations (including a post–World War II stint as a VA hospital), but it is now back to its original 1926 splendor. More intriguing than scary is the rumor that ghosts of wounded soldiers and even Al Capone, for whom the Everglades Suite is nicknamed, roam the halls here. But don't worry. The hotel is far from a haunted house. It is warm, welcoming, and extremely charming. Now under the management of the Westin Hotel group, the hotel boasts large Moorish-style rooms decorated with tasteful period reproductions and some high-tech amenities. Always a popular destination for golfers, including former President Clinton (who stays in the Al Capone suite), the Biltmore is situated on a lush, rolling 18-hole course that is as challenging as it is beautiful. The spa is fantastic and the enormous 21,000 square foot winding pool (surrounded by arched walkways and classical sculptures) is legendary—it's where a pre-*Tarzan* Johnny Weissmuller broke the world's swimming record.

1200 Anastasia Ave., Coral Gables, FL 33134. ⓒ **800/727-1926** or 305/445-1926; Westin 800/228-3000. Fax 305/442-9496. www.biltmorehotel.com. 275 units. Winter $339–$509. Off-season $259–$479. Additional person $20. Special packages available. AE, DC, DISC, MC, V. Valet parking $14; free self-parking. **Amenities:** 5 restaurants; 2 bars; outdoor pool; 18-hole golf course; 10 lighted tennis courts; state-of-the-art health club; full-service spa; sauna; concierge; car rental through concierge; elaborate business center and secretarial services; salon; 24-hr. room service; babysitting; laundry and dry-cleaning service. *In room:* A/C, TV, VCR on request, fax, dataport, minibar, hair dryer, iron, safe; kitchenette in tower suite.

EXPENSIVE

David William Hotel 👁👁   This sister hotel to the Biltmore shares many of the same amenities without the Biltmore's price. You can even take a shuttle to the Biltmore to play a round of golf, enjoy the health club and spa, play tennis, or take a dip in the pool. The luxurious one- and two-bedroom suites are extremely spacious and have eat-in kitchens for extended stays. For a spectacular view of Miami, go up to the roof and have a drink by the pool. The hotel, which has undergone a recent external renovation, is directly across the street from the Granada Golf Course, less than 5 miles from the airport, and only 20 minutes from Miami Beach. Donna's Bistro, a fusion restaurant with a homey feel, is spectacular. Executive chef Donna Wynter was the chef de cuisine at the Biltmore Hotel and has worked as a chef at New York's Tavern on the Green and Toscana Ristorante. If you want luxury without the price, this is your best alternative in the Gables.

700 Biltmore Way, Coral Gables, FL 33134. ⓒ **800/757-8073** or 305/445-7821. Fax 305/913-1943. www.davidwilliamhotel.com. 116 units. Winter $249–$489 double. Off-season $209–$269 double. AE, DISC, MC, V. Valet parking $9. **Amenities:** Restaurant; coffee shop; lounge; gourmet market; rooftop pool; limited room service. *In room:* A/C, TV, fax, kitchenette, minibar, coffeemaker, hair dryer, iron, safe.

Hotel Place St. Michel 👁👁👁   This European-style hotel in the heart of Coral Gables is one of the city's most romantic options. The accommodations and hospitality are straight out of Old World Europe, complete with dark wood-paneled walls, cozy beds, beautiful antiques, and a quiet elegance that seems startlingly out of place in trendy Miami. Everything here is charming—from the brass elevator and parquet floors to the paddle fans. One-of-a-kind furnishings make each room special. Bathrooms are on the smaller side but are hardly cramped. All have shower/tub combos except for two, which have either/or. If you're picky, request your preference. Guests are treated to fresh fruit baskets upon arrival and enjoy perfect service throughout their stay. The exceptional Restaurant St. Michel is a very romantic dining choice.

162 Alcazar Ave., Coral Gables, FL 33134. (?) **800/848-HOTEL** or 305/444-1666. Fax 305/529-0074. www.hotelplacestmichel.com. 27 units. Winter $165 double; $200 suite. Off-season $125 double; $160 suite. Additional person $10. Rates include continental breakfast and fruit basket upon arrival. AE, DC, MC, V. Self-parking $7. **Amenities:** Restaurant; lounge; access to nearby health club; concierge; room service; laundry and dry-cleaning service. *In room:* A/C, TV, data-port, hair dryer, iron (available upon request).

6 Coconut Grove

This waterfront village hugs the shores of Biscayne Bay, just south of U.S. 1 and about 10 minutes from the beaches. Once a haven for hippies, head shops, and arty bohemian characters, the Grove succumbed to the inevitable temptations of commercialism and has become a Gap nation, featuring a host of fun, themed restaurants, bars, a megaplex, and lots of stores. Outside of the main shopping area, however, you will find the beautiful remnants of old Miami in the form of flora, fauna, and, of course, water.

VERY EXPENSIVE

Grove Isle Club and Resort ★★★ Hidden away in the bougainvillea and lushness of the Grove, the Grove Isle Resort is off the beaten path on its own lushly landscaped 20-acre island, just outside the heart of Coconut Grove. The isolated exclusivity of this resort contributes to a country club vibe, though, for the most part, the people here aren't snooty; they just value their privacy and precious relaxation time. Everyone dresses in white and pastels, and if they're not on their way to a set of tennis, they're not in a rush to get anywhere. You'll step into rooms that are elegantly furnished with mosquito-netted canopy beds and a patio overlooking the bay. You'll need to reserve early here—rooms go very fast. Baleen, a fantastic yet pricey haute cuisinerie, serves fresh seafood and other regional specialties in an elegant dining room or outside on the water.

4 Grove Isle Dr., Coconut Grove, FL 33133. (?) **800/88-GROVE** or 305/858-8300. Fax 305/854-6702. www.groveisle.com. 49 units. Winter $350–$495 suite. Off-season $295–$475 suite. Rates include breakfast. Additional person $20. AE, DC, MC, V. Valet parking $15. **Amenities:** Restaurant; large outdoor heated pool; 12 outdoor tennis courts; deluxe health club; watersports rentals; concierge; secretarial services; salon; room service; in-room massage; babysitting; laundry and dry-cleaning service. *In room:* A/C, TV/VCR, video rental delivered to room for $5, dataport, mini-bar, hair dryer, iron, safe.

Mayfair House Hotel ★ *Overrated* This Gaudí-esque hotel, located within the deserted streets of Mayfair Mall (an outdoor shopping area), certainly makes you feel removed from the mayhem in the surrounding streets of the Grove, but to me, it's somewhat desolate. Each guest unit has been individually designed and was renovated in 1998. No two rooms are alike, though each room has its own Roman tub or whirlpool and private terrace. Some suites are downright opulent and include a private outdoor Japanese-style hot tub. The top-floor terraces offer good views, and all are hidden from the street by leaves and latticework. Since the lobby is in a shopping mall, recreation is confined to the roof, where you'll find a small pool, sauna, and snack bar. If you're looking for complete seclusion, the Mayfair is fine, but, for the money, the airier Wyndham Grand Bay is a better choice (see below).

3000 Florida Ave., Coconut Grove, FL 33133. ℂ 800/433-4555 or 305/441-0000. Fax 305/441-1647. www.mayfairhousehotel.com. 179 units. Winter $289–$379 suite. Off-season $169–$379 suite. Year-round $800 penthouse. Packages available. AE, DC, DISC, MC, V. Valet parking $15; self-parking $6. **Amenities:** Restaurant; rooftop snack bar; private nightclub; outdoor pool; access to nearby health club; Jacuzzi; concierge; elaborate business center and secretarial services; 24-hr. room service; dry cleaning. *In room:* A/C, TV/VCR, fax, dataport, minibar, coffeemaker, hair dryer.

Ritz-Carlton Coconut Grove

The third and smallest of Miami's Ritz-Carlton hotels, which opened in fall 2002, promises to be the most intimate of its properties, surrounded by 2 acres of tropical gardens and overlooking Biscayne Bay and the Miami skyline. Decorated in an Italian Renaissance design, the hotel's understated luxury will be a welcome addition to an area known for its gaudiness. Expect the Ritz-Carlton standard of service and comfort.

2700 Tigertail Ave., Coconut Grove, FL 33133. ℂ 800/241-3333 or 305/644-4680. Fax 305/644-4681. www.ritzcarlton.com. 115 units. Winter $385–$750 double. Off-season $245–$550 double. AE, DC, DISC, MC, V. Valet parking. **Amenities:** 2 restaurants; cigar bar; outdoor pool; health club; concierge, business center; 24-hr. room service. *In room:* A/C, TV, dataport, minibar, hair dryer.

Wyndham Grand Bay Hotel ✦✦✦

Grand in size and stature, the Grand Bay Hotel looks like it belongs in Acapulco with its ziggurat structure and tropical landscaping, but once you see the massive bright red sculpture/structure done by late Condé Nast editorial director Alexander Lieberman in the driveway, you know you're not in Mexico. Ultraluxurious, the Grand Bay is quietly elegant, and, as a result, has hosted the likes of privacy fanatics such as Michael Jackson. British singer George Michael filmed his "Careless Whisper" video here because of its sweeping views of Biscayne Bay. Rooms are superb, with views of the bay and the Coconut Grove Marina, and they're decorated in soft peach tones with a country French theme. Bathrooms are equally luxurious. Service is outstanding, and the clientele ranges from families to international jet-setters. Bice, a sublime Northern Italian restaurant, is the hotel's most popular dining option.

2669 S. Bayshore Dr., Coconut Grove, FL 33133. © 800/327-2788 or 305/858-9600. www.wyndham.com. 181 units. Winter $359–$400 suite. Off-season $279–$349 suite. Additional person $20. AE, DC, MC, V. Valet parking $16. **Amenities:** 4 restaurants; lounge serving afternoon tea; indoor heated pool and outdoor pool; 24-hr. health club; Jacuzzi; sauna; concierge; business center; babysitting. *In room:* A/C, TV, CD player, fax, dataport, minibar, coffeemaker, hair dryer, iron, safe.

7 West Miami/Airport Area

As Miami continues to grow at a rapid pace, expansion has begun westward, where land is plentiful. Several resorts have taken advantage of the space to build world-class tennis and golf courses. While there's no sea to swim in, a plethora of facilities makes up for the lack of an ocean view.

EXPENSIVE

Doral Golf Resort and Spa ⊛   This recently renovated 650-acre golf and tennis resort is in the middle of nowhere, but with all it's got, it really is a destination in itself. While the pampering in the spa is nothing to sneer at, the next-door golf resort hosts world-class tournaments and boasts the Great White Course—the Southeast's first desert-scape course, designed by the Shark himself, Greg Norman. *Note:* Repeat guests usually book the season well in advance. The Blue Lagoon water park features two 80,000-gallon pools with cascading waterfalls, a rock facade, and the 125-foot Blue Monster water slide. Rooms here, like the hotel itself, are spacious, all with private balconies, many overlooking a golf course or garden. Much-needed renovations to the rooms reveal a plantation-style decor with lots of wicker and wood. Spacious bathrooms are done up in marble. Enhancements to the golf courses, spa suites, and driving range have also brought the resort up to speed with its competition. The spa's restaurant serves tasty, healthy fare—so good you won't realize it's health food, actually. For a spa or golf vacation, the Doral is an ideal choice. Otherwise, consider investing your money in a hotel that's better located.

4400 NW 87th Ave., Miami, FL 33178. © 800/71-DORAL or 305/592-2000. Fax 305/594-4682. www.doralresort.com. 693 units. Winter $349 double; $439 suite; $565 1-bedroom suite; $909 2-bedroom suite. Off-season $155 double; $225 suite; $305 1-bedroom suite; $405 2-bedroom suite. Additional person $35. Golf and spa packages available. AE, DC, DISC, MC, V. Valet parking $15. **Amenities:** Restaurant; sports bar; 4 pools and a 125-ft. water slide; 5 golf courses and driving range; 10

tennis courts; health club and world-class spa; bike rental; concierge; business center; room service; babysitting; laundry and dry-cleaning service. *In room:* A/C, TV, CD player, dataport, minibar, coffeemaker, hair dryer, iron, safe.

MODERATE

Don Shula's Hotel and Golf Club   Guests come to Shula's mostly for the golf, but there's plenty here to keep nongolfers busy, too. Opened in 1992, Shula's resort is an all-encompassing oasis in the middle of the planned residential neighborhood of Miami Lakes, complete with a Main Street and nearby shopping facilities—a good thing, since the site is more than a 20-minute drive from anything. The guest rooms, located in the main building or surrounding the golf course, are plain but pretty in typical, uninspiring Florida decor—pastels, wicker, and light wood. As expected, the hotel's Athletic Club features state-of-the-art equipment and classes, but costs hotel guests $10 per day or $35 per week. The award-winning Shula's Steak House and the more casual Steak House Two get high rankings nationwide.

Main St., Miami Lakes, FL 33014. ℂ 800/24-SHULA or 305/821-1150. Fax 305/820-8190. 330 units. Winter $129–$289 suite. Off-season $99–$209 suite. Additional person $10. Business packages available. AE, DC, MC, V. **Amenities:** 6 restaurants; 2 bars; 2 pools; 2 golf courses and a driving range; 9 tennis courts; health club; saunas; sporting courts. *In room:* A/C, TV/VCR.

BARGAIN CHAINS

If you must stay near the airport, consider any of the dozens of moderately priced chain hotels. You'll find one of the cheapest and most recommendable options at either of the **Days Inn** locations at 7250 NW 11th St. or 4767 NW 36th St. (ℂ **800/329-7466** or 305/888-3661), each about 2 miles from the airport.

8 North Dade County

VERY EXPENSIVE

Turnberry Isle Resort & Club 🎔🎔🎔   One of Miami's classiest resorts, this gorgeous 300-acre compound, owned by the Mandarin Oriental Hotel group, has every possible facility for active guests, particularly golfers. You'll pay a lot to stay here—but it's worth it. The main attractions are two Trent Jones courses, available only to members and guests of the hotel. A new seven-story Jasmine wing looks like a Mediterranean village surrounded by tropical gardens that are joined by covered marble walkways to the other wings. Treat yourself to a "Turnberry Retreat" at the Turnberry Spa, which recently underwent a $10 million renovation. Impeccable service consistently brings loyal fans back to this resort for more. Its location in the well-manicured residential and shopping area of Aventura means you'll find excellent shopping and some of the best dining in Miami right in the neighborhood. Unless you're into boating, the higher-priced resort rooms (instead of the yacht club) are where you'll want to stay; you'll be steps from the spa facilities and the renowned Veranda restaurant. The well-proportioned rooms are gorgeously tiled to match the Mediterranean-style architecture. The huge bathrooms even have a color TV mounted within reach of the whirlpool bathtubs and glass-walled showers. The only drawback to this hotel is that you'll need to take a shuttle to the beach.

19999 W. Country Club Dr., Aventura, FL 33180. (☎ **800/327-7028** or 305/936-2929. Fax 305/933-6560. www.turnberryisle.com. 395 units. Winter $395–$495 double; $605–$1,200 suite; $3,000–$4,200 penthouse. Off-season $175–$275 double; $375–$730 suite; $2,500–$3,500 penthouse. AE, DC, DISC, MC, V. Valet parking $12; free self-parking. **Amenities:** 6 restaurants; numerous bars and lounges; 2 outdoor pools; 2 golf courses; 2 tennis complexes; state-of-the-art spa; extensive watersports equipment rental; concierge; secretarial services; 24-hr. room service; babysitting. *In room:* A/C, TV/VCR, CD player, fax, dataport, minibar, fridge and coffeemaker on request, hair dryer.

5

Where to Dine

Don't be fooled by the plethora of superlean model types you're likely to see posing throughout Miami: Contrary to popular belief, dining in this city is as much a sport as the in-line skating on Ocean Drive. With over 6,000 restaurants to choose from, dining out in Miami has become a passionate pastime for locals and visitors alike. Our star chefs have fused Californian-Asian with Caribbean and Latin elements to create a world-class flavor all its own: *Floribbean.* Think mango chutney splashed over fresh swordfish or a spicy sushi sauce served alongside Peruvian ceviche.

Formerly synonymous with early-bird specials, Miami's new-wave cuisine, 10 years in the making, now rivals that of San Francisco—or even New York. Stellar chefs such as Mark Militello, Allen Susser, Norman van Aken, and Jonathan Eismann remain firmly planted in the city's culinary scene, fusing local ingredients into edible masterpieces. Indulging in this New World cuisine is not only high in calories, it's high in price. But if you can manage to splurge at least once, it'll be worth it.

Thanks to a thriving cafe society in both South Beach and Coconut Grove, you can also enjoy a moderately priced meal and linger for hours without having a waiter hover over you. In Little Havana, you can chow down on a meal that serves about six for less than $10. And since seafood is plentiful, it doesn't have to cost you an arm and a leg to enjoy the appendages of a crab or lobster. Don't be put off by the looks of our recommended seafood shacks in places such as Key Biscayne—oftentimes these spots get the best and freshest catches.

Whatever you're craving, Miami's got it—with the exception of decent Chinese food and a New York–style slice of pizza. Like many cities in Europe and Latin America, it is fashionable to dine late in South Beach, preferably after 9pm, sometimes as late as midnight. Service on South Beach is notoriously slow and arrogant, but it comes with the turf. (Of course, it is possible to find restaurants that defy the notoriety and actually pride themselves on friendly service.) On the mainland—especially in Coral Gables, and, more recently, downtown and on Brickell Avenue—you can also experience fine, creative dining without the pretense.

The biggest complaint when it comes to Miami dining isn't the haughtiness, but rather the dearth of truly moderately priced restaurants, especially in South Beach and Coral Gables. It's either really cheap or really expensive; the in-between somehow gets lost in the culinary shuffle. Quick-service diners don't really exist here as they do in other cosmopolitan areas. I've tried to cover a range of cuisines in a range of prices. But with new restaurants opening on a weekly basis, you're bound to find a savory array of dining choices for every budget.

As far as dress is concerned, it all depends on where you eat. On South Beach, things tend to get a bit dressier, though jackets are never required and black is always the safest bet.

Many restaurants keep extended hours in season (roughly Dec–Apr), and may close for lunch and/or dinner on Monday, when the traffic is slower. Always call ahead, since schedules do change. Dining in Miami is no longer just an early bird's paradise. Thanks to Latin and European influences, there are now restaurants in which you can have your dinner at, say, 2am, if that's what appeals to you. Still hot in Miami are fusion, eclectic, and the South Florida–born New World cuisine.

Also, always look carefully at your bill—many South Beach restaurants include a 15% gratuity to your total due to the enormous influx of European tourists who are not accustomed to tipping. Keep in mind that this amount is only *suggested* and can be adjusted, either higher or lower, depending on your assessment of the service provided. Because of this tipping-included policy, South Beach wait staff are best known for their lax or inattentive service. Always be sure to look carefully at your bill to make sure you don't overtip.

1 South Beach

The renaissance of South Beach (which started in the early '90s and is still continuing, as classic cuisine gives in to mod-temptation by inevitably fusing with more chic, nouveau developments created by faithful followers and devotees of the Food Network school of cooking) has spawned dozens of first-rate restaurants. In fact, big-name restaurants from across the country have capitalized on South Beach's international appeal and opened, and continue to open, branches here with great success. A few old standbys remain from the *Miami Vice* days, but the flock of newcomers dominates the scene, with places going in and out of style as quickly as the tides.

The Lincoln Road area is packed with places offering good food and a great atmosphere. Since it's impossible to list them all, I recommend strolling and browsing. Most restaurants post a copy of their menu outside. With very few exceptions, the places on Ocean Drive are crowded with tourists and priced accordingly. You'll do better to venture a little farther onto the pedestrian-friendly streets just west of Ocean Drive.

VERY EXPENSIVE

BED 𝄢𝄢 ECLECTIC   BED—that's "Beverage. Entertainment. Dining"—is one of the most gimmicky dining lounges to land in South Beach in a very long time. An array of inviting mosquito-netted beds awaits diners. You'll rest your head against soft cushiony pillows. A DJ spins Euro mood music and some techno. You'll have no problem appreciating the taste and aroma of the exquisite (and exquisitely priced) cuisine, featuring dishes such as macadamia-nut-crusted swordfish with black-bean daikon sprout salad and peanut sauce. For dessert, try the Ménage à Trois—peanut butter mousse, homemade jam, and brittle all under a "blanket" of chocolate—or take a Roll in the Sack—an apple-cinnamon Swiss roll in a phyllo sack with vanilla ice cream. Beware of crumbs in the sheets, as they aren't always changed between customers, and for the agoraphobic, do not go to BED on a weekend night—it's a nightmare. This restaurant gets my approval for the stellar food, not as a night-club-esque hangout.

929 Washington Ave., South Beach. ✆ **305/532-9070.** Fax 305/532-7757. Reservations required, accepted only on the day you plan to dine there. Main courses $32–$40. AE, DC, MC, V. Wed–Sun: first lay (no actual seats) 8:30pm; second lay 10:30pm. Lounge 11pm–3am.

Blue Door 𝄢𝄢 FRENCH TROPICAL   It used to be that the Blue Door's greatest claim to fame was that Madonna was part owner. The food was unremarkable, but the eye candy was sickly sweet. When the material girl fled, so did others, leaving the Blue Door wide open for anything, as long as it was as fabulous as the hotel in which it sits. The most recent incarnation of the restaurant begs for superlatives more flattering than the standard "fabulous." The eye candy is still here, but now you have good reason to focus your eyes on the food rather than who's eating it. Thanks to award-winning chef Claude Troisgrois—a star in his own right—the menu frowns upon the ubiquitous fusion moniker in favor of a more classic French approach to tropical spices and ingredients. Ragout of Maine lobster in coconut-milk broth; sea bass with brown butter, cashews, and roasted hearts of palm; and ravioli stuffed with taro

South Beach Dining

To Central Miami Beach ↗

The Bass Museum of Art

COLLINS PARK

Miami Beach Convention Center

Jackie Gleason Theater of Performing Arts

Lincoln Road Mall

BELLE ISLAND

Venetian Causeway

FLAMINGO PARK

Española Way

Miami Beach Post Office

Beach Patrol Station

Art Deco Welcome Center

LUMMUS PARK

ATLANTIC OCEAN

SOUTH POINTE PARK

Government Cut

root mousseline are just a few of the Blue Door's tempting offerings. Service can be snippy, slow, and, at times, downright rude, but the food makes up for what the restaurant lacks in hospitality.

In the Delano Hotel, 1685 Collins Ave., South Beach. ℂ **305/674-6400.** Reservations recommended for dinner. Main courses $29–$46. AE, DC, MC, V. Daily 7am–4pm, 7pm–midnight (late-night menu 3–7am).

Joe's Stone Crab Restaurant ★★ SEAFOOD

Unless you grease the palms of one of the stone-faced maitre d's with some stone-cold cash, you'll be waiting for those famous claws for up to 2 hours—if not more. As much a Miami landmark as the beaches themselves, Joe's is a microcosm of the city, attracting everyone from T-shirted locals to a bejeweled Ivana Trump. Whatever you wear, however, will be eclipsed by a kitschy, unglamorous plastic bib that your waiter will tie on you unless you say otherwise. Open only during stone-crab season (Oct–May), Joe's reels in the crowds with the freshest, meatiest stone crabs and their essential accouterments: creamed spinach and excellent sweet potato fries. The claws come in medium, large, or jumbo. Some say size doesn't matter; others swear by the jumbo (and more expensive) ones. Whatever you choose, pair them with a savory mustard sauce (a mix of mayo and mustard) or hot butter. Not feeling crabby? The fried chicken and liver and onions on the regular menu are actually considered by many as far superior—they're definitely far cheaper—to the crabs. Also, save room for dessert. The Key lime pie here is the best in town. If you don't want to wait, try Joe's Takeaway, next door to the restaurant— it's a lot quicker and just as tasty.

11 Washington Ave. (at Biscayne St., just south of 1st St.), South Beach. ℂ **305/ 673-0365,** or 305/673-4611 for takeout. www.joesstonecrab.com. Reservations not accepted. Market price varies but averages $62.95 for a serving of jumbo crab claws, $38.95 for large claws. AE, DC, DISC, MC, V. Daily 11:30am–2:30pm; Sun–Thurs 5–10pm, Fri–Sat 5–11pm. Open mid-Oct to mid-May.

Kiss ★ STEAK

This is not your grandfather's steakhouse. Sure, you can order the same New York strip as at, say, the Palm, but at Kiss, you can also get a strip show with your strip steak. Yes, Kiss is a high-style, high-concept cabaret, with live entertainment that isn't necessarily as raw as you may like your meat, but it's certainly more sizzling than medium rare. The food is quite good here, especially the ridiculously priced Kiss exclusive magnum slow-roasted prime rib, served with a trio of sauces for $69.95, but you will be distracted by the circus-like atmosphere and cavalcade of club clowns who don't convene here for food, but for fanfare and, of course, lots of air kisses.

In the Albion Hotel, 301 Lincoln Rd., South Beach. ☏ **305/695-4445**. Reservations recommended. Main courses $22–$52. AE, MC, V. Mon–Thurs 7pm–1am, Fri–Sat 7pm–2am. Lounge open until 3am weekdays, 4am weekends.

Mark's South Beach ⭐⭐⭐ NEW WORLD/MEDITER-RANEAN Named after owner and chef Mark Militello, this is one of the best restaurants in all of Miami. A cozy, contemporary restaurant nestled in the basement of the quietly chic Hotel Nash, Mark's New World– and Mediterranean-influenced menu changes nightly. What doesn't change is the consistency and freshness of the restaurant's exquisite cuisine. The roasted rack of Colorado lamb with semolina gnocchi is exceptional and worth every bit of choles-terol it may have. Crispy-skin yellowtail snapper with shrimp, tomato, black olives, oregano, and crumbled feta cheese is in a school of its own. Desserts, including an impressive cheese cart, are outrageous, especially the pistachio cake with chocolate sorbet. Unlike many South Beach eating establishments, the knowledgeable servers are here because of their experience in the restaurant—not modeling—business.

In the Hotel Nash, 1120 Collins Ave., South Beach. ☏ **305/604-9050**. Reservations recommended. Main courses $16–$38. AE, DC, DISC, MC, V. Sun–Thurs 7–11pm, Fri–Sat 7pm–midnight.

Monty's Stone Crab Restaurant ⭐ SEAFOOD This restaurant is the antithesis of South Beach trendiness, with scrappy wood floors and a very casual raw bar set outside around a large swimming pool. The best deal in town is still the all-you-can-eat stone crabs—about $40 for the large ones and $35 for the mediums. That's about the same price that Joe's, located 2 blocks away, charges for just three or four claws. (But don't order stone crabs in summer—they aren't as fresh.) Enjoy the incredible views and off-season fish specialties, including the Maryland she-crab soup, rich and creamy without too much thick-ener. Beware of Friday nights, when the happy-hour crowds convene around (and sometimes in) the pool for postwork revelry.

300 Alton Rd., South Beach. ☏ **305/673-3444**. Reservations recommended. Main courses $20–$40. AE, DC, MC, V. Sun–Thurs 5:30–11pm, Fri–Sat 5:30pm–midnight.

Nemo ⭐⭐⭐ PAN-ASIAN What Wolfgang Puck is to foodies on the West Coast, Nemo's chef, Michael Schwartz, is to Miami. Hailing from Puck's lauded Chinois in L.A., Schwartz's Pan-Asian cuisine is masterful. Nemo is a funky, high-style eatery with an open kitchen and an outdoor courtyard canopied by trees and lined with an eclectic mix of people. Among the reasons to eat in this restaurant:

grilled Indian spiced pork chop; grilled mahimahi with citrus and grilled sweet onion salad; kimchi glaze, basil and crispy potatoes; and an inspired dessert menu by Hedy Goldsmith that's not for the faint of calories. Seating inside is comfy cozy, but borders on cramped. On Sunday mornings, the open kitchen is converted into a buffet counter for the restaurant's unparalleled brunch. Be prepared for a wait; the crowd tends to spill out onto the street.

100 Collins Ave., South Beach. ℂ **305/532-4550.** Reservations recommended. Main courses $22–$36; Sun brunch $26. AE, MC, V. Lunch Mon –Fri noon–3pm. Dinner Mon–Sat 7pm–midnight, Sun 6–11pm. Sun brunch 11am–3pm. Valet parking $10.

Nobu ⭐⭐⭐ SUSHI   When Madonna ate here, no one really noticed. Not because they were purposely trying not to notice, but because the real star at Nobu is the sushi. The raw facts: Nobu has been hailed as one of the best sushi restaurants in the world, with always-packed eateries in New York, London, and Los Angeles. The Omakase, or Chef's Choice—a multicourse menu entirely up to the chef for $70 per person and up—gets consistent raves. And although you won't wait long for your food to be cooked, you will wait forever to score a table here.

At the Shore Club Hotel, 1901 Collins Ave., South Beach. ℂ **305/695-3100.** Reservations for parties of 6 or more. Main courses $10–$30. AE, MC, V. Sun–Thurs 6pm–midnight, Fri–Sat 6pm–1am.

Pacific Time ⭐⭐⭐ PAN-ASIAN   Chef and co-owner Jonathan Eismann was awarded the Robert Mondavi Award for Culinary Excellence in June 1994, and his restaurant, Pacific Time, has been recognized by *Bon Appétit* and *Esquire* magazines as one of America's "Best New Restaurants." Eismann's dishes are stunning hybrids of Chinese, Japanese, Korean, Vietnamese, Mongolian, and Indonesian flavors. One of the best dishes is the Mongolian lamb salad, which has a lightly sweet, earthy taste with a crunchy kick of onion. For a main course, the ever-changing menu offers many locally caught fish specialties such as Szechuan grilled mahimahi served on a bed of shredded shallots and ginger with a sweet sake-infused sauce and tempura-dunked sweet potato slivers on the side. The famous chocolate bombe is every bit as decadent as they say, with hot bittersweet chocolate bursting from the cupcake-like center—order it as soon as you sit down. The wine list is quite extensive.

915 Lincoln Rd. (between Jefferson and Michigan aves.), South Beach. ℂ **305/534-5979.** Reservations recommended. Main courses $23.50–$32. AE, DC, MC, V. Sun–Thurs 6–11pm, Fri–Sat 6pm–midnight.

Tantra ★★★ ECLECTIC   Marrakesh meets Miami Beach in this truly original, outrageously priced exotic outpost devoted to the ancient Indian tantric philosophy of tempting the senses with all things pleasurable. Begin with your surroundings: a sultry interior of soft grass (yes, it's real; they resod weekly) and starry lights overhead. In the front room by the bar, there are low-lying couches and pillow-lined booths bolstered by drapes that can be closed for privacy. Belly dancers mix with cocktail waitresses singing the praises of Tantra's special aphrodisiac cocktails and offering you a puff of Turkish tobacco from the communal hookah pipe (they insist it's clean, but I'd be wary).

Tantra serves a combination of Middle Eastern, Mediterranean, and Indian dishes that really are divine. Consider the Tantra Love Apple (a ripe tomato layered with Laura Chenel goat cheese and basil oil, garnished with pomegranate seeds), or perhaps Nine Jewel Indian Spiced Rack of Lamb. The $52 filet mignon is delicious, but its price tag borders on obscene.

Don't come to Tantra looking for a serene vibe to match the setting and menu. Tantra practically turns into a nightclub after dinner, attracting a crowd of celebrities and scenesters.

1445 Pennsylvania Ave. (at Española Way), South Beach. (✆ **305/672-4765.** Reservations required. Main courses $24–$48. AE, DC, DISC, MC, V. Daily 7pm–5am. Late-night menu 1am to closing.

Touch ★★ ECLECTIC   Despite the presence of the ubiquitous velvet ropes out front and the loud soundtrack inside, Touch is not a nightclub. Located on busy Lincoln Road, Touch works harder to be something of a tropical supper club, complete with faux palm trees.

The food is a mod Southwestern, with dishes as dolled up as the restaurant's interior. Specialties include delicious Canadian elk chop, seared and served with black plum salad, Frangelico corn custard and Merlot plum demi-glacé; a red-peppercorn-crusted ahi tuna; and a pan-seared filet with vegetable sauté, wasabi mashed potatoes, and candied ginger. Despite the air of haughtiness you may receive out front at the ropes, service is actually quite good. If the noise inside is too loud, and it often is, request a table outside, ensconced safely behind the ropes, where you can watch the passersby try to put their fingers on what, exactly, Touch portends to be.

910 Lincoln Rd., South Beach. (✆ **305/532-8003.** Reservations required. Main courses $20–$75. AE, DC, MC, V. Sun–Thurs 7pm–midnight, Fri–Sat 7pm–1am.

Tuscan Steak ★★★ ITALIAN/STEAK   This excellent Northern Italian restaurant, a member of the China Grill scion, is all about meat served Italian style, in large family-style portions. With a rich wood interior, the atmosphere is reminiscent of the dining room of a well-connected family—ornate and very loud. The house salad is a massive undertaking of the classic antipasto, filled with shredded slices of salami and pepperoni, chunks of mozzarella, and a delicate vinaigrette. Be sure to order the sautéed spinach with garlic and the onion mashed potatoes with whichever steak you choose. All steaks are big enough for at least three people to share. The house specialty is a delicious T-bone steak served with pungent garlic purée. On any given weekend night, reservations are secondary to being friends with the ultratanned host, so expect a long wait for a table. The bar is the only place to wait . . . if you can find a spot there, and drinks are rather pricey. The background music is straight out of Studio 54 and so is the flashy crowd. Despite the long waits, after one meal here, you'll likely want to kiss the ring of the true boss of this culinary mob scene—the chef.

433 Washington Ave., South Beach. ✆ **305/534-2233.** Reservations strongly recommended on weekends. Main courses $20–$65. Family-style meals are $50 per person, including appetizer and main course. AE, DISC, MC, V. Sun–Thurs 6pm–midnight, Fri–Sat 6pm–1am.

Twelve Twenty ✸✸✸ AMERICAN PROGRESSIVE   Prepare to shell out a pretty penny for the very haute twist on American and international cuisine (portions are small and prices are big) that rolls out of this kitchen in the high and mighty Tides Hotel. The air of elegance (perhaps pickled by the scent of money) mixes with the fragrances of dishes such as the blue prawn risotto with black trumpet mushrooms and curry, and warm maple-and-bourbon-smoked salmon. Save room for dessert, because you will want to try the Baked Jamaica—a luscious concoction of coffee and banana macadamia ice creams, English toffee fudge, cinnamon meringue, and dark rum crème anglaise. Also worthy of dessert are the restaurant's signature Tropical Popsicle martinis, such as the apricot and ginger version that comes complete with a minipopsicle-cum-stirrer made of lychee; a pineapple basil martini comes with a Guanabana popsicle. There isn't much of a scene here other than a trickle of hotel guests who occasionally pass through the lobby. Despite its exposure, Twelve Twenty offers a fair share of privacy, which is good for the number of business power meals it hosts.

In the Tides Hotel, 1220 Ocean Dr., South Beach. ✆ **305/604-5130.** Reservations recommended. Main courses $26–$35. AE, MC, V. Sun–Thurs 7–11pm, Fri–Sat 7–midnight.

Wish ★★★ ECLECTIC/BRAZILIAN/FRENCH Wish got its start as a haute vegetarian restaurant, located in the stylish Todd Oldham–designed The Hotel. It was, and still is, a terrific setting (request an outside table in the serene, umbrellaed courtyard), but the foodies couldn't bear a meal without meat. First culinary whiz Andrea Curto came on board and redirected the meaty menu, and then passed her whisk onto E. Michael Reidt, one of *Food and Wine* magazine's "Ten Best New Chefs of 2001," whose own culinary wishes have come true in the form of fantastic French Brazilian cuisine. Two of Wish's finest are cachaca-marinated tuna over jicama quinoa salad on spicy charred watermelon, and pan-seared beef tenderloin on a truffled taro root purée with stewed carrots and grilled asparagus.

In The Hotel, 801 Collins Ave., South Beach. ✆ 305/531-2222. Reservations recommended. Main courses $16–$32. AE, DC, DISC, MC, V. Daily 6–10:30pm.

EXPENSIVE

Joia Restaurant and Bar ★★ ITALIAN Without harping on the service too much (it's quite leisurely), the pasta here is among the freshest anywhere on the beach. The chef is a native Italian and he takes great pride in crafting the perfect pasta no matter who's eating it. There is a laundry list of appetizers, salads, and pastas. Recommended dishes include the *rigatoni al funghi*, a mushroom-lover's delight, with large tube pasta filled with shiitake and porcini mushrooms; the *gnocchi di zucca*, homemade potato-and-pumpkin dumplings in a tomato or cheese sauce; and the *bauletti di pollo al funghi*, a folded chicken breast stuffed with Fontina cheese, mushrooms, and sage. The wine list is also exquisite.

150 Ocean Dr., South Beach. ✆ 305/674-8871. Reservations recommended. Main courses $12–$30. AE, DC, DISC, MC, V. Daily noon–4pm; Sun–Thurs 6pm–midnight, Fri–Sat 6pm–1am.

L'Entrecote de Paris ★★ FRENCH Everything in this little piece of Paris, a classy little (albeit recently expanded) bistro, is simple. For dinner, it's either steak, chicken, or seafood—I'd stick to the steaks, particularly the house special, L'Entrecote's French steak, with all-you-can-eat French fries (or *pommes frites*, rather). The salmon looks like spa cuisine, served with a pile of bald steamed potatoes and a salad with simple greens and an unmatchable vinaigrette. The steak, on the other hand, is the stuff cravings are made of, even if you're not a die-hard carnivore. Its salty sharp sauce is rich but not thick, and full of the beef's natural flavor. I loved the *profiteroles au chocolat*, a perfect puff pastry filled with vanilla ice cream and topped with a dark bittersweet chocolate sauce. Most diners are very Euro and pack a petit attitude. Servers, however, are superquick and professional, and almost friendly in a French kind of way, making up for the close quarters.

413 Washington Ave., South Beach. © **305/673-1002.** Reservations recommended on weekends. Main courses $16–$24. DC, MC, V. Sun–Thurs 6:30pm–midnight, Fri–Sat 6pm–1am.

Shoji Sushi ☆☆☆ SUSHI   Despite the sushi saturation on South Beach, Shoji stands apart from the typical sashimi-and-California-roll routine with expertly prepared, exquisitely fresh, and *innovative* top-notch rolls. The sleek sister to its next-door neighbor Nemo, Shoji is known for its authentic Japanese box sushi technique; the sushi, rice, and ingredients are packed into a tidy, tasty cake that won't crumble into your lap. Among the rolls I can't seem to get enough of here are the hamachi jalapeño—cilantro, daikon sprout, asparagus, avocado, and jalapeños—and the spicy lobster roll which consists of mango, avocado, scallion, shiso, salmon egg, and huge chunks of lobster. Wash it all down with the saketinis and my personal fave, the gingertini, which is made with ginger, vodka, triple sec, ginger ale, and pickled ginger juice.

100 Collins Ave., South Beach. © **305/532-4245.** Reservations recommended. Main courses $13–$21. AE, MC, V. Mon–Fri noon–3pm; daily 6pm–1am. Valet parking $10.

Sushi Samba Dromo ☆☆☆ SUSHI/CEVICHE   It's Brazilian, it's Peruvian, it's Japanese, it's super sushi! This multinational New York City import is definitely sceneworthy: it's a hipster's paradise. This stylish, sexy restaurant charges a pretty penny for some exotic sushi rolls such as the $14.50 soft-shell crab roll (a tasty combo of chives, jalapeño, and crab) and the $11.50 South Asian roll, with shrimp, tomato, cucumber, chives, cilantro, and onions. And while the sushi is top-notch, the sashimi ceviches are even better. An assortment of four—your choice of lobster, salmon, yellowtail, tuna, and fluke—is somewhat of a deal at $27, considering the fact that separately each can run you from $9 to $13.50. Main plates are equally exceptional, and while they have the usual haute dishes of snapper and Chilean sea bass, I'd try the churrasco a' Rio Grande, a divine assortment of meats served with rice, beans, collard greens, and chimichurri sauce. Come here for good food and an excellent scene.

600 Lincoln Rd., South Beach. © **305/673-5337.** Reservations recommended. Main courses $17–$27. AE, MC, V. Daily noon–2am.

MODERATE

Balan's ☆☆ MEDITERRANEAN   A direct import from London's hip Soho area, Balan's draws inspiration from various

Mediterranean and Asian influences, labeling its cuisine "MediterAsian." With a brightly colored interior straight out of a mod '60s flick, Balan's is a local favorite among the gay and arty crowds. The moderately priced food is rather good here—especially the sweet-potato soufflé with leeks and roasted garlic; fried goat cheese, and portobello mushrooms; and the Chilean sea bass with roasted tomato. When in doubt, the restaurant's signature lobster club sandwich is always a good choice.

1022 Lincoln Rd. (between Lenox and Michigan), South Beach. ⓒ **305/534-9191.** Reservations not accepted. Main courses $8–$18. AE, DISC, MC, V. Sun–Thurs 8am–midnight, Fri–Sat 8am–1am.

Big Pink ⓡ *(Kids)* AMERICAN   "Real Food for Real People" is the motto to which this restaurant strictly adheres. Located on what used to be a gritty corner of Collins Avenue, Big Pink is owned by the folks at the higher-end Nemo. Scooters and motorcycles line the streets surrounding the place, which is a favorite among beach bums, club kids, and those craving Big Pink's comforting and hugely portioned pizzas, sandwiches, salads, and hamburgers. The fare is above average at best, and the menu is massive, but it comes with a good dose of kitsch, such as their "gourmet" spin on the classic TV dinner, which is done perfectly, right down to the compartmentalized dessert. Televisions line the bar area and family-style table arrangement (there are several booths, too) promotes camaraderie among diners. Outdoor tables are available. Even picky kids will like the food here and parents can enjoy the family-friendly atmosphere (not the norm for South Beach) without worrying if their kids are making too much noise.

157 Collins Ave., Miami Beach. ⓒ **305/532-4700.** Main courses $12.50–$19.95. AE, DC, MC, V. Sun and Thurs 8am–2am, Mon–Wed 8am–midnight, Fri–Sat 8am–5am.

El Rancho Grande ⓡⓡ MEXICAN   Hidden just off Lincoln Road, El Rancho Grande was once a well-kept secret among devout Mexican food fanatics. It's not such a secret anymore. With a relatively restrained decor (clay pots, sponge-painted yellow walls), El Rancho Grande doesn't hold anything back when it comes to the cuisine. The Aztec Soup, a hot and spicy blend of chicken and tortilla strips, is some of the best I've had. Fresh, spicy salsa and expertly prepared, hugely portioned enchiladas, burritos, and fajitas are sensational. The scene is young and lively without being too rowdy. Margaritas are a little weak when frozen and better ordered on the rocks. Expect a wait at the small bar for your table, especially on weekends. Limited outdoor seating is available.

1626 Pennsylvania Ave., Miami Beach. © 305/673-0480. Main courses $10–$19. AE, DC, MC, V. Daily 11am–11pm.

Grillfish ☆☆ SEAFOOD Grillfish manages to pay the exorbitant South Beach rent with the help of a loyal local following who come for fresh, simple seafood in a relaxed but upscale atmosphere. The barroom seafood chowder is full of chunks of shellfish, as well as some fresh white fish fillets in a tomato broth. The small ear of corn, included with each entree, is about as close as you'll get to any type of vegetable offering besides the pedestrian salad. Still, at these prices, it's worth a visit to try some local fare including mako shark, swordfish, tuna, marlin, and wahoo. For the surf-and-turf lovers, Grillfish has taken the plunge into a meaty venture right next door, at Grillsteak (1438 Collins Ave., same hours, credit cards, price range, and reservation policy). The two get along with each other rather swimmingly.

1444 Collins Ave. (corner of Española Way), South Beach. © 305/538-9908. www.grillfish.com. Reservations for 6 or more only. Main courses $9–$26. AE, DC, DISC, MC, V. Sun–Thurs 6pm–11pm, Fri–Sat 6pm–midnight.

Joe Allen ☆☆ *Finds* AMERICAN It's hard to compete in a city with haute spots everywhere you look, but Joe Allen, a restaurant that has proven itself in both New York and London, has stood up to the challenge by establishing itself off the beaten path in the only area of South Beach that has managed to remain impervious to trendiness and overdevelopment. Located on the bay side of the beach, Joe Allen is in an unassuming building conspicuously devoid of neon lights, valet parkers, and fashionable pedestrians. Inside, however, one discovers a hidden jewel: a stark yet elegant interior and nononsense, fairly priced, ample-portioned dishes such as meatloaf, pizza, fresh fish, and salads. The scene has a homey feel flavored by locals looking to escape the hype without compromising quality.

1787 Purdy Ave./Sunset Harbor Dr. (3 blocks west of Alton Rd.), South Beach. © 305/531-7007. Reservations recommended, especially on weekends. Main courses $14.50–$25. MC, V. Mon–Fri 11:30am–11:45pm, Sat–Sun noon–11:45pm.

Larios on the Beach ☆ *Overrated* CUBAN If you're a fan of singer Gloria Estefan, you will definitely want to check out this restaurant, which she and her husband, Emilio, co-own; if not, you may want to reconsider, as the place is an absolute mob scene, especially on weekends. The classic Cuban dishes get a so-so rating from the Cubans, but a better one from those who aren't as well versed in the cuisine. The portions here are larger than life, as are some of the restaurant's patrons, who come here for the sidewalk scenery and the well-prepared black beans and rice. Inside, the restaurant turns into a makeshift salsa club, with music blaring over the animated conversations and the sounds of English clashing with Spanish. Because of its locale on Ocean Drive, Larios is a great place to bring someone who's never experienced the Cuban culture or tasted its cuisine.

820 Ocean Dr., South Beach. © 305/532-9577. Reservations recommended. Main courses $8–$27. AE, MC, V. Sun–Thurs 11:30am–midnight, Fri–Sat 11:30am–2am.

Spiga ☆☆ ITALIAN   This intimate Italian restaurant is cool without being pretentious, concentrating on the food rather than the fanfare that has become central to so many South Beach eateries. Like the hotel in which it resides, Spiga's atmosphere is wonderfully low-key, making it a quiet favorite with locals and some luminaries. The complimentary bruschetta with grilled eggplant, served to you at one of the few tables inside or out, is the first of many culinary treats. The garlicky gnocchi with tomato and basil is an incredible illustration of how simple doesn't have to mean bland. The pungent Gorgonzola polenta appetizer is a meal in itself, and the risotto with bay scallops is a rousing display of culinary precision. The place is vaguely reminiscent of a Florentine trattoria, and if you stop to listen, you'll notice the prevailing language here is, in fact, Italian.

Hotel Impala, 1228 Collins Ave., South Beach. © 305/534-0079. Reservations accepted. Main courses $7–$20. AE, DC, MC, V. Daily 6pm–midnight.

Tap Tap ☆ HAITIAN   The whole place looks like an overgrown tap tap, a brightly painted jitney common in Haiti. Every inch is painted in vibrant neon hues (blue, pink, purple, and so on) and the atmosphere is always fun. It's where the Haiti-philes and Haitians, from journalists to politicians, hang out.

The *lanbi nan citron,* a tart, marinated conch salad, is perfect with a tall tropical drink and maybe some lightly grilled goat tidbits, which are served in a savory brown sauce and are less stringy than a typical goat dish. Another supersatisfying choice is the pumpkin soup, a rich brick-colored purée of subtly seasoned pumpkin with a dash of pepper. An excellent salad of avocado, mango, and watercress is a great finish. Soda junkies should definitely try the watermelon soda. For the ethnophobic, there's a rather tasty vegetable stew, but I strongly recommend the goat—it tastes just like chicken.

819 5th St. (between Jefferson and Meridian aves., next to the Shell Station), South Beach. © 305/672-2898. Reservations accepted. Main courses $6–$17. AE, DC, DISC, MC, V. Mon–Thurs 5–11pm, Fri–Sat 5pm–midnight, Sun 5–10pm. Closed Aug.

Van Dyke Cafe ☆ AMERICAN   The younger, jazzier sibling of Ocean Drive's News Café, the Van Dyke is similar in spirit and cuisine but different in attitude. Unlike the much scenier and much more touristy News Café, Van Dyke is a locals' favorite, at which people-watching is also premium but attitude is practically non-existent. Both cafes have nearly the same menu, with decent salads, sandwiches, and omelets, but the Van Dyke's warm wood-floored interior, upstairs jazz bar, accessible parking, and intense chocolate soufflé make it a less taxing alternative. Also, unlike News, Van Dyke turns into a sizzling nightspot, featuring live jazz nearly every night of the week (a $5 cover charge is added to your bill if you sit at a table; the bar's free). Outside there's a tree-lined seating area.

846 Lincoln Rd., South Beach. ☎ 305/534-3600. Reservations recommended for dinner. Main courses $9–$17. AE, DC, MC, V. Daily 8am–2am.

INEXPENSIVE

11th Street Diner AMERICAN   Like many of Miami's residents, this retro-diner is a transplant from the Northeast. Uprooted from its 1948 Wilkes-Barre, Penn., foundation, the actual structure was dismantled and rebuilt on a bustling corner of Washington Avenue. It's a popular round-the-clock spot that attracts a friendly yet motley crew of locals, club kids, and curious tourists and is well known for its slow service and greasy diner fare. Come in for breakfast and you'll find bleary-eyed patrons chowing down after a night of partying.

1065 Washington Ave., South Beach. ☎ 305/534-6373. Items $8–$15. AE, MC. Daily 24 hr.

Front Porch Café ☆ AMERICAN   Located in an unassuming, rather dreary-looking Art Deco hotel, the Front Porch Café is a relaxed local hangout known for cheap breakfasts. While some of the wait staff might be a bit sluggish, it seems that nobody here is in a rush. If you are, this is *not* the place for you. Enjoy home-style French toast with bananas and walnuts, omelets, fresh fruit salads, pizzas, and classic breakfast pancakes.

In the Penguin Hotel, 1418 Ocean Dr., South Beach. ☎ 305/531-8300. Main courses $5–$16. AE, DC, DISC, MC, V. Daily 8:30am–10:30pm.

Lincoln Road Café ☆ *Value* CUBAN   A local favorite, this down-to-earth Cuban-accented cafe is very popular for its cheap breakfasts. For $6, you can indulge in a hearty portion of eggs any style, with bacon, ham, sausage, Cuban toast, and coffee. Lunch and dinner specials are delicious and very cheap as well; try the black beans and rice or a chicken fricassee with plantains. The few tables inside are usually passed up in favor of the several outdoors, but in the evenings the house is full inside and out, as talented Latin musicians perform out front.

941 Lincoln Rd., South Beach. ℂ 305/538-8066. Items $6–$11. AE, DC, MC, V.
Daily 8am–midnight.

News Café ✺ AMERICAN   In the late '80s, South Beach pio-
neer Mark Soyka opened this cafe on a depressed, decrepit Ocean
Drive, sparking what some now call the South Beach renaissance.
The thriving News has become part of Miami history and it still
draws locals onto what has become the most tourist-ridden street in
the area. Whether you come by foot, blade, Harley, or Ferrari, you
should wait for an outside table, which is where you need to be to
fully appreciate the experience. Service is notoriously slow and often
arrogant (perhaps because the tip is included), but the menu, while
not newsworthy, has some fairly good items, such as the Middle
Eastern platter of hummus, tahini, tabouli, and grape leaves; hamburgers; and omelets. If it's not too busy, you can enjoy a leisurely
cappuccino outside; creative types like to bring their laptops and sit
here all day (or all night—it's open 24 hr.). There's also an extensive
collection of national and international newspapers and magazines
at the in-house newsstand.

800 Ocean Dr., South Beach. ℂ 305/538-6397. Items $5–$20. AE, DC, MC, V.
Daily 24 hr.

Pizza Rustica ✺ PIZZA   Italians often scoff at the way Americans
have mangled their recipe for pizza. But at Pizza Rustica, even the
Italians marvel at these thin-crusted gourmet meals. This is the real
deal—no thick, doughy, greasy concoctions here. Instead, Rustica features several delicious, huge slices of gourmet, authentically Tuscan-
style pizza. Spinach and Gorgonzola cheese blend harmoniously with
a brush of olive oil and garlic on a slate of the delicious, crispy dough.
There's also a four-cheese, arugula, and rosemary potato slice, among
others. Check out their new location at 1447 Washington Ave.
(between 8th and 9th sts.), South Beach (ℂ **305/538-6009**).

863 Washington Ave., South Beach. ℂ 305/674-8244. Slice $4. No credit cards.
Daily 11am–6am.

Puerto Sagua ✺ CUBAN/SPANISH   This brown-walled diner is
one of the only old holdouts on South Beach. Its steady stream of
regulars ranges from *abuelitos* (little old grandfathers) to hipsters who
stop in after clubbing. It has endured because the food is good, if a
little greasy. Some of the less heavy dishes are a superchunky fish
soup with pieces of whole flaky grouper, chicken, and seafood paella,
or marinated kingfish. Also good are most of the shrimp dishes, especially the shrimp in garlic sauce, which is served with white rice and

salad. This is one of the most reasonably priced places left on the beach for simple, hearty fare. Don't be intimidated by the hunched, older waiters. Even if you don't speak Spanish, they're usually willing to do charades (plus the menu is translated into English). Hurry, before another boutique goes up in its place.

700 Collins Ave., South Beach. ℂ **305/673-1115.** Main courses $6–$24; sandwiches and salads $5–$10. AE, DC, MC, V. Daily 7:30am–2am.

Sport Café ℛ ITALIAN   When Sport Café first opened, way back when South Beach was still a fledgling in the trendoid business, it had a plain interior, wooden chairs, and a view of the parking lot. Televisions inside were tuned to soccer matches at all times—hence the name. The key to Sport's success was, and still is, its good, cheap, homemade Italian food—nothing fancy. Only now the cafe has moved up the block to a large corner space complete with private outdoor garden. The restaurant might have moved on to better digs, but one thing remains the same: The food is still great and the soccer matches continue to kick the crowd into a frenzy. Try the nightly specials, especially when the owners' mother is cooking her lasagna.

560 Washington Ave., South Beach. ℂ **305/674-9700.** Reservations accepted for 4 or more. Main courses $5–$18; sandwiches and pizzas $6–$9. AE, MC, V. Daily noon–1am.

Sushi Rock Café ℛ SUSHI   Perhaps it has something to do with its campy name, but for some reason almost every rock star that comes to town makes a requisite stop here for a sushi fix. Aerosmith's Joe Perry and Steven Tyler ate here almost every night during their Miami-based recording sessions, and David Lee Roth has been spotted here more than once. Sushi Rock is known for a sporadically fresh assortment of sushi, hand rolls, and traditional Japanese cuisine; funky atmosphere; and hip late-night crowds. What diners are to hamburgers, Sushi Rock is to raw fish—it's always consistent but will never appear on any "best of" lists.

1351 Collins Ave. (at 14th St.), South Beach. ℂ **305/532-2133.** Items $4–$19. AE, DC, MC, V. Sun–Thurs noon–midnight, Fri–Sat 2pm–1am.

2 Miami Beach: Surfside, Bal Harbour & Sunny Isles

The area north of the Art Deco District—from about 21st Street to 163rd Street—had its heyday in the 1950s when huge hotels and gambling halls blocked the view of the ocean. Now, many of the old hotels have been converted into condos or budget lodgings and the bay-front mansions have been renovated by and for wealthy entrepreneurs, families, and speculators. The area has many more residents, albeit seasonal, than visitors. On the culinary front, the result is a handful of superexpensive, traditional restaurants as well as a number of value-oriented spots. For restaurants in this section, see the map, "Miami Beach, Surfside, Bal Harbour & Sunny Isles Accommodations & Dining" on p. 65 of chapter 4.

VERY EXPENSIVE

The Forge Restaurant ⭐⭐⭐ STEAK/AMERICAN   English oak paneling and Tiffany glass suggest high prices and haute cuisine, and that's exactly what you get at the Forge. Each elegant dining room possesses its own character and features high ceilings, ornate chandeliers, and European artwork. The atmosphere is elegant but not too stuffy. On Wednesday night (the party night here), however, it's pandemonium as the who's who of Miami society gather for dinner, dancing, and schmoozing. Like the rest of the menu, appetizers are mostly classics, from beluga caviar to baked onion soup to shrimp cocktail and escargot. When they're in season, order the stone crabs. For the main course, any of the seafood, chicken, or veal dishes are recommendable, but the Forge is especially known for its award-winning steaks. Its wine selection is equally lauded—ask for a tour of the cellar.

432 Arthur Godfrey Rd. (41st St.), Miami Beach. ✆ **305/538-8533.** Reservations required. Main courses $21–$55. AE, DC, MC, V. Sun–Thurs 6pm–midnight, Fri–Sat 6pm–1am.

Shula's Steak House ⭐⭐ AMERICAN/STEAK   Climb a sweeping staircase in the Alexander All-Suite Luxury Hotel and go through the glass hallway—designed like an atrium, so exotic flora and fauna beckon from both within and without—and you'll find yourself in this magnificent restaurant that has been acclaimed as one of the greatest steak houses in all of North America. If you're feeling adventurous, try the 48-ounce club (you can get your name engraved on a gold plaque if you can finish this absolutely *huge* piece of meat) or settle for the 20-ounce Kansas City strip or the 12-ounce filet mignon. Fresh seafood abounds when in season, and the oysters Rockefeller are a particularly good choice.

In the Alexander Hotel, 5225 Collins Ave., Miami Beach. ✆ **305/341-6565.** Reservations recommended. Main courses $18–$58. AE, DISC, MC, V. Daily 11am–3:30pm and 6–11pm. Free valet parking.

EXPENSIVE

Atlantic Restaurant ⭐⭐ AMERICAN   If you didn't know any better, you'd think you were in Nantucket at this comfortable blue-and-white beach-style restaurant designed to make you feel like you're eating in someone's guest house kitchen. The food, however, isn't your typical hamburger-and-hot-dog-on-the-grill fare. Sure, you can get all-American mac and cheese, but the Atlantic's version comes with truffles. Thanks to the Beach House Bal Harbour's owner, Jennifer Rubell, Atlantic gets delightfully kitschy with special themed-dinner nights such as the clam bake, in which a slew of fresh, all-you-can-eat seafood is yours for the taking. Same goes for the meat and potatoes night. Brunches are particularly delicious here, too, as is the poolside and oceanfront seating.

In the Beach House Bal Harbour Hotel, 9449 Collins Ave., Bal Harbour. ✆ **305/695-7930.** Reservations recommended, required on weekends. Main courses $9.50–$22. AE, DC, MC, V. Daily 7am–11pm.

MODERATE

Cafe Prima Pasta ✿✿ ITALIAN   Proving that good things do come in small packages, this tiny corner cafe's home cooking draws nightly hordes of carbo-craving diners who don't seem to mind waiting for a table for upward of an hour. Choice ingredients include the ripest, freshest tomatoes, the finest olive oil, mozzarella that melts in your mouth, and fish that puts some seafood restaurants to shame. The spicy garlic-and-oil dip that comes with the bread is hard to resist and will likely linger with you for days, like the memory of this fine meal. Though tables are packed in, the atmosphere still manages to be romantic.

414 71st St. (half a block east of the Byron movie theater), Miami Beach. ✆ **305/867-0106.** Reservations not accepted. Main courses $9–$19; pastas $7–$9. No credit cards. Mon–Thurs noon–midnight, Fri noon–1am, Sat 1pm–1am, Sun 5pm–midnight.

Lemon Twist ✿✿ MEDITERRANEAN   In addition to great Mediterranean fare, there is a twist to this place in the form of a complimentary shot of the eponymous house spirit (a lemon vodka shot). But that comes after your meal. To start, you will receive a bowl of perfectly marinated olives, which can endanger your appetite, so go easy on them. Expect friendly service and excellent meat and pasta dishes at terrific prices. Specialties such as spinach lasagna with smoked salmon and shank of lamb caramelized with whole garlic are savored by a savvy crowd that has likely escaped South Beach for this refreshing change of scenery.

908 71st St. (off the 79th St. Causeway), Miami Beach/Normandy Isle. ✆ **305/868-2075.** Reservations recommended on weekends. Main courses $9–$18. AE, MC, V ($25 minimum). Tues–Sun 5:30pm–midnight. Closed July 4 weekend.

Wolfie Cohen's Rascal House ✿ DELI   Open since 1954 and still going strong, this historic, nostalgic culinary extravaganza is one of Miami Beach's greatest traditions. Scooch into one of the ancient vinyl booths—which have hosted many a notorious bottom, from Frank Sinatra to mob boss Sam Giancana—and review the huge menu that's loaded with authentic Jewish staples.

17190 Collins Ave. (at 163rd St.) Sunny Isles. ✆ **305/947-4581.** Main courses $8–$30. AE, MC, V. Daily 7am–1am.

INEXPENSIVE

Curry's *Value* AMERICAN   Established in 1937, this large dining room on the ocean side of Collins Avenue is one of Miami Beach's oldest, and kitschiest, restaurants. Neither the restaurant's name nor the tacky Polynesian wall decorations are indicative of its offerings, which are straightforwardly American and reminiscent of the area's heyday. Broiled and fried fish dishes are available, but the best selections, including steak, chicken, and ribs, come off the open charcoal grill perched by the front window. Prices are incredibly reasonable here, and include an appetizer, soup, or salad, as well as a potato or vegetable, dessert, and coffee or tea.

7433 Collins Ave., Miami Beach. ✆ **305/866-1571.** Reservations accepted. Main courses (including appetizer and dessert) $10–$20. MC, V. Tues–Sun 4–10pm.

Sheldon's Drugs ✿ *Value* AMERICAN   This typical old-fashioned drugstore counter was a favorite breakfast spot of Isaac Bashevis Singer. Consider stopping into this historic site for a good piece of pie and a side of history. According to legend, the author was sitting at Sheldon's eating when his wife got the call in 1978 that he had won the Nobel Prize for Literature. The menu hasn't changed much since then. You can get eggs and oatmeal and a good tuna melt. The food is pretty basic, but you can't beat the prices.

9501 Harding Ave., Surfside. ✆ **305/866-6251.** Main courses $4–$8; soups and sandwiches $2–$5. AE, DISC, MC, V. Mon–Sat 7am–9pm, Sun 7am–4pm.

3 Key Biscayne

Key Biscayne has some of the world's nicest beaches, hotels, and parks, yet it is not known for great food. Locals, or "Key rats" as they're known, tend to go off-island for meals or takeout, but here are some of the best on-the-island choices. For restaurants in this section, see the map, "Key Biscayne, Downtown, Little Havana, Coral Gables, Coconut Grove & West Miami/Airport Area" on p. 69 of chapter 4.

EXPENSIVE

Rusty Pelican ✿ SEAFOOD   The Pelican's private walkway leads over a lush waterfall into one of the most romantic dining rooms in the city, located right on beautiful blue-green Biscayne Bay. The restaurant's windows look out over the water onto the sparkling stalagmites of Miami's magnificent downtown. Inside, quiet wicker paddle fans whirl overhead and saltwater fish swim in pretty tableside aquariums. The restaurant's surf-and-turf menu features conservatively prepared prime steaks, veal, shrimp, and lobster. The food is good, but the atmosphere—the reason why you're here—is even better, especially at sunset, when the view is magical.

3201 Rickenbacker Causeway, Key Biscayne. ✆ **305/361-3818.** Reservations recommended. Main courses $16–$22. AE, DC, MC, V. Daily 11:30am–4pm; Sun–Thurs 5–11pm, Fri–Sat 5pm–midnight.

INEXPENSIVE

Bayside Seafood Restaurant and Hidden Cove Bar ✰ (Finds

SEAFOOD   Known by locals as "the Hut," this ramshackle restaurant and bar is a laid-back outdoor tiki hut and terrace that serves pretty good sandwiches and fish platters on paper plates. A blackboard lists the latest catches, which can be prepared blackened, fried, broiled, or in a garlic sauce. The fish dip is wonderfully smoky and moist, if a little heavy on mayonnaise. Local fishers and yachties share this rustic outpost with equal enthusiasm and loyalty. A completely new air-conditioned area for those who can't stand the heat is a welcome addition, as are the new deck and spruced-up decor. But behind it all, it's nothing fancier than a hut—if it was anything else, it wouldn't be nearly as appealing.

3501 Rickenbacker Causeway, Key Biscayne. ✆ **305/361-0808.** Reservations accepted for 15 or more. Appetizers, salads, and sandwiches $4.50–$8; platters $7–$13. AE, MC, V. Daily 11:30am until closing (which varies).

Jimbo's (Finds SEAFOOD

Locals like to keep quiet about Jimbo's, a ramshackle seafood shack that started as a gathering spot for fishermen and has since become the quintessential South Florida watering hole, snack bar, and hangout for those in the know. If ever Miami had a backwoods, this was it, right down to the smoldering garbage can, stray dogs, and chickens. Do *not* get dressed up to come here—you will get dirty. Go to the bathroom before you get here, too, because the porta-potties are absolutely rancid. Grab yourself a dollar can of beer (there's only beer, water, and soda, but you are allowed to bring your own choice of drink if you want) from the cooler and take in the view of the tropical lagoon. Jimbo's smoked fish—marlin or salmon—is the best in town, but be forewarned: There are no utensils or napkins. When I asked for some, the woman said, "Lady, this is a place where you eat with your hands." I couldn't have said it better.

Off the Rickenbacker Causeway at Sewerline Rd., Virginia Key. © **305/361-7026.** Smoked fish about $4. No credit cards. Daily 6am–6:30pm. Head south on the main road towards Key Biscayne, make a left just after the MAST Academy (there will be a sign that says Virginia Key), tell the person in the toll booth you're going to Jimbo's, and he'll point you in the right direction.

4 Downtown

Downtown Miami is a large sprawling area divided by the Brickell bridge into two distinct areas: Brickell Avenue and the bayfront area near Biscayne Boulevard. You shouldn't walk from one to the other—it's quite a distance and unsafe at night. Convenient Metromover stops do adjoin the areas, so for a quarter it's better to hop on the scenic sky tram (closed after midnight). For restaurants in this section, see the map, "Key Biscayne, Downtown, Little Havana, Coral Gables, Coconut Grove & West Miami/Airport Area" on p. 69 of chapter 4.

VERY EXPENSIVE

Azul ⭐⭐⭐ GLOBAL FUSION Executive chef Michelle Bernstein, Miami's wunderkind in the kitchen, creates a tour de force of international cuisine, inspired by Caribbean, French, Argentine, Asian, and even American flavors. Like a stunning designer gown, the restaurant's decor, with its waterfront view, high ceilings, walls burnished in copper, and silk-covered chairs, is complemented by sparkling jewels—in this case, the food. The *hamachi carpaccio* appetizer is a sumptuous arrangement of yellowtail (imported from Japan), shaved fennel, mixed greens, and cucumber. Entrees, or "plates of resistance" as they're called here, include braised langoustine open-faced ravioli; ginger-lemongrass-glazed Chilean sea bass served with black rice, kimchi, and Napa cabbage; and chicken with red Thai curry. Desserts range from fruity to chocolaty and shouldn't be skipped.

At the Mandarin Oriental, 500 Brickell Key Dr., Miami. © **305/913-8254.** Reservations strongly recommended. Main courses $24–$38. AE, DC, DISC, MC, V. Mon–Fri noon–3pm; Mon–Sat 7–11pm.

Capital Grille ⭐⭐ STEAK This place reeks of power. Wine cellars filled with high-end classics, dark wood paneling, pristine white tablecloths, chandeliers, and marble floors all contribute to the clubby atmosphere. For an appetizer, start with the lobster and crab cakes. If you're not in the mood for beef or lobster, try the pan-seared red snapper and asparagus covered with hollandaise. The wine cellars you're surrounded by are filled with about 5,000 bottles of wine—too extensive and rare to list. While some people prefer the more stalwart style and service of Morton's up the block, others find Capital to be a bit livelier. The food's pretty much the same between the two, though I find the steaks at Morton's to be a notch better; however, the atmosphere at the Capital Grille is *much* more inviting. Complimentary valet parking here as opposed to Morton's, which charges a fee, is another reason to visit.

444 Brickell Ave., Miami. © **305/374-4500**. Reservations recommended. Main courses $21–$35. AE, DC, DISC, MC, V. Mon–Fri 11:30am–3pm; Mon–Thurs 5–10:30pm, Fri 5–11pm, Sat 6–11pm, Sun 5–10pm.

Porcao 🌟🌟 BRAZILIAN   The name sounds eerily like "pork out," which is what you'll be doing at this exceptional Brazilian *churrascaria* (a Brazilian-style restaurant devoted mostly to meat— it's the Portuguese translation of steakhouse). For about $30, you can feast on salads and meats *after* you sample the unlimited gourmet buffet, which includes such fillers as pickled quail eggs, marinated onions, and an entire prosciutto. Do not stuff yourself here, as the next step is the meaty part: Choose as much lamb, filet mignon, chicken hearts, and steaks as you like, grilled, skewered, and sliced right at your table. Side dishes also come with the meal, including beans and rice and fried yucca.

801 Brickell Bay Dr., Miami. © **305/373-2777**. Reservations accepted. Prix fixe $31.50 per person, all you can eat. AE, DC, MC, V. Daily noon–midnight.

EXPENSIVE

Big Fish 🌟🌟 *Finds* SEAFOOD/ITALIAN   This scenic seafood shack on the Miami River is a real catch—if you can find it. Hard to locate but well worth the search, Big Fish's remote location keeps many people biting. In fact, Big Fish added some Italian options to its all-seafood menu in the hopes of luring more people, and that worked, too. Big Fish has a sweeping view of the Miami skyline and some of the freshest catch around; the pasta served with it is only a starchy diversion. But the spectacular setting may be the real draw, right there on the Miami River where freighters, fishing boats, dinghies, and sometimes yachts slink by to the amusement of the faithful diners who no longer have to fish around for a charming, serene seafood restaurant. Beware of Friday nights, when Big Fish turns into a big happy hour scene.

55 SW Miami Ave. Rd., Miami. © **305/373-1770**. Main courses $15–$28. AE, DC, MC, V. Daily 11am–11pm. Cross the Brickell Ave. Bridge heading south and take the first right on SW 5th St. The road narrows under a bridge. The restaurant is just on the other side.

MODERATE

5061 Eaterie & Deli 𝕲 AMERICAN/FRENCH/DELI This two-story, 1949 building on the up-and-coming 50s block of Biscayne Boulevard features a mind-numbing selection of generously portioned, uncomplicated cuisine (think American diner meets French bistro) with a lively, hip atmosphere to match. The urban industrial chic palette of muted tones, concrete floors, and subtle textures complement the leather sofas, animal-print recliners, and wooden chairs—all enhanced by an extensive menu and wine list. 5061 features a confusing selection of several types of fair-tasting cuisine—quiche, sandwiches, hamburgers, fish, pasta, salads—everything from cheese plates to cheeseburgers. Paté and terrine are made on site and are expertly prepared thanks to the fact that the restaurant's owner is Parisian. There's a large bar downstairs with an excellent wine list, as well as a second-floor bookstore/cafe in which only travel, food, and wine books are sold.

5061 Biscayne Blvd. (at 50th St.), Miami. 𝕔 **305/756-5051**. Main courses $9.95–$29.95. AE, DC, MC, V. Daily 10:30am–11:30pm, deli 6:30am–8:30pm.

Fishbone Grille 𝕲𝕲 SEAFOOD Fish are flying in the open kitchen of this extremely popular, reasonably priced seafood joint. Whether you take yours grilled, blackened, or sautéed, the chefs here work wonders with superfresh snapper, grouper, dolphin, tuna, sea bass, and shrimp, to name just a few. For nonfish eaters, there are delicious pizzas and an excellent New York strip steak. All meals come with salad and a fantastic slab of jalapeño cornbread. The interior is plain and simple; the only thing elaborate is the long list of daily specials.

650 S. Miami Ave., Miami. 𝕔 **305/530-1915**. Reservations recommended for 6 or more. Main courses $9–$20. AE, DC, DISC, MC, V. Mon–Thurs 11:30am–10pm, Fri 11:30am–11pm, Sat 5–11pm, Sun 5:30–9pm.

Soyka Restaurant & Café 𝕲 AMERICAN Brought to us by the same man who owns the News Café in South Beach, Soyka is a much-needed addition (though it's easy to miss) to the seedy area known as the Biscayne Corridor. The motif inside is industrial chic, reminiscent of a souped-up warehouse you might find in New York. Lunches focus on burgers, sandwiches, and wood-fired oven pizzas. Dinners include simple fare such as an excellent, massive Cobb salad or more elaborate dishes such as the delicious turkey Salisbury steak. The bar area offers a few comfy couches and bar stools and tables on which to dine, if you prefer not to sit in the open dining room. A children's menu is available for both lunch and dinner. A lively crowd of bohemian Design District types, professionals, and singles gather here for a taste of urban life. On weekends, the place is packed and very loud. Do not expect an after-dinner stroll around the neighborhood—it's still too dangerous for pedestrian traffic. Head over the causeway to South Beach and stroll there.

5556 NE 4th Court (Design District, off of Biscayne Blvd. and 55th St.), Miami. ℭ **305/759-3117.** Reservations recommended. Main courses $8–$26. AE, MC, V. Sun–Thurs 11am–11pm (bar open until midnight), Fri–Sat 11am–midnight (bar open until 1am). Happy hour Mon–Fri 4–7pm.

INEXPENSIVE

La Cibeles Café 🅐 *Value* CUBAN   This typical Latin diner serves some of the best food in town. Just by looking at the line that runs out the door every afternoon between noon and 2pm, you can see that you're not the first to discover it. Pay attention to the daily lunch specials and go with them. A pounded, tender chicken breast *(pechuga)* is smothered in sautéed onions and served with rice and beans and a salad. The trout and the roast pork are both very good. When available, try the *ropa vieja,* a shredded beef dish delicately spiced and served with peas and rice.

105 NE 3rd Ave. (1 block west of Biscayne Blvd.), Miami. ℭ **305/577-3454.** No credit cards. Main courses $5–$9. Mon–Sat 7:30am–7:30pm.

Latin American Cafeteria 🅐🅐 CUBAN   The name may sound a bit generic, but this no-frills indoor-outdoor cafeteria has the best Cuban sandwiches in the entire city. They're big enough for lunch and a doggy-bagged dinner, too. Service is fast, prices are cheap, but be forewarned: English is truly a second language at this chain, so have patience. It's worth it.

9796 Coral Way, Miami. ℭ **305/226-2393.** AE, MC, V. Main courses $5–$9. Daily 7:30am–11pm.

Perricone's Marketplace 🅐 ITALIAN   A large selection of groceries and wine, plus an outdoor porch and patio for dining, make this one of the most welcoming spots downtown. Its rustic setting in the midst of downtown is a fantastic respite from city life. Sundays offer buffet brunches and all-you-can-eat dinners, too. But it's most popular weekdays at noon, when the suits show up for delectable sandwiches, quick and delicious pastas, and hearty salads.

15 SE 10th St. (corner of S. Miami Ave.), Miami. ℭ **305/374-9693.** Sandwiches $6.95–$8.25; pastas $11.50–$16.95. AE, MC, V. Sun–Mon 7:30am–10:30pm, Tues–Sat 7:30am–midnight.

Tobacco Road AMERICAN   Miami's oldest bar is a bluesy Route 66–inspired institution favored by barflies, professionals, and anyone else who wishes to indulge in good and greasy bar fare—chicken wings, nachos, and so on—for a reasonable price in a down-home, gritty but charming atmosphere. The burgers are also good—particularly the Death Burger, a deliciously unhealthy combo of choice sirloin topped with grilled onions, jalapeños, and pepper-jack cheese—bring on the Tums! Also a live music venue, the Road, as it is known by locals, is well traveled, especially during Friday's happy hour and Tuesday's lobster night, when 100 1¼-pound lobsters go for only $10.99 apiece.

626 S. Miami Ave. ✆ **305/374-1198.** Main courses $7–$10. AE, DC, MC, V. Mon–Sat 11:30am–5am, Sun noon–5am. Cover charge $5 Fri–Sat night.

5 Little Havana

The main artery of Little Havana is a busy commercial strip called Southwest 8th Street, or *Calle Ocho*. Auto-body shops, cigar factories, and furniture stores line this street, and on every corner there seems to be a pass-through window serving superstrong Cuban coffee and snacks. In addition, many of the Cuban, Dominican, Nicaraguan, Peruvian, and other Latin American immigrants have opened full-scale restaurants ranging from intimate candlelit establishments to bustling stand-up lunch counters. For restaurants in this section, see the map, "Key Biscayne, Downtown, Little Havana, Coral Gables, Coconut Grove & West Miami/Airport Area" on p. 69 of chapter 4.

MODERATE

Hy-Vong ✿✿ VIETNAMESE   A must in Little Havana, expect to wait hours for a table, and don't even think of mumbling a complaint. Despite the poor service, it's worth it. Vietnamese cuisine combines the best of Asian and French cooking with spectacular results. Food at Hy-Vong is elegantly simple and super spicy. Appetizers include small, tightly packed Vietnamese spring rolls and kimchi, a spicy, fermented cabbage. Star entrees include pastry-enclosed chicken with watercress-cream-cheese sauce and fish in tangy mango sauce.

Enjoy the wait with a traditional Vietnamese beer and lots of company. Outside this tiny storefront restaurant, you'll meet interesting students, musicians, and foodies who come for the large delicious portions.

3458 SW 8th St. (between 34th and 35th aves.), Little Havana. ✆ **305/446-3674.** Reservations accepted for parties of 5 or more. Main courses $9–$19. AE, MC, DISC, V. Tues–Sun 6–11pm. Closed 2 weeks in Aug.

From Ceviche to Picadillo: Latin Cuisine at a Glance

In Little Havana and wondering what to eat? Many restaurants list menu items in English for the benefit of *norteamericano* diners. In case they don't, though, here are translations and suggestions for filling and delicious meals:

Arroz con pollo   Roast chicken served with saffron-seasoned yellow rice and diced vegetables.

Café Cubano   Very strong black coffee, served in thimble-size cups with lots of sugar. It's a real eye-opener.

Camarones   Shrimp.

Ceviche   Raw fish seasoned with spice and vegetables and marinated in vinegar and citrus to "cook" it.

Croquetas   Golden-fried croquettes of ham, chicken, or fish.

Paella   A Spanish dish of chicken, sausage, seafood, and pork mixed with saffron rice and peas.

Palomilla   Thinly sliced beef, similar to American minute steak, usually served with onions, parsley, and a mountain of french fries.

Pan Cubano   Long, white crusty Cuban bread. Ask for it *tostada* (toasted and flattened on a grill with lots of butter).

Picadillo   A rich stew of ground meat, brown gravy, peas, pimientos, raisins, and olives.

Plátano   A deep-fried, soft, mildly sweet banana.

Pollo asado   Roasted chicken with onions and a crispy skin.

Ropa vieja   A shredded beef stew whose name literally means "old clothes."

Sopa de pollo   Chicken soup, usually with noodles or rice.

Tapas   A general name for Spanish-style hors d'oeuvres, served in grazing-size portions.

INEXPENSIVE

La Esquina de Tejas Hondureña ★★ *Value* CUBAN   Best known as the diner where Ronald Reagan ate during his 1983 campaign in Miami, La Esquina de Tejas Hondureña has gained a national reputation for its great food and low prices. There's a shrine dedicated to the former president in the "Presidential Quarters," and the menu even has his signed autograph and the presidential seal of approval. This Cuban restaurant was recently bought by Hondurans, who serve its excellent food in either a Cuban or Honduran style, depending on your choice. There is also a completely new Honduran menu to choose from, featuring tacos, enchiladas, and *baleadas* (flour tortillas with butter, refried beans, and cheese). You must try the *arroz a la marinera,* the Cuban version of Spanish paella. It's filled with clams, oysters, mussels, lobster, shrimp, squid, snapper, stone crab, and scallops cooked in fresh seafood broth. If you're not in the mood for seafood, try the *vaca frita,* a grilled, shredded flank steak served with moro rice (black beans cooked with white rice) and *maduros* (sweet, fried plantains). You won't regret a trip here.

101 SW 12th Ave., Little Havana. ✆ **305/545-0337.** Daily specials $7–$15; appetizers 75¢–$5.50. AE, MC, V. Daily 8am–5pm.

Versailles ✿✿ CUBAN   Versailles is the meeting place of Miami's Cuban power brokers, who convene daily over *cafe con leche* to discuss the future of the exiles' fate. A glorified diner, the place sparkles with glass, chandeliers, murals, and mirrors meant to evoke the French palace. There's nothing fancy here—nothing French, either—just straightforward food from the home country. The menu is a veritable survey of Cuban cooking and includes specialties such as Moors and Christians (flavorful black beans with white rice), ropa vieja (shredded beef stew), and fried whole fish. Whereas La Esquina de Tejas Hondureña is known more for its food and Ronald Reagan than its atmosphere, Versailles is the place to come for mucho helpings of Cuban kitsch.

3555 SW 8th St., Little Havana. ✆ **305/444-0240.** Soup and salad $2–$10; main courses $5–$20. DC, DISC, MC, V. Mon–Thurs 8am–2am, Fri 8am–3:30am, Sat 8am–4:30am, Sun 9am–1am.

6 Coral Gables

Coral Gables is a foodie's paradise—a city in which you certainly won't go hungry. What Starbucks is to most major cities, excellent gourmet and ethnic restaurants are to Coral Gables, where there's a restaurant on every corner, and everywhere in between. For restaurants in this section, see the map, "Key Biscayne, Downtown, Little Havana, Coral Gables, Coconut Grove & West Miami/Airport Area" on p. 69 of chapter 4.

VERY EXPENSIVE

Christy's 𝄞𝄞 STEAK/AMERICAN   Power is palpable at this elegant English-style restaurant where an ex-president could be sitting at one table and a rock star at another. But Christy's is the kind of place where conversations are at a hush and no one seems to care whom they're sitting next to. The selling point here, rather, is the corn-fed beef and calf's liver, not to mention the broiled lamb chops, prime rib of beef with horseradish sauce, teriyaki-marinated filet mignon, and perfectly tossed Caesar salad. Baked sweet potatoes and a sublime blackout cake are also yours for the taking. For a little drama, order the cruise-ship-esque baked Alaska. It livens up the staid place. Just like a fine wine or the typical Christy's customer, the meat here is aged a long time. Located on a nondescript corner, you know you've arrived at the right place if you can count the Rolls Royces parked out front.

3101 Ponce de León Blvd., Coral Gables. ✆ **305/446-1400.** Reservations recommended. Main courses $20–$35. AE, DC, MC, V. Mon–Thurs 11:30am–10pm, Fri 11:30am–11pm, Sat 5–11pm, Sun 5–10pm.

Le Festival 𝄞𝄞 FRENCH   Le Festival's contemporary pink awning hangs over one of Miami's most traditional Spanish-style buildings. Shrimp and crab cocktails, fresh patés, and an unusual cheese soufflé are star appetizers. Both meat and fish are either simply seared with herbs and spices or doused in wine and cream sauces. Dessert can be a delight if you plan ahead: Grand Marnier and chocolate soufflés are individually prepared and must be ordered at the same time as the entrees. There's also a wide selection of other homemade sweets. If you go on a Monday, you'll get a complimentary soufflé. Not a bad way to start the week.

2120 Salzedo St. (right above Alhambra Circle), Coral Gables. ✆ **305/442-8545.** Reservations required for dinner. Main courses $30–$60. AE, DC, DISC, MC, V. Mon–Fri 11:45am–2:30pm; Mon–Thurs 6–10:30pm, Fri–Sat 6–11pm.

Norman's 𝄞𝄞𝄞 NEW WORLD CUISINE   *Gourmet* magazine called Norman's the best restaurant in South Florida, but many disagree: They think it's the best restaurant in the entire United States. Gifted chef and cookbook author Norman van Aken takes New World Cuisine (which, along with chef Allen Susser, he helped create) to another plateau with dishes that have landed him on such shows as the Discovery Channel's *Great Chefs of the South* and on the wish lists of gourmands everywhere. The open kitchen invites you to marvel at the mastery that lands on your plate in the form of pan-roasted swordfish with black-bean *muneta;* stuffed baby bell pepper in cumin-scented tomato broth with avocado *crema;* chargrilled New York strip steak with *chimichurri* sabayon, *pommes frites,* and Creole-mustard-spiced caramelized red onions; plantain-crusted dolphin; or chicken and tiny shrimp paella with garbanzo beans and chorizo mojo, to name a few.

The staff is adoring and professional and the atmosphere is tasteful without being too formal. The portions are realistic, but still, be careful not to overdo it. You'll want to try some of the funky, fantastic desserts.

21 Almeria Ave. (between Douglas and Ponce de León), Coral Gables. © 305/446-6767. Reservations highly recommended. Main courses $22–$38. AE, DC, MC, V. Mon–Thurs 6–10:30pm, Fri–Sat 6–11pm. Bar opens at 5:30pm.

EXPENSIVE

Caffe Abbracci 🍷🍷 ITALIAN   You'll understand why this restaurant's name means "hugs" in Italian the moment you enter the dark romantic enclave: Your appetite will be embraced by the savory scents of fantastic Italian cuisine wafting through the restaurant. The homemade black-and-red ravioli filled with lobster in pink sauce, risotto with porcini and portobello mushrooms, and the house specialty—grilled veal chop topped with tricolor salad—are irresistible and perhaps the culinary equivalent of a warm, embracing hug. A cozy bar and lounge was added recently.

318 Aragon Ave. (1 block north of Miracle Mile, between Salzedo St. and Le Jeune Rd.), Coral Gables. © 305/441-0700. Reservations recommended for dinner. Main courses $16–$26.50; pastas $15.50–$19.50. AE, DC, MC, V. Mon–Fri 11:30am–3pm, Sun–Thurs 6–11:30pm, Fri–Sat 6pm–12:30am.

MODERATE

Brasserie Les Halles 🍷🍷 FRENCH   Known especially for its fine steaks and delicious salads, this very welcome addition to the Coral Gables dining scene does a brisk business. The modest and moderately priced menu is particularly welcome in an area of overpriced, stuffy restaurants. For starters, try the mussels in white wine sauce and the escargot. For a main course, the duck confit is an unusual and rich choice. Pieces of duck meat wrapped in duck fat are slow-cooked and served on salad frissé with baby potatoes with garlic. Service by the young French staff is polite but a bit slow. The tables tend to be a little too close, although there is a lovely private balcony space overlooking the dining room where groups can gather.

2415 Ponce de León Blvd. (at Miracle Mile), Coral Gables. © 305/461-1099. Reservations recommended on weekends. Main courses $12.50–$22.50. AE, DC, DISC, MC, V. Daily 11:30am–midnight.

Ortanique on the Mile ★★ NEW WORLD CARIBBEAN
You'll be greeted as you walk in by soft spiderlike lights and
canopied mosquito netting that will make you wonder whether
you're on a secluded island or inside one of King Tut's temples. Chef
Cindy Hutson has truly perfected her tantalizing New World
Caribbean menu. For starters, an absolute must is the pumpkin
bisque with a hint of pepper sherry. Afterward, move on to the tropical mango salad with fresh marinated Sable hearts of palm, julienne
mango, baby field greens, toasted Caribbean candied pecans, and
passion-fruit vinaigrette. For an entree, I recommend the pan-
sautéed Bahamian black grouper marinated in teriyaki and sesame
oil. It's served with an ortanique (an orange-like fruit) orange
liqueur sauce and topped with steamed seasoned chayote, zucchini,
and carrots on a lemon-orange boniato sweet-plantain mash. For
dessert, try the chocolate mango tower—layers of brownie, chocolate mango mousse, meringue, and sponge cake, accompanied by
mango sorbet and tropical fruit salsa. Entrees may not be cheap, but
they're a lot less than airfare to the islands, from where most, if not
all, the ingredients used here hail.

278 Miracle Mile (next to Actor's Playhouse), Coral Gables. ⓒ **305/446-7710.**
Reservations requested. Main courses $11–$29. AE, DC, MC, V. Mon–Tues 6–10pm,
Wed–Sat 6–11pm, Sun 5:30–9:30pm.

INEXPENSIVE

Biscayne Miracle Mile Cafeteria ★ *Value* AMERICAN   Here
you'll find great Southern-style cooking at unbelievably low prices.
The menu changes, but roast beef, baked fish, and barbecued ribs are
typical entrees, few of which exceed $5. Food is picked up cafeteria
style (no frills at all) and brought to one of the many unadorned
Formica tables. The restaurant is always busy. The kitschy 1950s
decor is an asset in this last of the old-fashioned cafeterias, where the
gold-clad staff is proud and attentive. Enjoy it while it lasts.

147 Miracle Mile, Coral Gables. ⓒ **305/444-9005.** Main courses $3.50–$4.50.
MC, V. Daily 11am–8:30pm.

Miss Saigon Bistro ★★ VIETNAMESE   Miss Saigon is small,
quiet, and not at all flashy. Servers at this family-run restaurant will
graciously offer to recommend dishes or even to custom-make
something for you. The menu is varied and reasonably priced and
the portions are huge—large enough to share. Noodle dishes and
soup bowls are hearty and flavorful; caramelized prawns are fantastic, as is the whole snapper with lemongrass and ginger sauce.
Despite the fact that there are few tables inside and a hungry crowd

usually gathers outside in the street, they will not at all rush you through your meal, which is worth savoring.

146 Giralda Ave. (at Ponce de León and 37th Ave.), Coral Gables. ℂ **305/446-8006**. Main courses $4–$17. AE, DC, DISC, MC, V. Mon–Thurs 11am–3pm and 5:30–10pm, Fri–Sat 5:30–11pm, Sun 5:30–10pm.

7 Coconut Grove

Coconut Grove was long known as the artists' haven of Miami, but the rush of developers trying to cash in on the laid-back charm of this old settlement has turned it into something of an overgrown mall. Still, there are several great dining spots both in and out of the confines of Mayfair or CocoWalk. For restaurants in this section, see the map, "Key Biscayne, Downtown, Little Havana, Coral Gables, Coconut Grove & West Miami/Airport Area" on p. 69 of chapter 4.

VERY EXPENSIVE

Baleen 𝕱𝕱𝕱 SEAFOOD/MEDITERRANEAN   While the prices aren't lean, the cuisine here is worth every pricey, precious penny. Oversized crab cakes, oak-smoked diver scallops, and steakhouse-quality meats are among Baleen's excellent offerings. The lobster bisque is the best on Biscayne Bay. Everything here is a la carte, so order wisely, as it tends to add up quickly. The restaurant's spectacular waterfront setting makes Baleen a true knockout. Brunch is particularly noteworthy as well.

4 Grove Isle Dr. (in the Grove Isle Hotel), Coconut Grove. ℂ **305/858-8300**. Reservations recommended. Main courses $18–$34. AE, DC, MC, V. Sun–Wed 7am–10pm, Thurs–Sat 7am–11pm.

EXPENSIVE

Anokha 𝕱𝕱𝕱 INDIAN   This is the best Indian restaurant in Miami. Anokha's motto is "a guest is equal to God and should be treated as such," and they do stick to it. They have fantastic tandooris, curries, and stews. The restaurant's location, at the end of a quiet stretch of Coconut Grove, is especially enticing because it prevents the throngs of pedestrians from overtaking what some people consider a diamond in the rough.

3195 Commodore Plaza (between Main Hwy. and Grand Ave.), Coconut Grove. ℂ **786/552-1030**. Main courses $10–$30. AE, DC, MC, V. Tues–Sun 11:30am–10:30pm.

Le Bouchon du Grove 𝕱𝕱 FRENCH   This very authentic, exceptional bistro is French right down to the wait staff. The food, prepared by an animated French (what else?) chef, is superb. An excellent starter is the wonderful *gratinée Lyonnaise* (traditional French onion soup). Fish is brought in fresh daily; try the Chilean sea bass when in season *(filet de loup poele)*. Though it is slightly heavy on the oil, it is delivered with succulent artichokes, tomato confit, and seasoned roasted garlic that is a gastronomic triumph. The *carre d'agneau roti* (roasted rack of lamb with Provence herbs) is served warm and tender, with an excellent amount of seasoning.

3430 Main Highway, Coconut Grove. ℂ **305/448-6060.** Reservations recommended. Main courses $18–$25. AE, MC, V. Mon–Fri 10am–3pm; Mon–Thurs 5–11pm, Fri 5pm–midnight, Sat 8am–midnight, Sun 8am–11pm.

MODERATE

Paulo Luigi's ℱ ITALIAN   Paulo Luigi's serves rich dishes that include cold and hot appetizers, homemade soups and salads, pastas, and pizzas. Owners Paul and Lola Shalaj, restaurant entrepreneurs for the past 27 years, have gained and kept a large devoted clientele with their tasty light Italian cuisine, generous portions, and friendly environment that has served as the perfect fine-dining hideaway for both local and national customers alike.

A favorite is the *jumbo rigatti rubino,* a chicken dish with a side of sausages, asparagus, and portobello mushrooms in light marinara sauce. There's also *chicken Marsala, linguine al frutti di mare* (for poultry and seafood lovers), and a special children's menu.

3324 Virginia St., Coconut Grove. ℂ **305/445-9000.** Reservations recommended. Main courses $9–$17. AE, MC, V. Daily noon–4pm and 5–11pm; Fri–Sat 5pm–1am.

Señor Frogs ℱ MEXICAN   Filled with a collegiate crowd, this restaurant is known for a raucous good time, a mariachi band, and powerful margaritas. The food at this rocking cantina is a bit too cheesy, but it's tasty, if not exactly authentic. The mole enchiladas, with 14 different kinds of mild chiles mixed with chocolate, is as flavorful as any I've tasted. Almost everything is served with rice and beans in quantities so large that few diners are able to finish.

3480 Main Hwy., Coconut Grove. ℂ **305/448-0999.** Reservations not accepted. Main courses $12–$17. AE, DC, MC, V. Mon–Sat 11:30am–2am, Sun 11:30am–1am.

INEXPENSIVE

Cafe Tu Tu Tango ℱ SPANISH/INTERNATIONAL   This restaurant in the bustling CocoWalk is designed to look like a disheveled artist's loft. Dozens of original paintings—some only half-finished—hang on the walls and on studio easels. Seating is either inside, among the clutter, or outdoors, overlooking the Grove's main drag. Flamenco and other Latin-inspired tunes complement a menu with a decidedly Spanish flare. Hummus spread on rosemary flat bread and baked goat cheese in marinara sauce are two good starters. Entrees include roast duck with dried cranberries, toasted pine nuts, and goat cheese, plus Cajun chicken egg rolls filled with corn, cheddar cheese, and tomato salsa. Pastas, ribs, fish, and pizzas round out the eclectic offerings, and several visits have proved each consistently good. Try the sweet, potent sangria and enjoy the warm, lively atmosphere from a seat with a view.

3015 Grand Ave. (on the second floor of CocoWalk), Coconut Grove. ℂ **305/ 529-2222.** Reservations not accepted. Tapas $3–$9.50. AE, MC, V. Sun–Wed 11:30am–midnight, Thurs 11:30am–1am, Fri–Sat 11:30am–2am.

8 North Miami Beach

Although there aren't many hotels in North Dade, the population in the winter months explodes due to the onslaught of seasonal residents from the Northeast. A number of exclusive condominiums and country clubs, including William's Island, Turnberry, and the Jockey Club, breed a demanding clientele, many of whom dine out nightly. That's good news for visitors, who can find superior service and cuisine at value prices.

VERY EXPENSIVE

Chef Allen's ✮✮✮ NEW WORLD CUISINE If anyone deserves to have a restaurant named after him, it's chef Allen Susser, winner of the esteemed James Beard Award for Best American Chef in the Southeast—the Academy Award of cuisine—and practically every other form of praise and honor awarded by the most discriminating palates. It is under Chef Allen's magic that ordinary Key limes and mangoes reappear in the form of succulent salsas and sauces. A traditional antipasto is transformed into a Caribbean one, with papaya-pineapple barbecue shrimp, jerk calamari, and charred rare tuna. Whole yellowtail in coconut milk and curry sauce is a particularly spectacular entree. Unlike other restaurants where location is key, Chef Allen's, located in the rear of a strip mall, could be in the desert, and hordes of people would still make the trek.

19088 NE 29th Ave. (at Biscayne Blvd.), North Miami Beach. ℂ **305/935-2900.** Reservations recommended. Main courses $22–$40. AE, DC, MC, V. Sun–Thurs 6–10pm, Fri–Sat 6–11pm.

INEXPENSIVE

Laurenzo's Café ✮✮ ITALIAN This recently expanded lunch counter in the middle of a chaotic grocery store has been serving delicious buffet lunches to the *paesanos* for years. New additions include an open kitchen and wood-burning pizza oven. A meeting place for the growing Italian population in Miami, the store has been open for more than 40 years. Daily specials usually include lasagna or eggplant parmigiana and two or three salad options. Also good are the rustic pizzas. Choose a wine from the vast selection and take your meal to go, or sit in the trellis-covered area amid busy shoppers buying their evening's groceries. You'll get to eavesdrop on some great conversations over your plastic tray of real Southern Italian–style cooking.

16385 W. Dixie Hwy. (south of corner of 163rd St.), North Miami Beach. © 305/945-6381. Main courses $4–$8, salads $2–$5. No credit cards. Mon–Fri 11am–7:30pm, Sat 11am–7pm; Sun 11am–4pm.

9 South Miami & West Miami

Though mostly residential, these areas nonetheless have several eating establishments worth the drive.

EXPENSIVE

Tropical Chinese 🦋🦋 CHINESE   This strip mall restaurant way out there in West Miami Dade is hailed as the best Chinese restaurant in the city. While the food is indeed very good—certainly more interesting than at your typical beef-and-broccoli shop—it still seems somewhat overpriced. Garlic spinach and prawns in a clay pot is delicious with the perfect mix of garlic cloves, mushrooms, and fresh spinach, but it's not cheap at $16.99. And unlike most Chinese restaurants, the dishes here are not large enough to share. Sunday afternoon dim sum is extremely popular and lines often snake around the shopping center.

7991 Bird Rd., West Miami. © 305/262-7576. Reservations highly recommended. Main courses $10–$25. AE, DC, MC, V. Mon–Fri 11:30am–10:30pm, Sat 11am–10:30pm, Sun 10:30am–10pm. Take U.S. 1 to Bird Rd. and go west on Bird, all the way down to 78th Ave. The restaurant is between 78th and 79th on Bird Rd. on the north side of the road.

INEXPENSIVE

Shorty's 🦋 BARBECUE   A Miami tradition since 1951, this log cabin is still serving some of the best ribs and chicken in South Florida. People line up for the smoke-flavored, slow-cooked meat that's so tender it seems to fall off the bone. The secret, however, is to ask for your order with sweet sauce. The regular stuff tastes bland and bottled. All the side dishes, including the coleslaw, corn on the cob, and baked beans, look commercial but are necessary to complete the experience. This is a jeans and T-shirt kind of place, but you may want to wear an elastic waistband, as overeating is not uncommon.

9200 S. Dixie Hwy. (between U.S. 1 and Dadeland Blvd.), South Miami. © 305/670-7732. Main courses $5–$9. DISC, MC, V. Mon–Thurs 11am–10pm, Fri–Sat 11am–11pm.

Tea Room ✸ ENGLISH TEA   Do stop in for a spot of tea at this recently rebuilt tearoom in historic Cauley Square off U.S. 1. The little lace-curtained room is an unusual site in this heavily industrial area better known for its warehouses than its doilies.

Try one of the simple sandwiches, such as the turkey club with potato salad and a small lettuce garnish, or onion soup full of rich brown broth and stringy cheese. Daily specials, such as spinach and mushroom quiche, and delectable desserts are a must before beginning your explorations of the old antiques and art shops in this little enclave of civility down south.

12310 SW 224th St. (at Cauley Square), South Miami. © 305/258-0044. Sandwiches and salads $7–$12; soups $3–$4. AE, DISC, MC, V. Mon–Sat 11am–4pm. Take 836 West (Dolphin Expressway) toward Miami International Airport. Take Palmetto Expressway South ramp toward Coral Way. Merge onto 826 South. Follow signs to Florida Turnpike toward Homestead. Take Turnpike South and exit at Caribbean Blvd. (#12). Go about a mile on Caribbean Blvd. Turn left on S. Dixie Hwy. and then right at SW 224th St. Then turn left onto Old Dixie Hwy. and a slight right onto SW 224th St. The restaurant is at Cauley Square Center.

6

What to See & Do in Miami

If there's one thing Miami doesn't have, it's an identity crisis. In fact, it's the city's vibrant, multifaceted personality that attracts millions each year, from all over the world. South Beach may be on the top of many Miami to-do lists, but the rest of the city, a fascinating assemblage of multicultural neighborhoods, should not be overlooked or neglected. Once considered "God's Waiting Room," the Magic City now attracts an eclectic mix of old and young, celebs and plebes, American and international, and geek and chic with an equally varied roster of activities.

For starters, Miami boasts some of the most natural beauty there is, with blinding blue waters, fine, sandy beaches, and lush tropical parks. The city's man-made brilliance, in the form of Crayola-colored architecture, never seems to fade in Miami's unique Art Deco District. For cultural variation, you can also experience the tastes, sounds, and rhythms of Cuba in Little Havana.

Lose yourself in the city's nature and its neighborhoods, and, best of all, its people—a sassy collection of artists and intellectuals, beach bums and international transplants, dolled-up drag queens and bodies beautiful. No wonder celebrities love to vacation here—the spotlight is on the city and its residents. And unlike most stars, Miami is always ready for its close-up. With so much to do and see, Miami is a virtual amusement park that's bound to entertain all those who pass through its palm-lined gates.

1 Miami's Beaches

Perhaps Miami's most popular attraction is its incredible 35-mile stretch of beachfront, which runs from the tip of South Beach north to Sunny Isles and circles Key Biscayne and the numerous other pristine islands dotting the Atlantic. The characteristics of Miami's many beaches are as varied as the city's population: There are beaches for swimming, socializing, or serenity; for family, seniors, or gay singles; some to make you forget you're in the city, others darkened by huge condominiums. Whatever type of beach vacation you're looking for, you'll find it in one of Miami's two distinct beach areas: Miami Beach and Key Biscayne. For a list of my picks for the best beaches in Miami, see chapter 1, "The Best of Miami."

MIAMI BEACH'S BEACHES   Collins Avenue fronts more than a dozen miles of white-sand beach and blue-green waters from 1st to 192nd streets. Although most of this stretch is lined with a solid wall of hotels and condos, beach access is plentiful. There are lots of public beaches here, wide and well maintained, complete with lifeguards, bathroom facilities, concession stands, and metered parking (bring lots of quarters). Except for a thin strip close to the water, most of the sand is hard-packed—the result of a $10 million Army Corps of Engineers Beach Rebuilding Project meant to protect buildings from the effects of eroding sand.

In general, the beaches on this barrier island (all on the eastern, ocean side of the island) become less crowded the farther north you go. A wooden boardwalk runs along the hotel side of the beach from 21st to 46th streets—about 1½ miles—offering a terrific sun-and-surf experience without getting sand in your shoes. Miami's lifeguard-protected public beaches include 21st Street, at the beginning of the boardwalk; 35th Street, popular with an older crowd; 46th Street, next to the Fontainebleau Hilton; 53rd Street, a narrower, more sedate beach; 64th Street, one of the quietest strips around; and 72nd Street, a local old-timers' spot.

KEY BISCAYNE'S BEACHES   If Miami Beach doesn't provide the privacy you're looking for, try Virginia Key and Key Biscayne. Crossing the Rickenbacker Causeway ($1 toll), however, can be a lengthy process, especially on weekends, when beach bums and tan-o-rexics flock to the Key. The 5 miles of public beach there, however, are blessed with softer sand and are less developed and more laid-back than the hotel-laden strips to the north.

2 The Art Deco District (South Beach)

"You know what they used to say? 'Who's Art?'" recalls Art Deco revivalist Dona Zemo, "You'd say, 'This is an Art Deco building,' and they'd say, 'Really, who is Art?' These people thought 'Art Deco' was some guy's name."

How things have changed. This guy Art has become one of the most popular Florida attractions since, well, that mouse Mickey. The district is roughly bounded by the Atlantic Ocean on the east, Alton Road on the west, 6th Street to the south, and Dade Boulevard (along the Collins Canal) to the north.

Miami Area Attractions & Beaches

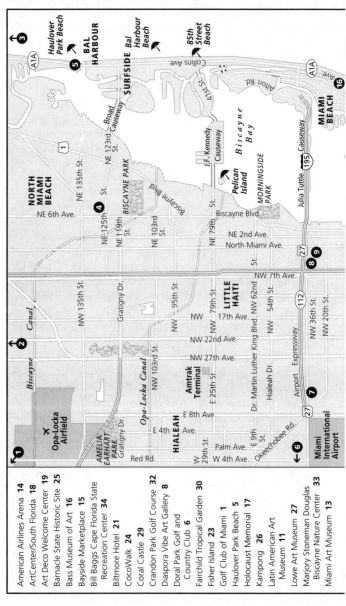

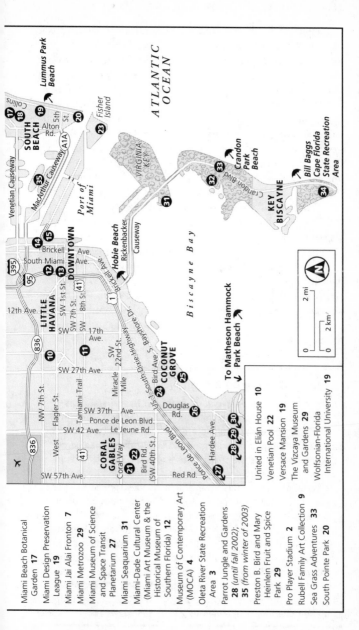

ATLANTIC OCEAN

Lummus Park Beach

SOUTH BEACH

Collins

Alton Rd.

5th St.

Fisher Island

Venetian Causeway

MacArthur Causeway (A1A)

Port of Miami

VIRGINIA KEY

Crandon Park Beach

Crandon Blvd

KEY BISCAYNE

Bill Baggs Cape Florida State Recreation Area

Brickell
South Miami
DOWNTOWN

Hobie Beach

Rickenbacker Causeway

Brickell Ave.

Biscayne Bay

395
95
12th Ave.
NW. 7th St.
Flagler St.
Tamiami Trail
836

LITTLE HAVANA

SW 1st St.
SW 7th St.
SW 8th St. (41)
1
SW 17th Ave.
SW 22nd St.
Bird Ave.

COCONUT GROVE

SW 27th Ave.

Miracle Mile

S. Bayshore Dr.

US-South Dixie Highway

To Matheson Hammock Park Beach

CORAL GABLES

SW 37th Ave.
Ponce de Leon Blvd.
SW 42 Ave. Le Jeune Rd.

Coral Way
Bird Rd. (SW 40th St.)
Red Rd.

Douglas Rd.

Hardee Ave.

Ponce de Leon Blvd

West
SW 57th Ave.
(41)

N

0   2 mi
0   2 km

Simply put, Art Deco is a style of architecture that, in its heyday of the 1920s and '30s, used to be considered ultramodern. Today, fans of the style consider it retro-fabulous. And while some people may not consider the style fabulous, it's undoubtedly retro. According to the experts, Art Deco made its debut in 1925 in an exposition in Paris in which it set a stylistic tone, with buildings based on early neoclassical styles with the application of exotic motifs like flora, fauna, and fountains based on geometric patterns. In Miami, Art Deco is marked by the pastel-hued buildings that line South Beach and Miami Beach. But it's a lot more than just color. If you look carefully, you will see the intricacies and impressive craftsmanship that went into each building back in the day—which, in Miami's case, was the '20s, '30s, and '40s, and now, thanks to intensive restoration, today.

Most of the finest examples of the whimsical Art Deco style are concentrated along three parallel streets—Ocean Drive, Collins Avenue, and Washington Avenue—from about 6th to 23rd streets.

After years of neglect and calls for the wholesale demolition of its buildings, South Beach got a new lease on life in 1979. Under the leadership of Barbara Baer Capitman, a dedicated crusader for the Art Deco region, and the Miami Design Preservation League, founded by Baer Capitman and five friends, an area made up of an estimated 800 buildings was granted a listing on the National

---

Finds **Walking by Design**

The Miami Design Preservation League offers several tours of Miami Beach's historic architecture, which all leave from the Art Deco Welcome Center, located at 1001 Ocean Dr. in Miami Beach. A self-guided audio tour (available 7 days a week, from 10am–4pm) turns the streets into a virtual outdoor museum, taking you through Miami Beach's Art Deco district at your own leisure, with tours in several languages for just $10 per person. Guided tours conducted by local historians and architects offer an in-depth look at the structures and their history. The 90-minute Ocean Drive and Beyond tour (offered every Sat at 10:30am) takes you through the district, pointing out the differences between Mediterranean Revival and Art Deco for $15 per person. If you're not blinded by neon, the Thursday night Art Deco District Up-to-Date tour (leaving at 6:30pm) will whisk you around for 90 minutes. Cost is $15. For more information on tours or reservations, call ☎ **305/672-2014.**

Register of Historic Places. Designers then began highlighting long-lost architectural details with soft sherbet shades of peach, periwinkle, turquoise, and purple. Developers soon moved in, and the full-scale refurbishment of the area's hotels was under way.

Today, hundreds of new establishments—hotels, restaurants, and nightclubs—have renovated, or are in the process of renovating, these older, historical buildings and are moving in, making South Beach on the cutting edge of Miami's cultural and nightlife scene.

EXPLORING THE AREA

If you're touring this unique neighborhood on your own, start at the **Art Deco Welcome Center,** 1001 Ocean Dr. (*(C)* **305/531-3484**), which is run by the Miami Design Preservation League. The only beachside building across from the Clevelander Hotel and bar, the center gives away lots of informational material, including maps and pamphlets, and runs guided tours about the neighborhood. Art Deco books (including *The Art Deco Guide,* an informative compendium of all the buildings here), T-shirts, postcards, mugs, and other paraphernalia are for sale. It's open Monday to Saturday from 9am to 6pm, sometimes later.

Take a stroll along **Ocean Drive** for the best view of sidewalk cafes, bars, colorful hotels, and even more colorful people. Another great place for a walk is **Lincoln Road,** which is lined with boutiques, large chain stores, cafes, and funky art and antiques stores. The Community Church, at the corner of Lincoln Road and Drexel Avenue, is the neighborhood's first church and one of its oldest surviving buildings, dating from 1921.

3 Miami's Museum & Art Scene

Miami has never been known as a cultural mecca as far as museums are concerned. Though several exhibition spaces have made forays into collecting nationally acclaimed work, limited support and political infighting have made it a difficult proposition. Recently, however, things have changed as museums such as the Wolfsonian, the Museum of Contemporary Art, the Bass Museum of Art, and the Miami Art Museum have gotten on the bandwagon, boasting collections and exhibitions high on the list of art aficionados. It's now safe to say that world-class exhibitions start here. Listed below are the most lauded museums that have become a part of the city's cultural heritage, and as such, are as diverse as the city itself.

IN SOUTH BEACH

ArtCenter/South Florida ☀ Not exactly a museum in the classic sense of the word, ArtCenter/South Florida is a multichambered space where local artists display their works in all mediums—from photography and sculpture to video and just about anything else that might exemplify their artistic nature. Admission is free and it's quite fun to mosey through the space viewing the various artists at work in their studios. Of course, all the art is for sale, but there's no pressure to buy. Just wander and enjoy.

800–924 Lincoln Rd. (at Meridian Ave.), South Beach. ✆ **305/674-8278.** www.art centersf.org. Free admission. Daily 11am–11pm.

Bass Museum of Art ☀☀☀ The Bass Museum of Art has expanded and received a dramatically new look (plus triple the amount of exhibition space), rendering it Miami's most progressive art museum. In addition to providing space in which to show the permanent collection, exhibitions of a scale and quality not previously seen in Miami will now be featured at the Bass. The museum's permanent collection includes European paintings from the 15th through the early 20th centuries with special emphasis on Northern European art of the Renaissance and baroque periods, including Dutch and Flemish masters such as Bol, Flinck, Rubens, and Jordaens.

2121 Park Ave. (1 block west of Collins Ave.), South Beach. ✆ **305/673-7530.** www.bassmuseum.org. Admission $6 adults, $4 students and seniors, free for children 6 and under. Tues–Wed and Fri–Sat 10am–5pm, Thurs 10am–9pm, Sun 11am–5pm. Closed Mon.

Holocaust Memorial ☀☀☀ This heart-wrenching memorial is hard to miss and would be a shame to overlook. The powerful centerpiece, Kenneth Triester's *Sculpture of Love & Anguish,* depicts victims of the concentration camps crawling up a giant, yearning hand, stretching up to the sky, marked with an Auschwitz number tattoo. Along the reflecting pool is the story of the Holocaust, told in cut marble slabs. Inside the center of the memorial is a tableau that is one of the most solemn and moving tributes to the millions of Jews who lost their lives in the Holocaust I've seen. You can walk through an open hallway lined with photographs and the names of concentration camps and their victims. From the street, you'll see the outstretched arm, but do stop and tour the sculpture at ground level.

1933 Meridian Ave. (at Dade Blvd.), South Beach. ✆ **305/538-1663.** http://miami. travelape.com/attractions/holocaust-memorial/. Free admission. Daily 9am–9pm.

Roadside Attraction

Morbid curiosity has led hordes of people—tourists and locals—to the **Versace Mansion (Amsterdam Palace),** the only private home on Ocean Drive. If you can get past the fact that the late designer was murdered on the steps of this palatial estate, you should definitely observe the intricate Italian architecture that makes this house stand out from its streamlined deco neighbors. Built in the 1930s as a replica of Christopher Columbus's son's palace in Santo Domingo, the house was originally called Casa Casuarina (House of the Pine), but was rechristened the Amsterdam Palace in 1935 when George Amsterdam purchased it. While there were rumors that the mansion was to be turned into a Versace museum, it was, instead, purchased by a private citizen from Texas. Located at the northwest corner of Ocean Drive and 11th Street, South Beach.

Wolfsonian-Florida International University &&& (Finds

Mitchell Wolfson Jr., heir to a family fortune built on movie theaters, was known as an eccentric, but I'd call him a pack rat. A premier collector of propaganda and advertising art, Wolfson was spending so much money storing his booty that he decided to buy the warehouse that was housing it. It ultimately held more than 70,000 of his items, from controversial Nazi propaganda to King Farouk of Egypt's match collection. Thrown in the eclectic mix are also zany works from great modernists such as Charles Eames and Marcel Duchamp. He then gave this incredibly diverse collection to Florida International University. The former 1927 storage facility has been transformed into a museum that is the envy of curators around the world. The museum is unquestionably fascinating and hosts lectures and rather swinging events surrounding particular exhibits.

1001 Washington Ave., South Beach. © 305/531-1001. www.wolfsonian.fiu.edu. Admission $5 adults; $3.50 seniors, students with ID, and children 6–12; by donation Thurs 6–9pm. Mon, Tues, Fri, and Sat 11am–6pm, Thurs 11am–9pm, Sun noon–5pm.

Diaspora Vibe Art Gallery && This art complex, housed in an

old bakery, is a funky artist hangout and is the home to some of the greatest artworks of Miami's diverse Caribbean, Latin American, and African-American cultures. The gallery has two seasons of shows, often focusing on emerging artists. During the winter, three artists are selected by the gallery to travel to and exhibit their works in Paris. On the last Friday of every month, from May through October, the gallery holds its fabulous "Final Fridays." A new artist's work is spotlighted inside, while outside in the courtyard are live music performances and readings of poetry and folk tales. Delicious Caribbean cuisine is also served. The who's who of Miami's cognoscenti gather here to recharge their cultural batteries.

561 NW 32nd St., Studio 48 (Bakehouse Art Complex), Miami. ℂ 305/759-1110. www.diasporavibe.com. Free admission. "Final Fridays" events $15. Mon–Fri by appointment; Sat–Sun 1–6pm; Final Fridays events May–Oct last Fri of the month 7–11pm.

Latin American Art Museum   In addition to the permanent collection of contemporary artists from Spain and Latin America, this museum hosts monthly exhibitions of works from Latin America and the Caribbean Basin. It's not a major attraction, but worth a stop if you're interested in Latin American art.

2206 SW 8th St., Little Havana. ℂ **305/644-1127.** Free admission. Tues–Fri 11am–5pm, Sat 11am–4pm. Closed Aug and major holidays.

Lowe Art Museum 𝕂𝕂   Located on the University of Miami campus, the Lowe Art Museum has a dazzling collection of 8,000 works that include American paintings, Latin American art, Navajo and Pueblo Indian textiles, and Renaissance and baroque art. Traveling exhibits such as *Rolling Stone* magazine's photo collection also stop here. For the most part, the Lowe is known for its collection of Greek and Roman antiquities, and, as compared to the more modern MOCA, Bass, and Miami Art Museum, features mostly European and international art hailing back to ancient times.

University of Miami, 1301 Stanford Dr. (at Ponce de León Blvd.), Coral Gables. ℂ 305/284-3603. www.lowemuseum.org. Admission $5 adults, $3 seniors and student with ID. Donation day is first Tues of the month. Tues, Wed, Fri, and Sat 10am–5pm, Thurs noon–7pm, Sun noon–5pm.

Miami Art Museum at the Miami–Dade Cultural Center 𝕂𝕂𝕂   The Miami Art Museum (MAM) features an eclectic mix of modern and contemporary works by such artists as Eric Fischl, Max Beckmann, Jim Dine, and Stuart Davis. Rotating exhibitions span the ages and styles, and often focus on Latin American or Caribbean artists. There are also fantastic themed exhibits such as the Andy Warhol exhibit, which featured all-night films by the artist, make-your-own pop art, cocktail hours, and parties with local deejays.

101 W. Flagler St., Miami. ℂ **305/375-3000.** www.miamiartmuseum.org. Admission $5 adults, $2.50 seniors and students, free for children under 12. Tues–Fri

10am–5pm; third Thurs of each month 10am–9pm; Sat–Sun noon–5pm. Closed major holidays. From I-95 south, exit at Orange Bowl–NW 8th St. and continue south to NW 2nd St.; turn left at NW 2nd St. and go 1½ blocks to NW 2nd Ave.; turn right.

Miami Museum of Science and Space Transit Planetarium 🐾🐾 (Kids)

The Museum of Science features more than 140 hands-on exhibits that explore the mysteries of the universe. Live demonstrations and collections of rare natural history specimens make a visit here fun and informative. Many of the demos involve audience participation, which can be lots of fun. There is also the Wildlife Center, with more than 175 live reptiles and birds of prey. The adjacent Space Transit Planetarium projects astronomy and laser shows as well as interactive demonstrations of upcoming computer technology and cyberspace features. Call, or visit their website, for a list of upcoming exhibits and laser shows.

3280 S. Miami Ave. (just south of the Rickenbacker Causeway), Coconut Grove. 𝓒 **305/646-4200** for general information or 305/854-2222 for planetarium show times. www.miamisci.org. $10 adults, $8 seniors and students, $6 children 3–12, free for children 2 and under; laser shows $6 adults, $3 seniors and children 3–12. After 4:30pm, ticket prices are half price. 25% discount for AAA members. Ticket prices include entrance to all museum galleries, planetarium shows, and the Wildlife Center. Museum of Science, daily 10am–6pm; call for planetarium show times (last show is at 4pm weekdays and 5pm on weekends). Closed Thanksgiving and Christmas days.

Museum of Contemporary Art (MOCA) 🐾🐾🐾

MOCA boasts an impressive collection of internationally acclaimed art with a local flavor. It is also known for its forward thinking and ability to discover and highlight new artists. A high-tech screening facility allows for film presentations to complement the exhibitions. You can see works by Jasper Johns, Roy Lichtenstein, Larry Rivers, Duane Michaels, and Claes Oldenberg, plus there are special exhibitions by such artists as Yoko Ono, Sigmar Polke, John Baldessari, and Goya.

770 NE 125th St., North Miami. 𝓒 **305/893-6211.** Fax 305/891-1472. www.mocanomi.org. Admission $5 adults, $3 seniors and students with ID, free for children 12 and under. Tues by donation. Tues–Sat 11am–5pm, Sun noon–5pm. Closed Mon and major holidays.

Rubell Family Art Collection 🐾🐾🐾 (Finds)

This impressive collection, owned by the Miami hotelier family, the Rubells, is housed in a two-story 40,000-square-foot former Drug Enforcement Agency warehouse in a sketchy area north of downtown Miami. The building looks like a fortress, which is fitting: Inside is a priceless collection of more than a thousand works of contemporary art, by the likes of Keith Haring, Damien Hirst, Julian Schnabel, Jean-Michel Basquiat, Paul McCarthy, Charles Ray, and Cindy Sherman. But be forewarned: Some of the art is extremely graphic and may be off-putting to some. The gallery changes exhibitions twice yearly and there is a seasonal program of lectures, artists' talks, and performances by prominent artists. As of press time, the gallery was looking to enlarge the current facility in order to accommodate this ever-growing, ever-impressive collection.

95 NW 29th St. (on the corner of NW 1st Ave. near the Design District), Miami. ✆ 305/573-6090. Free admission. Thurs–Sat 9am–9pm and by appointment.

4 Historic Homes & Sites

South Beach's well-touted Art Deco District is but one of many colorful neighborhoods that can boast dazzling architecture. The rediscovery of the entire Biscayne Corridor (from downtown to about 80th St. and Biscayne Blvd.) has given light to a host of ancillary neighborhoods on either side that are filled with Mediterranean-style homes and Frank Lloyd Wright gems. Coral Gables is home to many large and beautiful homes, mansions, and churches that reflect architecture from the 1920s, '30s, and '40s. Some of the homes, or portions of their structures, have been created from coral rock and shells.

Barnacle State Historic Site ★★ The former home of naval architect and early settler Ralph Middleton Munroe is now a museum in the heart of Coconut Grove. It's the oldest house in Miami and it rests on its original foundation, which sits on 5 acres of hardwood and landscaped lawns. The house's quiet surroundings, wide porches, and period furnishings illustrate how Miami's first snowbird lived in the days before condo-mania and luxury hotels. Enthusiastic and knowledgeable state park employees offer a wealth of historical information.

3485 Main Hwy. (1 block south of Commodore Plaza), Coconut Grove. ✆ 305/448-9445. Fax 305/448-7484. Admission $1. Concerts $5, free for children under 10. Fri–Mon 9am–4pm. Tours Fri–Sun at 10am, 11:30am, 1pm, and 2:30pm. From downtown Miami, take U.S. 1 south to 27th Ave., make a left, and continue to S. Bayshore Dr.; then make a right, follow to the intersection of Main Hwy., and turn left.

Coral Castle ★★ (Finds) There's plenty of competition, but Coral Castle is probably the strangest attraction in Florida. In 1923, the story goes, a 26-year-old crazed Latvian, suffering from unrequited love of a 16-year-old who left him at the altar, immigrated to South Miami and spent the next 25 years of his life carving huge boulders into a prehistoric-looking roofless "castle." It seems impossible that one rather short man could have done all this, but there are scores of affidavits on display from neighbors who swear it happened. An interesting 25-minute audio tour guides you through the spot, now in the National Register of Historic Places. Although Coral Castle is overpriced and undermaintained, it's worth a visit when in the area, about 37 miles from Miami.

28655 S. Dixie Hwy., Homestead. ⓒ 305/248-6345. www.coralcastle.com. Admission $9.75 adults, $6.50 seniors, $5 children 7–12. Daily 7am–9pm. Take 836 West (Dolphin Expressway) toward Miami International Airport. Merge onto 826 South (Palmetto Expressway) and take it to the Florida Turnpike toward Homestead. Take the 288th St. exit (#5) and then take a right on South Dixie Hwy., a left on SW 157th Ave., and then a sharp left back onto South Dixie Hwy. Coral Castle is about .05 miles down on the left side of the street.

United in Elián House   It was only a matter of time. After Elián González was rescued from a raft off the coast of Fort Lauderdale in November 1999, he lived in this modest, now famous, house with relatives for 5 months before being reunited with his father and returned to Cuba in a storm of controversy. For Cuban nationals, the house became a shrine and the boy became a symbol for their struggle. See where Elián lived, played, breathed, and ate. See Elián's toys. See where the international media camped out. See where relatives cried for the cameras. You get the picture.

2319 NW 2nd St., Little Havana. No tel. Sunday 10am–6pm. Free admission.

Venetian Pool ⭐⭐⭐ *Kids*   Miami's most beautiful and unusual swimming pool, dating from 1924, is hidden behind pastel stucco walls and is honored with a listing in the National Register of Historic Places. Underground artesian wells feed the free-form lagoon, which is shaded by three-story Spanish porticos and features both fountains and waterfalls. It can be cold in the winter months. During summer, the pool's 800,000 gallons of water are drained and refilled nightly thanks to an underground aquifer, ensuring a cool, *clean* swim. Visitors are free to swim and sunbathe here.

2701 DeSoto Blvd. (at Toledo St.), Coral Gables. ⓒ 305/460-5356. www.venetian pool.com. Admission and hours vary seasonally. Nov–Mar $5.50 for those 13 and older, $2.50 children under 13; April–Oct, $8.50 for those 13 and older, $4.50 children under 13. Children must be 3 years old and provide proof of age with birth certificate, or 38 inches tall to enter. Hours are at least 11am–4:30pm, but are often longer. Call for more information.

The Vizcaya Museum and Gardens ⭐⭐⭐   Sometimes referred to as the "Hearst Castle of the East," this magnificent villa is more Gatsby-esque than anything else you'll find in Miami. It was built in 1916 as a winter retreat for James Deering, co-founder and former vice president of International Harvester. The industrialist was fascinated by 16th-century art and architecture and his ornate mansion, which took 1,000 artisans 5 years to build, became a celebration of that period. If you love antiques, this place is a dream come true, packed with European relics and works of art from the 16th to the 19th centuries. Most of the original furnishings, including dishes and paintings, are still intact. You will see very early versions of a telephone switchboard, central vacuum cleaning system, elevators, and fire sprinklers. A free guided tour of the 34 furnished rooms on the first floor takes about 45 minutes. The second floor, which consists mostly of bedrooms, is open to tour on your own. The spectacularly opulent villa wraps itself around a central courtyard. Outside, lush formal gardens front an enormous swath of Biscayne Bay. Definitely take the tour of the rooms, but immediately thereafter, you will want to wander and get lost in the gardens.

3251 S. Miami Ave. (just south of Rickenbacker Causeway), North Coconut Grove. © 305/250-9133. www.vizcayamuseum.com. Admission $10 adults, $5 children 6–12, free for children 5 and under. Villa daily 9:30am–5pm (ticket booth closes at 4:30pm); gardens daily 9:30am–5:30pm.

5 Nature Preserves, Parks & Gardens

The Miami area is a great place for outdoors types, with beaches, parks, nature preserves, and gardens galore.

At the historic **Bill Baggs Cape Florida State Park** ⚓, 1200 Crandon Blvd. (© **305/361-5811**), at the southern tip of Key Biscayne about 20 minutes from downtown Miami, you can explore the unfettered wilds and enjoy some of the most secluded beaches in Miami. There's also a historic lighthouse that was built in 1825, which is the oldest lighthouse in South Florida. The lighthouse was damaged during the Second Seminole War (1836) and again in 1861 during the Civil War. Out of commission for a while, in 1978 the U.S. Coast Guard restored it to working lighthouse condition. A rental shack leases bikes, hydrobikes, kayaks, and many more water toys. It's a great place to picnic, and a newly constructed restaurant serves homemade Latin food, including great fish soups and sandwiches. Just be careful that the raccoons don't get your lunch—the furry black-eyed beasts are everywhere. Wildlife aside, however, Bill Baggs has been consistently rated as one of the top 10 beaches in the U.S. for its 1¼ miles of wide, sandy beaches and its secluded, serene atmosphere. Admission is $4 per car with up to eight people. Open daily from 8am to sunset. Tours of the lighthouse are available every Thursday through Monday at 10am and 1pm. Arrive at least half an hour early to sign up—there is only room for 10 people on each. Take I-95 to the Rickenbacker Causeway and take that all the way to the end.

Fairchild Tropical Garden ★★★, at 10901 Old Cutler Rd. in South Miami (© **305/667-1651;** www.ftg.org), is the largest of its kind in the continental United States. A veritable rain forest of both rare and exotic plants, as well as 11 lakes and countless meadows, are spread across 83 acres. Palmettos, vine pergola, palm glades, and other unique species create a scenic, lush environment. More than 100 species of birds have been spotted at the garden (ask for a check-list at the front gate), and it's home to a variety of animals. You should not miss the 30-minute narrated tram tour (tours leave on the hour 10am–3pm weekdays and 10am–4pm weekends) to learn about the various flowers and trees on the grounds. There is also a museum, a cafe, a picnic area, and a gift shop with fantastic books on gardening, cooking, and edible gifts. The 2-acre rain-forest exhibit, Windows to the Tropics, will save you a trip to the Amazon. Expect to spend a minimum of 2 hours here.

Admission is $8 for adults and free for children 12 and under accompanied by an adult. Open daily, except Dec. 25, from 9:30am to 4:30pm. Take I-95 south to U.S. 1, turn left onto Le Jeune Road, and follow it straight to the traffic circle; from there, take Old Cutler Road 2 miles to the park.

Located on Biscayne Bay in Coconut Grove (4013 Douglas Rd.; www.ntbg.org/kampong.html), the **Kampong** ★★ is a 7-acre botanical garden featuring a stunning array of flowering trees and tropical fruit trees including mango, avocado, and pomelos. In the early 1900s, noted plant explorer David Fairchild traveled the world seeking rare plants of economic and aesthetic value that might be cultivated in the United States. In 1928, he and his wife, Marian (daughter of Alexander Graham Bell), built a two-story residence here (listed on the National Register of Historic Places) amid some of his collections, borrowing the Malaysian word *kampong* for his home in a garden. It's a must-see for those interested in horticulture. Tours are by appointment only, from Monday to Friday. For tour information, call © **305/442-7169.** Admission is $10 a person. Take U.S. 1 to Douglas Road (SW 37th Ave.). Go east on Douglas Road for about a mile. The Kampong will be on your left.

Named after the late champion of the Everglades, the **Marjory Stoneman Douglas Biscayne Nature Center** ★, 6767 Crandon Blvd., Key Biscayne (© **305/361-6767;** www.biscaynenature center.org), has just moved into a brand-new $4 million facility and offers hands-on marine exploration, hikes through coastal hammocks, bike trips, and beach walks. Local environmentalists and historians lead intriguing trips through the local habitat. Call to reserve a spot on a regularly scheduled weekend tour or program. Be sure to wear comfortable closed-toe shoes for hikes through wet or rocky terrain. Open daily 10am to 7pm Memorial Day through Labor Day; daily 10am to 4pm the rest of year. Admission to park is $4 per person; admission to nature center free. Call for weekend programs. To get there, take I-95 to the Rickenbacker Causeway Exit (#1) and take the causeway all the way until it becomes Crandon Boulevard. The center is on the east side of the street (the Atlantic Ocean side). Driving time is about 25 minutes from downtown Miami.

Because so many people are so focused on the beach itself, the **Miami Beach Botanical Garden,** 2000 Convention Center Dr., Miami Beach (© **305/673-7256**), remains a mostly secret garden. The lush, tropical 4½-acre garden is a fabulous, all-natural retreat from the city. Open Monday through Friday from 8:30am to 5pm, Saturday and Sunday from 9:30am to 5pm. Admission is free.

The **Oleta River State Recreation Area** 𝕽𝕽, 3400 NE 163rd St., North Miami (© **305/919-1846**), consists of 993 acres—the largest urban park in the state—on Biscayne Bay. With miles of bicycle and canoe trails, a sandy swimming beach, shaded picnic pavilions, and a fishing pier, Oleta River State Recreation Area offers visitors an outstanding outdoor recreational experience cloistered from the confines of the big city. Open daily from 8am to sunset. Admission for pedestrians and cyclists is $1 per person; by car: driver plus car, $2; driver plus up to 7 passengers and car, $4. Take 1-95 to exit 17 (SR 826 East), and go all the way east until just before the causeway. The park entrance is on your right. Driving time from downtown Miami is about a half hour.

A testament to Miami's unusual climate, the **Preston B. Bird and Mary Heinlein Fruit and Spice Park** 𝕽, 24801 SW 187th Ave., Homestead (© **305/247-5727**), harbors rare fruit trees that cannot survive elsewhere in the country. If a volunteer is available, you'll learn some fascinating things about this 30-acre living plant museum, where the most exotic varieties of fruits and spices—ackee, mango, Ugli fruits, carambola, and breadfruit—grow on strange-looking trees with unpronounceable names. There are also original coral rock buildings dating back to 1912.

The best part? You're free to take anything that *naturally* falls to the ground. You'll also find samples of interesting fruits and jellies made from the park's bounty as well as exotic ingredients and cookbooks in the gift store.

Admission to the spice park is $3.50 for adults and $1 for children under 12. It's open daily from 10am to 5pm; closed major holidays.

Tours are included in the price of admission and are offered at 11am, 1pm, and 2:30pm. Take U.S. 1 south, turn right on SW 248th Street, and go straight for 5 miles to SW 187th Avenue. The drive from Miami should take 45 minutes to an hour.

6 Sightseeing Cruises & Organized Tours
BOAT & CRUISE-SHIP TOURS

You don't need a boating license or a zillion-dollar yacht to explore Miami by boat. Thanks to several enterprising companies, boat tours are easy to find, affordable, and are an excellent way to see the city from a more liquid perspective.

Bay Escape ⍟ This 1-hour air-conditioned cruise will take you past Millionaires' Row and the Venetian Islands for just $10. There's also a food stand and cash bar. The tours are bilingual.

Bayside Marketplace Marina, 401 Biscayne Blvd., Downtown. ℭ **305/373-7001.** All tickets $10; free for children 12 and under. Millionaires' Row tour daily 1, 3, 5, and 7pm. Evening party cruise (music and cash bar) Fri–Sat 9–11pm.

***Heritage Miami II* Topsail Schooner** This relaxing ride aboard Miami's only tall ship is a fun way to see the city, since it's on a schooner (as opposed to the other tour company's cruising boats), which gives you more of a feel of the water. The 2-hour cruise passes by Villa Vizcaya, Coconut Grove, and Key Biscayne and puts you in sight of Miami's spectacular skyline and island homes. Call to make sure the ship is running on schedule. On Friday, Saturday, and Sunday evenings, there are 1-hour tours to see the lights of the city, leaving at 6:30pm, for $10 per person.

Bayside Marketplace Marina, 401 Biscayne Blvd., Downtown. ℭ **305/442-9697.** Fax 305/442-0119. Tickets for day tours $15 adults, $10 children 12 and under. Sept–May only. Tours leave daily at 1:30, 4, and 6:30pm and Fri–Sun also at 9, 10, and 11pm.

Water Taxi ⍟⍟⍟ *Value* Not exactly a tour, per se, the Water Taxi is a cheap and fantastic way to see the city via local waterways. The two major routes run between Bayside Marketplace and the 5th Street Marina on South Beach; the second is basically a downtown water shuttle service between the various hotels in downtown as well as the Port of Miami, the Hard Rock Cafe at Bayside, East Coast Fisheries, and Fisher Island. Cost is $7 one way, $12 round trip, and $15 for an all-day pass. The Bayside/South Beach trip is the best one to take because there aren't as many stops.

ℭ **305/467-6677.** www.watertaxi.com.

Tips **Go Ahead, Act Like a Tourist!**

The Miami Tourist Bus may sound like a savvy traveler's worst nightmare, but if you want to see the city London-style on a double-decker diesel bus *and* get a tan, this is your best bet. Running daily from Aventura to Miami's Kendall suburb, the bus allows unlimited hop-on/hop-off service at popular stops such as Sunset Place, CocoWalk, and Bayside, and has on-board commentary and history as you're being driven through the city. The bus also takes you through the Art Deco District and the tony Bal Harbour Shops, all for a $20 day pass. Weeklong passes are also available for $45. For more information, call ℭ **305/573-8687** or log onto www.miamitouristbus.com.

SIGHTSEEING TOURS

While there are several sightseeing tour operators in Miami, most, unfortunately, either don't speak English or are just plain shoddy. The following is the one we'd recommend:

Miami Nice Excursion Travel and Service ℱ   Pick your destination, and the Miami Nice tours will take you to the Everglades, Fort Lauderdale, South Beach, the Seaquarium, Key West, Cape Canaveral, or wherever else you desire. The best trip for first-timers is the City Tour, a comprehensive tour of the entire city and its various neighborhoods. If you've got the time, you will definitely want to add on a side trip to the Everglades and/or Key West (though I suggest exploring the Everglades on your own). Included in most Miami trips is a fairly comprehensive city tour narrated by a knowledgeable guide. The company is one of the oldest in town.

18430 Collins Ave., Miami Beach. ℭ **305/949-9180.** http://miaminicetours.com. Tours are $29–$55 adults, $25 children. Daily 7am–10pm. Call ahead for directions to various pickup areas.

SPECIALIZED TOURS

In addition to those listed below, a great option for seeing the city is to take a tour led by **Dr. Paul George.** Dr. George is a history teacher at Miami–Dade Community College and a historian at the Historical Museum of Southern Florida. He also happens to be "Mr. Miami." There's a set calendar of tours (including the Mystery, Murder, and Mayhem Bus Tour detailed below), and all of them are fascinating to South Florida buffs. Tours focus on neighborhoods, such as Little Havana, Brickell Avenue, or Key Biscayne, and on themes, such as Miami cemeteries and the Miami River. The often long-winded discussions can be a bit much for those who just want a quick look around, but Dr. George certainly knows his stuff. The cost is $15 to $25; reservations are required (℃ **305/375-1621**). Tours leave from the Historical Museum at 101 W. Flagler St., Downtown.

Biltmore Hotel Tour ★★★ *Value*   Take advantage of these free Sunday walking tours to enjoy the hotel's beautiful grounds. The Biltmore is chock-full of history and mystery, including a few ghosts; go out there and see for yourself. In addition, there are also free weekly fireside sessions that are open to the public and presented by Miami Storytellers. Learn about the hotel's early days and rich stories of the city's past. These wonderful sessions are held in the main lobby by the fireplace and are accompanied by a glass of champagne. Call ahead to confirm.

1200 Anastasia Ave., Coral Gables. ℃ 305/445-1926. www.biltmorehotel.com. Free admission. Tours depart on Sun at 1:30, 2:30, and 3:30pm. Call for times of storytelling sessions.

Miami Design Preservation League ★★   On Thursday evenings and Saturday mornings, the Design Preservation League sponsors walking tours that offer a fascinating inside look at the city's historic Art Deco District. Tour-goers meet for a 1½-hour walk through some of America's most exuberantly "architectured" buildings. The league led the fight to designate this area a National Historic District and is proud to share the splendid locale with visitors. Also, see p. 117 for more information.

Art Deco Welcome Center, 1001 Ocean Dr., South Beach. ℃ 305/672-2014. www. mdpl.org. Walking tours $10 per person. Tours leave Sat at 10:30am and Thurs at 6:30pm. Self-guided audio tours also available daily for $10. No reservations necessary. Call ahead for updated schedules.

Mystery, Murder, and Mayhem Bus Tour ★★★   Visit the past by video and bus to Miami–Dade's most celebrated crimes and criminals from the 1800s to the present. From the murder spree of the Ashley Gang to the most notorious murders and crimes of our century, including the murder of designer Gianni Versace, historian Paul George conducts a most fascinating 3-hour tour of scandalous proportions.

Leaves Sat at 10pm from the Dade Cultural Center, 101 W. Flagler St., Miami. Tickets $35. Advance reservations required; call ℃ 305/375-1621.

7 Watersports

There are many ways to get well acquainted with Miami's wet look. Choose your own adventure from the suggestions listed below.

BOATING

Private rental outfits include **Boat Rental Plus,** 2400 Collins Ave., Miami Beach (🕿 **305/534-4307**), where 50-horsepower 18-foot powerboats rent for some of the best prices on the beach. There's a 2-hour minimum and rates go from $99 to $449, including taxes and gas. They also have great specials on Sundays. A $250 cash or credit card deposit is required. Cruising is permitted only in and around Biscayne Bay. Ocean access is prohibited. Renters must be over 21. The rental office is at 23rd Street, on the inland waterway in Miami Beach. It's open daily from 10am to sunset. If you want a specific type of boat, call ahead to reserve. Otherwise, show up and take what's available.

Club Nautico of Coconut Grove, 2560 S. Bayshore Dr. (🕿 **305/858-6258**), rents high-quality powerboats for fishing, water-skiing, diving, and cruising in the bay or ocean. All boats are Coast Guard equipped, with VHF radios and safety gear. Rates range from $199 for 4 hours and $299 for 8 hours, to as much as $419 on weekends. Club Nautico is open daily from 9am to 5pm (weather permitting). Other locations include the Crandon Park Marina, 4000 Crandon Blvd., Key Biscayne (🕿 **305/361-9217**), with the same rates and hours as the Coconut Grove location; and the Miami Beach Marina, Pier E, 300 Alton Rd., South Beach (🕿 **305/673-2502**), where rates range from $229 for 4 hours and from $299 for 8 hours. Nautico on Miami Beach is open daily from 9am to 5pm. For money-saving coupons, log on to www.boatrent.com.

JET SKIS/WAVERUNNERS

Don't miss a chance to tour the islands on the back of your own powerful watercraft. Bravery is, however, a prerequisite, as Miami's waterways are full of speeding jet-skiers and boaters who think they're in the Indy 500. Many beachfront concessionaires rent a variety of these popular (and loud) water scooters. The latest models are fast and smooth. Try **Tony's Jet Ski Rentals,** 3601 Rickenbacker Causeway, Key Biscayne (🕿 **305/361-8280**), one of the city's largest rental shops, located on a private beach in the Miami Marine Stadium lagoon. There are three models available accommodating up to three people. Rates range from $45 for a half hour to $80 for a full hour, depending on the number of riders. Tony's is open daily from 10:30am to 6:30pm.

SAILING

You can rent sailboats and catamarans through the beachfront concessions desk of several top resorts, such as the **Doral Golf Resort and Spa** (see p. 77).

Sailboats of Key Biscayne Rentals and Sailing School, in the Crandon Marina (next to Sundays on the Bay), 4000 Crandon Blvd., Key Biscayne (℗ **305/361-0328** days, 305/279-7424 evenings), can also get you out on the water. A 22-foot sailboat rents for $27 an hour or $81 for a half day. A Cat-25 or J24 is available for $35 an hour or $110 for a half day. If you've always had a dream to win the America's Cup but can't sail, the able teachers at Sailboats will get you started. They offer a 10-hour course over 5 days for $300 for one person or $400 for you and a buddy.

SCUBA DIVING & SNORKELING

In 1981, the U.S. government began a wide-scale project designed to increase the number of habitats available to marine organisms. One of the program's major accomplishments has been the creation of nearby artificial reefs, which have attracted all kinds of tropical plants, fish, and animals.

Diver's Paradise of Key Biscayne, 4000 Crandon Blvd. (℗ **305/ 361-3483**), offers two dive expeditions daily to the more than 30 wrecks and artificial reefs off the coast of Miami Beach and Key Biscayne. You can take a 3-day certification course for $399, which includes all the dives and gear. If you already have your C-card, a dive trip costs about $90 if you need equipment and only $35 if you bring your own gear. It's open Monday to Friday from 10am to 6pm and Saturday and Sunday from 8am to 6pm. Call ahead for times and locations of dives. For snorkeling, they will also set you up with equipment and maps on where to see the best underwater sights. Rental for mask, fins, and snorkel is $15.

South Beach Divers, 850 Washington Ave., Miami Beach (℗ **305/531-6110**) will also be happy to tell you where to go under the sea and will provide you with rental equipment as well for $30, which includes the mask, fins, and snorkel. They also do dive trips to Key Largo three times a week and do dives off Miami on Sundays at $95 for a two-tank dive.

WINDSURFING

Many hotels rent windsurfers to their guests, but if yours doesn't have a watersports concession stand, head for Key Biscayne.

Sailboards Miami, Rickenbacker Causeway, Key Biscayne (℗ **305/361-SAIL**), operates out of big yellow trucks on Hobie Beach, the most popular windsurfing spot in the city. For those who've never ridden a board but want to try it, they offer a 2-hour lesson for $69 that's guaranteed to turn you into a wave warrior or you get your money back. After that, you can rent a board for $26 an hour or $38 for 2 hours. If you want to make a day of it, a 10-hour prepaid card costs $150. These cards require you to prepay, but they also reduce the price by about $70 for the day. You can use the card all year, until the time on it runs out. Open daily from 10am to 5:30pm. Make your first right after the tollbooth (at the beginning of the causeway—you can't miss it) to find the outfitters.

8 More Ways to Play, Indoors & Out

BIKING

Biking note: Children under the age of 16 are required by Florida law to wear a helmet, which can be purchased at any bike store or retail outlet selling biking supplies. The cement promenade on the southern tip of South Beach is a great place to ride. Biking up the beach (on either the beach or along the beach on a cement pathway—which is a lot easier!) is great for surf, sun, sand, exercise, and people-watching—just be sure to keep your eyes on the road, as the scenery can be most distracting. Most of the big beach hotels rent bicycles, as does the **Miami Beach Bicycle Center,** 601 5th Street, South Beach (*②* **305/674-0150**), which charges $5 per hour or $14 per day. It's open Monday to Saturday from 10am to 7pm, Sunday from 10am to 5pm.

Bikers can also enjoy more than 130 miles of paved paths throughout Miami. The beautiful and quiet streets of Coral Gables and Coconut Grove are great for bicyclists. Several bike trails are spread throughout these neighborhoods, where old trees form canopies over wide, flat roads lined with grand homes and quaint street markers.

The terrain in Key Biscayne is perfect for biking, especially along the park and beach roads. If you don't mind the sound of cars whooshing by your bike lane, **Rickenbacker Causeway** is also fantastic, since it is one of the only bikeable inclines in Miami from which you get fantastic elevated views. However, be warned that this is a grueling ride, especially going up the causeway. **Key Biking,** 61 Harbor Dr., Key Biscayne (*②* **305/361-0061**), rents mountain bikes for $5 an hour or $15 a day. It's open Monday through Friday from 10am to 7pm, Saturday from 10am to 6pm, and Sunday from 11am to 4pm.

FISHING

Fishing licenses are required in Florida. If you go out with one of the fishing charter boats listed below, you are automatically accredited, because the companies are. If you go out on your own, however,

you must have a Florida fishing license, which costs $16.50. Call
© **888/FISH-FLORIDA** for more information.

Some of the best surf casting in the city can be had at **Haulover
Beach Park** at Collins Avenue and 105th Street, where there's a
bait-and-tackle shop right on the pier. **South Pointe Park,** at the
southern tip of Miami Beach, is another popular fishing spot and
features a long pier, comfortable benches, and a great view of the
ships passing through Government Cut, the deep channel made
when the port of Miami was dug.

Key Biscayne offers deep-sea fishing to those willing to get their
hands dirty and pay a bundle. The competition among the boats is
fierce, but the prices are basically the same no matter which you
choose. The going rate is about $400 to $450 for a half day and
$600 to $700 for a full day of fishing. These rates are usually for a
party of up to six, and the boats supply you with rods and bait as
well as instruction for first-timers. Some will take you out to the
Upper Keys if the fish aren't biting in Miami.

You might also consider the following boats, all of which sail out
of the Key Biscayne marina and are in relatively good shape and
nicer than most out there: *Sunny Boy III* (*©* **305/361-2217**),
Queen B (*©* **305/361-2528**), and *L & H* (*©* **305/361-9318**). Call
for reservations.

Bridge fishing in Biscayne Bay is also popular in Miami; you'll see
people with poles over almost every waterway. But look carefully for
signs telling you whether it's legal to do so wherever you are. Some
bridges forbid fishing.

GOLF

There are more than 50 private and public golf courses in the Miami
area. Contact the **Greater Miami Convention and Visitors Bureau**
(*©* **800/933-8448**; www.miamiandbeaches.com) for a list of courses
and costs.

The best hotel courses in Miami are found at the **Doral Golf
Resort and Spa** (see p. 77), home of the legendary Blue Monster
course as well as the Gold Course, designed by Raymond Floyd; the
Great White Shark Course; and the Silver Course, refinished by
Jerry Pate.

Other hotels with excellent golf courses include the **Turnberry
Isle Resort & Club** (see p. 78), with two Robert Trent
Jones–designed courses for guests and members, and the **Biltmore
Hotel** ☆☆ (see p. 73), which is my pick for best public golf course,

because of its modest greens fees and an 18-hole par-71 course located on the hotel's spectacular grounds. It must be good: Despite his penchant for privacy, former President Bill Clinton prefers teeing off at this course over any other in Miami!

Otherwise, the following represent some of the area's best public courses. **Crandon Park Golf Course,** formerly known as the Links, 6700 Crandon Blvd., Key Biscayne (© **305/361-9129**), is the number one ranked municipal course in the state and one of the top five in the country. The park is situated on 200 bayfront acres and offers a pro shop, rentals, lessons, carts, and a lighted driving range. The course is open daily from dawn to dusk; greens fees (including cart) are $86 per person during the winter and $45 per person during the summer. Special twilight rates are available.

One of the most popular courses among real enthusiasts is the semi-private **Doral Park Golf and Country Club,** 5001 NW 104th Ave., West Miami (© **305/591-8800**); it's not related to the Doral Hotel or spa. Call to book in advance, since this challenging 18-holer is extremely popular. The course is open from 6:30am to 6pm during the winter and until 7pm during the summer. Cart and greens fees vary, so call © **305/594-0954** for information.

Known as one of the best in the city, the **Golf Club of Miami,** 6801 Miami Gardens Dr., at NW 68th Avenue, North Miami (© **305/829-8456**), has three 18-hole courses of varying degrees of difficulty. You'll encounter lush fairways, rolling greens, and some history to boot. The west course, designed in 1961 by Robert Trent Jones and updated in the 1990s by the PGA, was where Jack Nicklaus played his first professional tournament and Lee Trevino won his first professional championship. The course is open daily from 6:30am to sunset. Cart and greens fees are $45 to $75 per person during the winter, and $20 to $34 per person during the summer. Special twilight rates are available.

Golfers looking for some cheap practice time will appreciate **Haulover Park Beach,** 10800 Collins Ave., Miami Beach (© **305/940-6719**), in a pretty bayside location. The longest hole on this par-27 course is 125 yards. It's open daily from 7:30am to 5:30pm during the winter, and until 7:30pm during the summer. Greens fees are $5 per person during the winter and $4 per person during the summer. Handcarts cost $1.40.

IN-LINE SKATING

Miami's consistently flat terrain makes in-line skating a breeze. Lincoln Road, for example, is a virtual skating rink as bladers compete with bikers and walkers for a slab of slate. But the city's heavy traffic and construction do make it tough to find long routes suitable for blading.

Because of the popularity of blading and skateboarding, the city has passed a law prohibiting skating on the west side (the cafe-lined strip) of Ocean Drive in the evenings, as well as a law that all bladers must skate slowly and safely. Also, if you're going to partake in the sport, remember to keep a pair of sandals or sneakers with you, since many area shops won't allow you inside with skates on.

Despite all the rules, you can still have fun, and the following rental outfit can help chart an interesting course for you and supply you with all the necessary gear. In South Beach, **Fritz's Skate Shop,** 726 Lincoln Rd. Mall (© **305/532-1954**), rents top-quality skates, including safety pads, for $8 per hour, $24 per day, and $34 overnight. If you're an in-line skater newbie, an instructor will hold your hand for $25 an hour. The shop also stocks gear and clothing.

SWIMMING

There is no shortage of water in the Miami area. See the **Venetian Pool** listing (p. 127), the "Miami's Beaches" section earlier in this chapter, and chapter 1, "The Best of Miami" for descriptions of good swimming options.

TENNIS

Hundreds of tennis courts in the area are open to the public for a minimal fee. Most courts operate on a first-come, first-served basis, and are open from sunrise to sunset. For information and directions, call the **City of Miami Beach Recreation, Culture, and Parks Department** (© **305/673-7730**) or the **City of Miami Parks and Recreation Department** (© **305/575-5256**).

Of the 590 public tennis courts throughout Miami, the three hard courts and seven clay courts at the **Key Biscayne Tennis Association,** 6702 Crandon Blvd. (© **305/361-5263**), are the best and most beautiful. Because of this, they often get crowded on weekends. There's a pleasant, if limited, pro shop, plus many good pros. Only four courts are lit at night, but if you reserve at least 48 hours in advance, you can usually take your pick. They cost $6 per person per hour. Courts are open daily from 8am to 9pm.

Other courts are pretty run of the mill and can be found in most neighborhoods. I do, however, recommend the **Miami Beach public courts at Flamingo Park,** 1001 12th St. in South Beach (© **305/673-7761**), where there are 19 clay courts that cost $2.50

per person an hour during the day and $3 per person an hour at night. It's first come, first serve.

Hotels with the best tennis facilities are the Biltmore, Turnberry Isle Resort and Spa, and the Doral Resort and Spa. See chapter 4, "Where to Stay," for information about these accommodations.

9 Spectator Sports

Check the *Miami Herald*'s sports section for a daily listing of local events and the paper's Friday "Weekend" section for comprehensive coverage and in-depth reports. For last-minute tickets, call the venue directly, since many season ticket holders sell singles and return unused tickets.

BASEBALL

The **Florida Marlins** shocked the sports world in 1997 when they became the youngest expansion team to win a World Series, but then floundered as their star players were sold off by former owner Wayne Huizenga. As long as the rebuilding process continues and the Marlins continue to struggle, tickets are easy to come by. If you're interested in catching a game, be warned: The summer heat in Miami can be unbearable, even in the evenings.

Home games are held at the **Pro Player Stadium,** 2267 NW 199th St., North Miami Beach (✆ **305/626-7426**). Tickets range from $4 to $50. Box office hours are Monday to Friday from 8:30am to 6pm, Saturday from 8:30am to 4pm, and before games; tickets are also available through Ticketmaster.

BASKETBALL

The **Miami Heat** (✆ **305/577-HEAT** or 305/835-7000), now led by celebrity coach Pat Riley, made its NBA debut in November 1988 and their games remain one of Miami's hottest tickets. Courtside seats are full of visiting celebrities from Puff Daddy to Madonna. The season lasts from October to April, with most games beginning at 7:30pm. They play in the brand-new waterfront **American Airlines Arena** located downtown on Biscayne Boulevard. Tickets are $14 to $50. Box office hours are Monday to Friday from 10am to 4pm (until 8pm on game nights); tickets are also available through Ticketmaster.

FOOTBALL

Miami's golden boys are the **Miami Dolphins,** the city's most recognizable team, followed by thousands of "dolfans." The team plays at least eight home games during the season, between September and December, at **Pro Player Stadium,** 2267 NW 199th St., North Miami Beach (☎ **305/620-2578**). Tickets cost between $20 and $40. The box office is open Monday to Friday from 8:30am to 5:30pm; tickets are also available through Ticketmaster.

JAI ALAI

Jai alai, sort of a Spanish-style indoor lacrosse, was introduced to Miami in 1924 and is regularly played in two Miami-area frontons (the buildings in which jai alai is played). Although the sport has roots stemming from ancient Egypt, the game, as it's now played, was invented by Basque peasants in the Pyrenees Mountains during the 17th century.

Players use woven baskets, called *cestas,* to hurl balls, called *pelotas,* at speeds that sometimes exceed 170 mph. Spectators, who are protected behind a wall of glass, place bets on the evening's players. The Florida Gaming Corporation owns the jai alai operations throughout the state, making betting on this sport as legal as buying a lottery ticket.

The **Miami Jai Alai Fronton,** 3500 NW 37th Ave., at NW 35th Street (☎ **305/633-6400**), is America's oldest fronton, dating from 1926. It schedules 13 games per night, which typically last 10 to 20 minutes, but can go much longer. Admission is $1 to the grandstand, $5 to the clubhouse. There are year-round games on Monday and Wednesday to Saturday at 7pm, and matinees on Monday, Wednesday, and Saturday at noon. This is the main location where jai alai is played in Miami. The other South Florida jai alai venue is in Dania, near the Fort Lauderdale Hollywood International Airport.

10 Animal Parks

For a tropical climate, Miami's got a lot of nontropical animals to see, and we're not talking about the motorists on I-95. Everything from dolphins and alligators to lions, tigers, and bears call Miami home (most in parks, some in nature). Call the parks to inquire about discount packages or coupons, which may be offered at area retail stores or in local papers.

Miami Metrozoo 𝒦𝒦 (Kids) This 290-acre, sparsely landscaped complex (it was devastated by Hurricane Andrew) is quite a distance from Miami proper and the beaches—about 45 minutes—but worth the trip. Isolated and never really crowded, it's also completely cageless—animals are kept at bay by cleverly designed moats. This is a fantastic spot to take younger kids (the older ones seem bored and unstimulated here); there's a wonderful petting zoo and play area, and the zoo offers several daily programs designed to educate and entertain. Residents include two rare white Bengal tigers, a Komodo dragon, rare koala bears, a number of kangaroos, and an African meerkat. The air-conditioned Zoofari Monorail tour offers visitors a nice overview of the park. An Andean Condor · exhibit opened in 2000, and the zoo is always upgrading its facilities, including the impressive aviary. *Note:* The distance between animal habitats can be great, so you'll be doing *a lot* of walking here. Also, because the zoo can be miserably hot during summer months, plan these visits in the early morning or late afternoon. Expect to spend about 3 hours here.

12400 SW 152nd St., South Miami. ℂ **305/251-0400.** www.zsf.org. Admission $8.95 adults, $4.75 children 3–12. Daily 9:30am–5:30pm (ticket booth closes at 4pm). Free parking. From U.S. 1 south, turn right on SW 152nd St. and follow signs about 3 miles to the entrance.

Miami Seaquarium *(Kids* *(Overrated*   If you've been to Orlando's SeaWorld, you may be disappointed with Miami's version, which is considerably smaller and not as well maintained. It's hardly a sprawling seaquarium, but you will want to arrive early to enjoy the effects of its mild splash. You'll need at least 3 hours to tour the 35-acre oceanarium and see all four daily shows starring a number of showy ocean mammals. You can cut your visit to 2 hours if you limit your shows to the better, albeit corny, Flipper Show and Killer Whale Show. The highly regarded Water and Dolphin Exploration Program (WADE) allows visitors to touch and swim with dolphins in the Flipper Lagoon. The program costs $125 per person and is offered twice daily, Wednesday through Sunday. Children must be at least 52 inches tall to participate. Reservations are necessary for this program. Call ℂ **305/365-2501** in advance for reservations.

4400 Rickenbacker Causeway (south side), en route to Key Biscayne. ℂ **305/361-5705.** www.miamiseaquarium.com. Admission $23.95 adults, $18.95 children 3–9, free for children under 3. Daily 9:30am–6pm (ticket booth closes at 4:30pm).

Parrot Jungle and Gardens *(Kids*   This Miami institution will take flight from its current location in South Miami in the fall of 2002 and head north in the winter of 2003 to a new $46 million home on Watson Island, along the MacArthur Causeway near Miami Beach. While the island will double as a protected bird sanctuary, the jungle's soon-to-be former digs in the heart of South Miami in a circa-1900 coral rock structure are a lot more charming and kitschier. The new 18.6-acre park will feature an Everglades exhibit, a petting zoo, and several theaters, jungle trails, and aviaries. Watch your heads because flying above are hundreds of parrots, macaws, peacocks, cockatoos, and flamingos. Continuous shows star roller-skating cockatoos, card-playing macaws, and numerous stunt-happy parrots. There are also tortoises, iguanas, and a rare albino alligator on exhibit.

Until the move: 11000 SW 57th Ave., Southern Miami–Dade County. ℭ **305/666-7834**. After the move: 1111 Parrot Jungle Trail, Watson Island (on the north side of MacArthur Causeway/I-395). ℭ **305/372-3822**. www.parrotjungle.com. Admission $15.95 adults, $13.95 seniors, $10.95 children 3–10. Daily 9:30am–6pm. Cafe opens at 8am. Take U.S. 1 south and turn left at SW 57th Ave., or exit Kendall Dr. from the Florida Turnpike and turn right on SW 57th Ave.

Sea Grass Adventures ✸ (Value (Kids) Even better than the Seaquarium is Sea Grass Adventures, in which a naturalist will introduce kids and adults to an amazing variety of creatures that live in the sea grass beds of the Bear Cut Nature Preserve near Crandon Beach on Key Biscayne. Not just a walking tour, you will be able to wade in the water with your guide and catch an assortment of sea life in nets provided by the guides. At the end of the program, participants gather on the beach while the guide explains what everyone's just caught, passing the creatures around in miniature viewing tanks. Call for available dates and reservations.

Marjory Stoneman Douglas Biscayne Nature Center, 6767 Crandon Blvd., Key Biscayne. ℭ **305/361-6767**. $10 per person. Daily 10am–4pm.

7

Shopping

Miami is one of the world's premier shopping cities; more than 10 million visitors came here last year and they spent in excess of $13 billion. People come to Miami from all over—from Latin America to Hong Kong—in search of some products that are all-American (i.e., Levi's, Nikes, etc.).

So if you're not into sunbathing and outdoor activities, or you just can't take the heat, you'll be in good company in one of Miami's many malls—and you are not likely to emerge empty-handed. In addition to the strip malls, Miami offers a choice of megamalls, from the upscale Shops at Sunset to the mammoth Aventura Mall to the ritzy Bal Harbour Shops (just to name a few).

Miami also offers more unique shopping spots, such as Bayside's Marketplace, where you can buy such eclectic items as handcrafted tropical birds or jewelry made of precious stones, and Little Havana, where you can buy hand-rolled cigars and *guayabera* shirts.

You may want to order the Greater Miami Convention and Visitors Bureau's "Shop Miami: A Guide to a Tropical Shopping Adventure." Although it is limited to details on the bureau's paying members, it provides some good advice and otherwise unpublished discount offers. The glossy little pamphlet is printed in English, Spanish, and Portuguese and provides information about transportation from hotels, translation services, and shipping. Call © **800/ 283-2707** or 305/539-3034 for more information.

1 The Shopping Scene

Below, you'll find descriptions of some of the more popular retail areas, where many stores are conveniently clustered together to make browsing easier.

As a general rule, shop hours are Monday through Saturday from 10am to 6pm and Sunday from noon to 5pm. Many stores stay open late (until 9pm or so) one night of the week (usually Thurs). Shops in Coconut Grove are open until 9pm Sunday through Thursday and even later on Friday and Saturday nights. South

Beach's stores also stay open later—as late as midnight. Department stores and shopping malls also keep longer hours, with most staying open from 10am to 9 or 10pm Monday through Saturday, and noon to 6pm on Sunday. With all these variations, call ahead to specific stores to find out what their hours are.

The 6.5% state and local sales tax is added to the price of all non-food purchases. Food and beverage in hotels and restaurants are taxed via the resort tax, which is 3% in Miami/South Beach and Bal Harbour, 4% in Surfside, and 2% in the rest of Miami–Dade County.

Most Miami stores can wrap your purchase and ship it anywhere in the world via United Parcel Service (UPS). If they can't, you can send it yourself, either through UPS (© **800/742-5877**) or through the U.S. Mail (see the Post Office Section under "Fast Facts: Miami" in chapter 3, "Getting to Know Miami").

SHOPPING AREAS

Most of Miami's shopping happens at the many megamalls scattered from one end of the county to the other; however, there is also some excellent boutique shopping and browsing to be done in the following areas (see "The Neighborhoods in Brief" in chapter 3 for more information):

AVENTURA   On Biscayne Boulevard between Miami Gardens Drive and the county line at Hallandale Beach Boulevard is a 2-mile stretch of major retail stores including Best Buy, Borders, Circuit City, Linens N' Things, Marshall's, Sports Authority, and more. Also here is the mammoth Aventura Mall, housing a fabulous collection of shops and restaurants.

CALLE OCHO   For a taste of Little Havana, take a walk down 8th Street between SW 27th Avenue and SW 12th Avenue, where you'll find some lively street life and many shops selling cigars, baked goods, shoes, furniture, and record stores specializing in Latin music. For help, take your Spanish dictionary.

COCONUT GROVE   Downtown Coconut Grove, centered on Main Highway and Grand Avenue and branching onto the adjoining streets, is one of Miami's most pedestrian-friendly zones. The Grove's wide sidewalks, lined with cafes and boutiques, can provide hours of browsing pleasure. Coconut Grove is best known for its chain stores (Gap, Banana Republic, etc.) and some funky holdovers from the days when the Grove was a bit more bohemian, plus excellent sidewalk cafes centered on CocoWalk and the Streets of Mayfair.

MIRACLE MILE (CORAL GABLES) Actually only a half-mile long, this central shopping street was an integral part of George Merrick's original city plan. Today, the strip still enjoys popularity, especially for its bridal stores, ladies' shops, haberdashers, and gift shops. Recently, newer chain stores, like Barnes & Noble, Old Navy, and Starbucks, have been appearing on the Mile. **Merrick Park,** a mammoth, 850,000-square-foot upscale outdoor shopping complex between Ponce de León Boulevard and Le Jeune Road, just off the Mile, opened in the Fall of 2002 with Nordstrom, Neiman Marcus, Armani, and Yves St. Laurent on board, to name a few.

DOWNTOWN MIAMI If you're looking for discounts on all types of goods—especially watches, fabric, buttons, lace, shoes, luggage, and leather—Flagler Street, just west of Biscayne Boulevard, is the best place to start. I wouldn't necessarily recommend buying expensive items here, as many stores seem to be on the shady side and do not understand the word *warranty.* However, you can still have fun here as long as you are a savvy shopper and don't mind haggling with people who may not have the firmest grasp on the English language. Most signs are printed in English, Spanish, and Portuguese; however, many shopkeepers may not be entirely fluent in English.

SOUTH BEACH Slowly but surely South Beach has come into its own as far as shopping is concerned. While the requisite stores—Gap, Banana Republic, et al.—have anchored here, several higher-end stores have also opened on the southern blocks of Collins Avenue, which has become the Madison Avenue of Miami. For the hippest clothing boutiques (including Armani and Armani Exchange, Ralph Lauren, Versace, Benetton, Agnes B, Guess?, Club Monaco, Kenneth Cole, and Nicole Miller, among others), stroll along this pretty strip of the Art Deco District.

For those who are interested in a little more fun with their shopping, consider South Beach's legendary Lincoln Road. This pedestrian mall, originally designed in 1957 by Morris Lapidus, recently underwent a multimillion-dollar renovation, restoring it to its former glory. Here, shoppers find an array of clothing, books, tchotchkes, and art as well as a menagerie of sidewalk cafes flanked on one end by a multiplex movie theater, and at the other, the Atlantic Ocean.

2 Shopping A to Z
ANTIQUES/COLLECTIBLES
Miami's antiques shops are scattered in small pockets around the city. Many that feature lower-priced furniture can be found in North

Miami, in the 1600 block of NE 123rd Street, near West Dixie Highway. About a dozen shops sell china, silver, glass, furniture, and paintings. But you'll find the bulk of the better antiques in Coral Gables and in Southwest Miami along Bird Road between 64th and 66th avenues and between 72nd and 74th avenues. For international collections from Bali to France, check out the burgeoning scene in the Design District centered on Northeast 40th Street west of 1st Avenue. Miami also hosts several large antiques shows each year. In October and November, the most prestigious one—the **Antique Show**—hits the Miami Beach Convention Center (② 305/754-4931). Exhibitors from all over come to display their wares, including jewelry. There's also a decent monthly show at the **Coconut Grove Convention Center** (② 305/444-8454). Miami's huge concentration of Art Deco buildings from the '20s and '30s makes this the place to find the best selections of Deco furnishings and decorations. A word to the serious collectors: Dania Beach, up in Broward County, about half an hour from downtown Miami, is the best place for antiques (it's known as the antiques capital of South Florida), so you may want to consider browsing in Miami and shopping up there.

Architectural Antiques   A great place to browse—if you don't mind a little dust—this huge warehouse has an impressive stash of ironwork, bronzes, paintings, lamps, furniture, and sculptures which have been salvaged from estates worldwide. Don't be surprised to find odd items, too, like an old British phone booth or a pair of gargoyles off an ancient church. 2500 SW 28th Lane (just west of U.S. 1), Miami. ② 305/ 285-1330. archantique@earthlink.net.

Miami Twice   While they are not technically antiques yet, the Old Florida furniture and decorations from the '30s, '40s, and '50s are great fun (and collectible). In addition to loads of Deco memorabilia, there are also vintage clothes, shoes, and jewelry. 6562 SW 40th St., South Miami. ② 305/666-0127. Fax 305/661-1142.

Modernism Gallery   Specializing in 20th-century furnishings from Gilbert Rohde, Noguchi, and Heywood Wakefield, this shop has some of the most beautiful examples of Deco goods from France and the United States. If they don't have what you're looking for, ask. They possess the amazing ability to find the rarest items. 1622 Ponce de León Blvd., Coral Gables. ② 888/217-2760.

Senzatempo *Finds*   If the names Charles Eames, George Nelson, or Gio Ponti mean anything to you, then this is where you'll want to visit. There's retro, Euro fabulous designer furniture and decorative arts from 1930 to 1960, as well as collectible watches, timepieces, and clocks. 1655 Meridian Ave. (at Lincoln Rd.), South Beach. ✆ 305/534-5588. www.senzatempo.com.

BOOKS

Barnes & Noble *Kids*   With half a dozen outlets in the area (Aventura, South Miami, Kendall, etc.) and more on the way, this huge chain offers anything readers could ask for, including a comfortable cafe, a large children's section, and tons of magazines. Plus, the chain gives you a 10% discount on all bestsellers and has incredible closeout specials. They often schedule readings with noted authors, too. Of the Miami-area locations, this branch has an especially nice little scene, featuring local intellectuals, students, and professors from the nearby University of Miami. 152 Miracle Mile, Coral Gables. ✆ 305/446-4152. www.bn.com.

Books & Books   A dedicated following turns out to browse at this warm and wonderful little independent shop. Enjoy the upstairs antiquarian room, which specializes in art books and first editions. If that's not enough intellectual stimulation for you, the shop hosts free lectures from noted authors, experts, and personalities almost nightly, from Monica Lewinsky to Martin Amis. At another location (933 Lincoln Rd., South Beach; ✆ 305/532-3222), you'll rub elbows with tanned and buffed South Beach bookworms sipping cappuccinos at the Russian Bear Cafe inside the store. This branch stocks a large selection of gay literature and also features lectures. 265 Aragon Ave., Coral Gables. ✆ 305/442-4408. www.booksandbooks.com.

Kafka's Cyberkafe   Check your e-mail and surf the Web while you sip a latte or snack on a sandwich or pastry with friendly neighborhood regulars. This popular used bookstore also stocks a wide range of foreign and domestic magazines and caters to an international-youth-hostel-type crowd. 1464 Washington Ave., South Beach. ✆ 305/673-9669.

CIGARS

Although it is illegal to bring Cuban cigars into the United States, somehow, forbidden *Cohibas* show up at every dinner party and nightclub in town. Not that I condone it, but if you hang around the cigar smokers in town, no doubt one will be able to tell you where you can get some of the highly prized contraband. Be careful, however, of counterfeits, which are typically Dominican cigars posing as Cubans. Cuban cigars are illegal and unless you go down a sketchy alley to buy one from a dealer (think of it as shady as a drug deal), you are going to be smoking Dominican ones.

The stores listed below sell excellent hand-rolled cigars made with domestic- and foreign-grown tobacco. Many of the *viejos* (old men) got their training in Cuba working for the government-owned factories in the heyday of Cuban cigars.

La Gloria Cubana This tiny storefront shop employs about 45 veteran Cuban rollers who sit all day rolling the very popular torpedoes and other critically acclaimed blends. They're usually back-ordered, but it's worth stopping in: They will sell you a box and show you around. 1106 SW 8th St., Little Havana. ✆ 305/858-4162.

Mike's Cigars *(Finds* Mike's recently moved to this new location, but it's one of the oldest and best smoke shops in town. Since 1950, Mike's has been selling the best from Honduras, the Dominican Republic, and Jamaica, as well as the very hot local brand, La Gloria Cubana. Many say it has the best prices, too. Mike's has the biggest selection of cigars in town and the employees speak English. 1030 Kane Concourse (at 96th St.), Bay Harbor Island. ✆ 305/866-2277. www.mikescigars.com.

COSMETICS, FRAGRANCES & BEAUTY PRODUCTS

Brownes & Co. *(Finds* Designed to look like an old-fashioned apothecary, this recently expanded beauty emporium combines the best selection of makeup and hair products—MAC, Shu Uemura, Kiehl's, Stila, Molton Brown, Francois Nars, and Dr. Hauschka, just to name a few—with lots of delicious-smelling bath and body stuff, plus a full-service beauty salon. Feel free to browse and sample here, as perfume-spritzing salespeople won't bother you. If you do need help, the staff is a collection of experts when it comes to beauty and hair products. Upstairs is the renowned salon, Some Like It Hot, in which you can get fabulously coiffed, colored, buffed, and waxed. If you do want to get waxed, make sure to ask for the city's best waxer, Latecia. 841 Lincoln Rd., South Beach. ✆ 305-532-8703. www.brownes beauty.com.

FASHION: CLOTHING & ACCESSORIES

Miami didn't become a fashion capital until—believe it or not—the pastel-hued, Armani-clad cops on *Miami Vice* had their close-ups on the tube. Before that, Miami was all about old men in white patent leather shoes and well-tanned women in bikinis. How things have changed! Miami is now a fashion mecca in its own right, with some of the same high-end stores you'd find on Rue de Fauborg St. Honore in Paris or Bond Street in London. You'll find all the chichi labels, including Prada and Gucci, right here at the posh Bal Harbour Shops.

For funkier frocks, South Beach is the place, where designers such as Cynthia Rowley, Betsey Johnson, and Giorgio Armani compete for window shoppers with local up-and-coming designers, some of whom design for drag queens and club kids only. The strip on Collins Avenue between 7th and 10th streets has become quite upscale, including such shops as Armani Exchange and Nicole Miller, along with the inescapable Gap and Banana Republic. Of course, there's also more mainstream (and affordable) shopping in the plethora of malls and outdoor shopping and entertainment complexes that are sprinkled throughout the city (see the section on malls below).

UNISEX

Agnes B   This fabulous French import features unique women's, men's, and children's high fashion at high prices. If you don't have carte blanche, however, the best buy in the store is the one-of-a-kind Agnes B perfume, in a lovely heart bottle, for just $20. 640 Collins Ave., South Beach. © 305/604-8705.

Base   A beautiful store featuring one-of-a-kind clothing made in St. Vincent that's light, breezy, fashionable, and, of course, pricey. Keep on the lookout for excellent sales. 939 Lincoln Rd., South Beach. © 305/531-4982.

Glitzy Tartz   The name alone says it all. This outlandish boutique features everything you'd want if you were a go-go boy or girl, in vinyl, mesh, and lamé—all in several sizes way too tight to accentuate the, uh, positive. 1251 Washington Ave., South Beach. © 305/535-0068.

Island Trading   Part of music mogul Chris Blackwell's empire, Island sells everything you'd need to wear in a tropical resort town: batik sarongs, sandals, sundresses, bathing suits, cropped tops, and more. Many of the unique styles are created on the premises by a team of young, innovative designers. 1332 Ocean Dr., South Beach. © 305/673-6300.

Laundry Industry   If you're colorblind, from New York, or just can't be bothered with coordinating your colors, Laundry Industry is for you, with the most chic (and priciest) black-and-white-only threads for men and women this side of SoHo. 666 Collins Ave., South Beach. © 305/531-2277.

WOMEN'S

Alice's Day Off   For beachwear, Alice's is the place. Season after season, you'll find pretty and flattering floral patterns and many flashy bikinis. If an itsy-bitsy bikini is not your style, Alice's also has a range of more modest cuts. Three locations: Miami International Mall, 1455 NW 107th Ave., Miami © **305/477-0393**; Dadeland Mall, 7223 SW 88th St., Miami © **305/663-7299**; and 5900 SW 72nd St., South Miami © **305/284-0301**. www.alicesdayoff.com.

Intermix   Pretty young things can get all dolled up thanks to Intermix's fun assortment of hip women's fashions, from Stella McCartney's pricey rhinestone T-shirts to the latest jeans worn by everyone at the MTV Awards. 634 Collins Ave., South Beach. © **305/ 531-5950**.

La Perla   The only store in Florida that specializes in superluxurious Italian intimate apparel. Of course, you could fly to Milan for the price of a few bras and a nightgown, but you can't find better quality. 9700 Collins Ave. (in the Bal Harbour Shops), Bal Harbour. © **305/ 864-2070**.

Place Vendome   For cheap and funky club clothes from zebra-print pants to bright, shiny tops. Two locations: 934 Lincoln Rd., South Beach © **305/673-4005**, and Aventura Mall, North Miami Beach © **305/ 932-8931**.

Therapy   Opened by Ellen Lansburgh, who ran successful shops in Aspen and New York that catered to a famous clientele, this intimate boutique offers one-of-a-kind pieces. The clothes, made of luxurious fabrics such as silk, taffeta, and tulle, are elegant and comfortable and are all the rage for the ladies-who-lunch crowd. 1065 Kane Concourse, Bay Harbor Islands. © **305/861-6900**.

MEN'S

Giorgio's   One of the finest custom men's stores in Miami, Giorgio's features an extensive line of Italian suits and all the latest by Canelli. 208 Miracle Mile, Coral Gables. © **305/448-4302**.

La Casa de las Guayaberas *Finds*   Miami's premier purveyor of the traditional yet retro-hip Cuban shirt known as the *guayabera*—a loose-fitting, pleated, button-down shirt—was founded by Ramon Puig, who emigrated to Miami over 40 years ago. He still uses the same scissors he did back then, only now he's joined by a team of seamstresses who hand-sew 20 shirts a day in all colors and styles. Prices range from $15 to $375. 5840 SW 8th St., Little Havana. © **305/266-9683**.

Wilke Rodriguez   Miami designer Eddie Rodriguez is a Latin Hugo Boss, with high-fashion suits in linens and light wool blends made especially for warmer climates. Cool T-shirts, shorts, and jackets are also part of this line, which is a local status symbol for many of Miami's fashion-conscious males. Prices range from the high $50s for T-shirts to $275 and up for jackets. 801 Washington Ave., South Beach. © 305/534-4030.

ACCESSORIES

Crybaby   Like a shop straight off of Melrose in Los Angeles or Magazine Street in New Orleans, this funky, kitschy tchotchke store carries whimsical toys, accessories, gifts, and clothing bearing the likenesses of the queen of kitsch, Hello Kitty, and much more, made by neo-pop artists such as Paul Frank (whose work entails Julius the monkey!). 6669 Biscayne Blvd., Miami. © 305/754-4279.

Simons and Green   Fantastic sterling silver jewelry, leather goods, and other assorted high-end tchotchkes and gift items are what you'll find in this quaint mainstay on South Miami's Sunset Drive. 5842 Sunset Dr., South Miami. © 305/667-1692.

JEWELRY

For name designers like Gucci and Tiffany & Co., go to the Bal Harbour Shops (see "Malls," below).

International Jeweler's Exchange   At least 50 reputable jewelers hustle their wares from individual counters at one of the city's most active jewelry centers. Haggle your brains out for excellent prices on timeless antiques from Tiffany's, Cartier, or Bulgari, or on unique designs you can create yourself. 18861 Biscayne Blvd. (in the Fashion Island), North Miami Beach. © 305/931-7032.

Seybold Building   Jewelers who specialize in an assortment of goods (diamonds, gems, watches, rings, etc.) gather here daily to sell diamonds and gold. With 300 jewelry stores located inside this independently owned and operated multilevel treasure chest, the glare is blinding as you enter. Here, you'll be sure to see handsome and up-to-date designs, but not too many bargains. 36 NE 1st St., Downtown. © 305/374-7922.

MALLS

There are so many malls in Miami and more being built all the time that it would be impossible to mention them all. What follows is a list of the biggest and most popular. You can find any number of nationally known department stores including Saks Fifth Avenue, Macy's, Lord & Taylor, Sears, and JCPenney in the Miami malls listed below, but Miami's own is **Burdines,** at 22 E. Flagler St., Downtown (© **305/835-5151**) and 1675 Meridian Ave. (just off

Lincoln Rd.) in South Beach (© **305/674-6311**). One of the oldest and largest department stores in Florida, Burdines specializes in good-quality home furnishings and fashions.

Aventura Mall *(Kids*   A multimillion-dollar makeover has made this spot one of the premier places to shop in South Florida. With more than 2.3 million square feet of space, this airy, Mediterranean-style mall has a 24-screen movie theater and more than 250 stores, including megastores JCPenney, Lord & Taylor, Macy's, Bloomingdale's, Sears, and Burdines. The mall offers moderate to high-priced merchandise and is extremely popular with families. A large indoor playground, Adventurer's Cove, is a great spot for kids, and the mall frequently offers activities and entertainment for children. There are numerous theme restaurants and a food court that eschews the usual suspects in favor of local operations. 19501 Biscayne Blvd. (at 197th St. near the Dade–Broward County line), Aventura. © **305/935-1110**. www.shopaventura mall.com.

Bal Harbour Shops   One of the most prestigious fashion meccas in the country, Bal Harbour offers the best-quality goods from the finest names. Giorgio Armani, Dolce & Gabbana, Christian Dior, Fendi, Joan & David, Krizia, Rodier, Gucci, Brooks Brothers, Waterford, Cartier, H. Stern, Tourneau, and many others are sandwiched between Neiman Marcus and a newly expanded Saks Fifth Avenue. Well-dressed shoppers stroll in a pleasant open-air emporium featuring several good cafes, covered walkways, and lush greenery. Parking costs $1 an hour with a validated ticket. You can stamp your own at the entrance to Saks Fifth Avenue, even if you don't make a purchase. 9700 Collins Ave. (on 97th St., opposite the Sheraton Bal Harbour Hotel), Bal Harbour. © **305/866-0311**. www.balharbourshops.com.

Bayside Marketplace   A popular stop for cruise-ship passengers, this touristy waterfront marketplace is filled with the usual suspects of chain stores as well as a slew of tacky gift shops and carts hawking assorted junk in the heart of downtown Miami. The second-floor food court is stocked with dozens of fast-food choices and bars. Most of the restaurants and bars stay open later than the stores. There's Lomardi's Conga Bar, Dick's Last Resort, Hard Rock Cafe, Fat Tuesday, Sharkey's, and Let's Make a Daiquiri. Parking is $1 per hour. While we wouldn't recommend you necessarily drop big money at Bayside, you should go by just for the view (of Biscayne Bay and the Miami skyline) alone. Beware of the adjacent amphitheater known as Bayfront Park, which usually hosts large-scale concerts and festivals, causing major pedestrian and vehicle traffic jams. 401 Biscayne Blvd., Downtown. ⓒ 305/577-3344. www.baysidemarketplace.com.

CocoWalk CocoWalk is a lovely outdoor Mediterranean-style mall with the usual fare of Americana: Gap, Banana Republic, etc. Its open-air style architecture is inviting not only for shoppers but also for friends or spouses of shoppers who'd prefer to sit at an outdoor cafe while said shopper is busy in the fitting room. A multiplex movie theater is also here, which comes in handy when there are big sales going on and the stores are mobbed. 3015 Grand Ave., Coconut Grove. ⓒ 305/444-0777. www.cocowalk.com.

Dadeland Mall One of the county's first malls, Dadeland features more than 175 specialty shops, anchored by four large department stores: Burdines, JCPenney, Lord & Taylor, and Saks Fifth Avenue. Sixteen restaurants serve from the adjacent Treats Food Court. New retail stores are constantly springing up around this centerpiece of South Miami suburbia. If you're not in the area, however, the mall is not worth the trek. Additionally, many non-Spanish-speaking people are put off by Dadeland because of the predominance of Spanish-speaking store employees. 7535 N. Kendall Dr. (intersection of U.S. 1 and SW 88th St., 15 min. south of Downtown), Kendall. ⓒ 305/665-6226.

Dolphin Mall As if Miami needed another mall, this $250 million megamall and amusement park rivals Broward County's monstrous Sawgrass Mills outlet. The 1.4-million-square-foot outlet mall features outlets such as Off Saks (Fifth Avenue), plus several discount shops, a 28-screen movie theater, and, not to be outdone by the Mall of America in Minnesota, a roller coaster. Florida Turnpike at S.R. 836, West Miami. ⓒ 305/365-7446.

The Falls Traffic to this mall borders on brutal, but once you get there, you'll feel a slight sense of serenity. Tropical waterfalls are the setting for this outdoor shopping center with dozens of moderately priced and slightly upscale shops. Miami's first Bloomingdale's is here, as are Polo, Ralph Lauren, Caswell-Massey, and more than 60 other specialty shops. A recent renovation added Macy's, Crate & Barrel, Brooks Brothers, and Pottery Barn, among others. If you are planning to visit any of the nearby attractions, which include Metro Zoo and Monkey Jungle, check with customer service for information on discount packages. 8888 Howard Dr. (at the intersection of U.S. 1 and 136th St., about 3 miles/4.6km south of Dadeland Mall), Kendall. ⓒ 305/255-4570. www.shopthefalls.com.

Sawgrass Mills   Just as some people need to take a tranquilizer to fly, others need one to traipse through this mammoth mall—the largest outlet mall in the country. Depending on what type of shopper you are, this experience can either be blissful or overwhelming. If you've got the patience, it is worth setting aside a day to do the entire place. Though it's located in Broward County, it is a phenomenon that attracts thousands of tourists and locals sniffing out bargains. From Miami, buses run three times daily; the trip takes just under an hour. Call **Coach USA** (ⓒ **305/887-6223**) for exact pickup points at major hotels. The price is $10 for a round-trip ticket. If you are driving, take I-95 north to 595 west to Flamingo Road. Exit and turn right, driving 2 miles to Sunrise Boulevard. You can't miss this monster on the left. Parking is free, but don't forget where you parked your car or you might spend a day looking for it. 12801 W. Sunrise Blvd., Sunrise (west of Fort Lauderdale). ⓒ **954/846-2300**. www.millscorp.com.

Shops at Sunset Place   Completed in early 1999 at a cost of over $140 million, this sprawling outdoor shopping complex offers more than just shopping. Visitors experience high-tech special effects, such as daily tropical storms (minus the rain) and the electronic chatter of birds and crickets. In addition to a 24-screen movie complex and an IMAX theater, there's a GameWorks (Steven Spielberg's Disney-esque playground for kids and adults), a Virgin Records store, and a NikeTown as well as mall standards such as Victoria's Secret, Gap, Urban Outfitters, bebe, etc. 5701 Sunset Dr. (at 57th Ave. and U.S. 1, near Red Rd.), South Miami. ⓒ **305/663-0482**.

Streets of Mayfair   This sleepy, desolate, labyrinthine shopping area conceals a movie theater, several top-quality shops, a bookstore, restaurants, art galleries, bars, and nightclubs. It was meant to compete with the CocoWalk shopping complex (just across the street), but its structure is very mazelike. Though it is open air, it is not wide open like CocoWalk and pales in comparison to that more populated neighbor. 2911 Grand Ave. (just east of Commodore Plaza), Coconut Grove. ⓒ **305/448-1700**.

MUSIC STORES
Blue Note Records *Finds*   Here for more than 18 years, Blue Note is music to the ears of music fanatics with a good selection of hard-to-find progressive and underground music. There are new, used, and discounted CDs and old vinyl, too. Call to find out about performances. Some great names show up occasionally.

A second location features jazz and LPs only. 16401 NE 15th Ave., North Miami Beach. ℂ **305/940-3394.** For jazz/LPs: 2299 NE 164th St., North Miami Beach ℂ **305/354-4563.** www.bluenoterecords.com.

Casino Records Inc. The young, hip salespeople here speak English and tend to be music buffs. This store has the largest selection of Latin music in Miami, including pop icons such as Willy Chirino, Gloria Estefan, Albita, and local boy Nil Lara. Their slogan translates to "If we don't have it, forget it." Believe me, they've got it. 1208 SW 8th St., Little Havana. ℂ **305/856-6888.**

Esperanto Music *(Finds* According to the experts, this independently owned record store boasts the city's best collection of Cuban and Latin music. 513 Lincoln Rd., Miami Beach. ℂ **305/ 534-2003.**

Revolution Records and CDs Here you'll find a fairly well-organized collection of CDs, from hard-to-find jazz to original recordings of Buddy Rich. They'll search for anything and let you hear whatever you like. 1620 Alton Rd., Miami Beach. ℂ **305/673-6464.**

THRIFT STORES/RESALE SHOPS

Children's Exchange *(Kids* Selling everything from layettes to overalls, this pleasant little shop is chock-full of good Florida-style stuff for kids to wear to the beach and in the heat. 1415 Sunset Dr., Coral Gables. ℂ **305/666-6235.**

Douglas Gardens Jewish Home and Hospital Thrift Shop Prices here are no longer the major bargain they once were, but for housewares and books, you can do all right. Call to see if they are offering any specials for seniors or students. 5713 NW 27th Ave., North Miami Beach. ℂ **305/638-1900.**

Rags to Riches This is an old-time consignment shop where you might find some decent rags, and maybe even some riches. Though not as upscale as it used to be, this place is still a good spot for costume jewelry and shoes. 12577 Biscayne Blvd., North Miami. ℂ **305/891-8981.**

Red White & Blue *(Finds* Miami's best-kept secret is this mammoth thrift store that is meticulously organized and well stocked. You've got to search for great stuff, but it is there. There are especially good deals on children's clothes and housewares. 12640 NE 6th Ave., North Miami. ℂ **305/893-1104.**

8

Miami After Dark

With all the hype, you'd expect Miami to have long outlived its 15 minutes of fame by now. But you'd be wrong. Miami's nightlife, especially in South Beach, is hotter than ever before— and still getting hotter.

Practically every club in the area has installed closely guarded velvet ropes to create an air of exclusivity. Don't be fooled or intimidated by them—*anyone* can go clubbing in the Magic City, and throughout this chapter, I've provided tips to ensure you gain entry to the venue you want to go to.

South Beach is certainly Miami's uncontested nocturnal nucleus, but more and more diverse areas, such as the Design District, South Miami, and even Little Havana, are increasingly providing fun alternatives without the ludicrous cover charges, "fashionably late" hours of operation (things don't typically get started on South Beach until after 11pm), the lack of sufficient self-parking, and outrageous drink prices that come standard in South Beach.

And while South Beach dances to a more electronic beat, other parts of Miami dance to a Latin beat—from salsa and merengue to tango and cha cha. However, if you're looking for a less frenetic good time, Miami's bar scene offers something for everyone, from haute hotel bars to sleek, loungey watering holes.

If the possibility of a celebrity sighting doesn't fulfill your cultural needs, Miami also offers a variety of first-rate diversions in theater, music, and dance, including a world-class ballet under the aegis of Edward Villella, a recognized symphony, and a talented opera company.

For up-to-date listing information, and to make sure time hasn't elapsed for the club of the moment, check the *Miami Herald's* "Weekend" section, which runs on Friday, or the more comprehensive listings in *New Times,* Miami's free alternative weekly, available each Wednesday, or visit www.miami.citysearch.com online.

1 Bars & Lounges

There are countless bars in and around Miami, with the highest concentration on trendy South Beach. The selection listed here is a mere sample. Keep in mind that many of the popular bars—and the easiest to get into—are in hotels. For a clubbier scene, if you don't mind making your way through hordes of inebriated club kids, a stroll on Washington Avenue will provide you with ample insight into what's hot and what's not. Just hold onto your bags. It's not dangerous, but occasionally, a few shady types manage to slip into the crowd. Another very important tip when in a club: *Never put your drink down out of your sight*—there have been unfortunate incidents in which drinks have been spiked with illegal chemical substances.

For a less hard-core, collegiate nightlife, head to Coconut Grove. Most require proof that you are over 21 to enter. Oh, yes, and when going out in South Beach, make sure to take a so-called disco nap, as things don't get going until at least 11pm. If you go earlier, be prepared to face an empty bar or club. Off of South Beach and in hotel bars in general, the hours are fashionably earlier, with the action starting as early as, say, 7pm.

Clevelander If wet T-shirt contests and a fraternity party atmosphere are your thing, then this Ocean Drive mainstay is your kind of place. Popular with tourists and locals who like to pretend they're tourists, the Clevelander attracts a lively, sporty, adults-only crowd (the burly bouncers *will* confiscate fake IDs) who have no interest in being part of a scene, but, rather, taking in the very revealing scenery. A great time to check out the Clevelander is on a weekend afternoon, when beach Barbies and Kens line the bar for a post-tanning beer or frozen cocktail. 1020 Ocean Dr., South Beach. ✆ 305/531-3485. No cover.

Forge The Forge lounge hosts an unusual mix of the uptight and those who wear their clothes too tight. It's also where surgically altered ladies look for their cigar-chomping sugar daddies in a setting that somehow reminds me of *Dynasty*. Call well in advance if you want to watch the parade of characters from a dinner table (see p. 97). The Forge people also own a ritzier nightclub (which is attached to the club), reminiscent of a cruise-ship lounge, called Jimmy'z (they say it's a private club, but if you dine at the restaurant or are acquainted with someone in the know, you can get in). 432 41st St., Miami Beach. ✆ 305/538-8533. No cover (though door policy tends to be a bit exclusive; dress up and you should have no problem).

To Central Miami Beach ↑ **①** **②**

22nd St. **③**

The Bass Museum of Art

COLLINS PARK

Dade Boulevard

20th St.

19th St.

Purdy Ave.

Dade Boulevard

Venetian Causeway

18th St.

Miami Beach Convention Center

James Ave.

Collins Ave.

Washington Ave.

④

17th St. **⑤**

Lincoln Rd.

Lincoln Road Mall **⑥** **⑦** **⑧** **⑨** **⑩** **⑪**

⑫

BELLE ISLAND

HISTORIC ART DECO DISTRICT

16th St.

Bay Rd.

Alton Rd.

West Ave.

Drexel Ave.

15th St.

⑬

Española Way

⑭

⑮

Lenox Ave.

Michigan Ave.

Jefferson Ave.

Meridian Ave.

14th St.

Miami Beach Post Office

⑯ **⑰**

13th St.

Biscayne Bay

West Ave.

12th St.

⑱

FLAMINGO PARK

11th St.

Beach Patrol Station

Euclid Ave.

Pennsylvania Ave.

Washington Ave.

⑲

⑳

Art Deco Welcome Center

10th St.

9th St.

8th St.

7th St.

6th St.

Michigan Ave.

㉑

LUMMUS PARK

Ocean Dr.

Collins Ave.

5th St.

4th St.

3rd St.

2nd St.

ATLANTIC OCEAN

1st St.

Washington Ave.

Collins Ave.

Ocean Dr.

㉒

㉓

Commerce St.

Biscayne St.

SOUTH POINTE PARK

Government Cut

FISHER ISLAND

0   0.25 mi

0   0.25 km

Impressions

There are two shifts in South Beach. There's nine to five.
And then there's nine to five.

—South Beach artist Stewart Stewart

Fox's Sherron Inn *(Finds* The spirit of Frank Sinatra is alive and well at this dark and smoky watering hole that dates back to 1946. Everything down to the vinyl booths and the red lights make Fox's a retro fabulous dive bar. Cheap drinks, couples cozily huddling in booths, and a seasoned staff of bartenders and barflies make Fox's the perfect place to retreat from the trenches of trendiness. Oh, and the food's actually good here, too. 6030 S. Dixie Hwy. (at 62nd Ave.), South Miami. ⓒ 305/661-9201. No cover.

Lola *(Finds* Lola redefines the neighborhood bar, striking the perfect balance between chill and chic. This bar, located away from the South Beach mayhem, is a showgirl in her own right—a swank, sultry lounge where people are encouraged to come as they are, leaving the attitude at home. Attracting a mixed crowd of gay, straight, young, and old(er), Lola reinvents itself each night with DJs spinning everything from retro '80s music to hard rock and classic oldies. On Tuesdays, the bar's most popular—and populated—night, it gets mobbed inside and outside, so they tend to keep a crowd at the ropes before letting them all in like cattle. 247 23rd St., South Beach. ⓒ 305/695-8697. No cover.

Mac's Club Deuce Standing on its own amidst an oasis of trendiness, Mac's Club Deuce is the quintessential dive bar, with cheap drinks and a cast of characters ranging from your typical barfly to your atypical drag queen. It's got a well-stocked jukebox, friendly bartenders, a pool table, and best of all, it's an insomniac's dream, open daily from 8am to 5am. 222 14th St., South Beach. ⓒ 305/673-9537. No cover.

Mynt This hyper-stylish, hip lounge is reminiscent of a space-age cafeteria. A massive 6,000-square-foot space, Mynt is nothing more than a huge living room in which models, celebrities, and assorted hangers-on bask in the green glow to the beats of very loud lounge and dance music. If you want to dance—or move, for that matter—this is not the place in which to do so. It's all about striking a pose in here. 1921 Collins Ave., South Beach. ⓒ 786/276-6132. Cover $10–$20.

Piccadilly Garden Lounge *(Finds* Hardly anyone in Miami knows that this completely off-the-beaten-path Design District lounge exists, which makes it that much cooler. A young, alternative crowd (bordering on Gothic) gathers in this garden every Saturday night for what is known as Pop Life, a musical homage to the sounds of British pop and alternative music. While the dank interior resembles a stuffy old Holiday Inn lounge, the music and the crowd is very mod. 35 NE 40th St., Design District. ✆ 305/573-8221. Cover $5 Sat.

Rose Bar at the Delano   If every rose has its thorn, the thorn at this painfully chic hotel bar is the excruciatingly high-priced cocktails. Otherwise, the crowd here is full of the so-called glitterati, fabulatti, and other assorted poseurs who view life through (Italian-made) rose-colored glasses. 1685 Collins Ave., South Beach. ✆ 305/672-2000. No cover.

2 Dance Clubs, Live Music, the Gay & Lesbian Scene & Latin Clubs

DANCE CLUBS

Clubs are as much a cottage industry in Miami as is, say, cheese in Wisconsin. Clubland, as its known, is not just a nocturnal theme park but a way of life for some. On any given night in Miami, there's something going on—no excuses are needed to throw a party here. Short of throwing a glammy event for the grand opening of a new gas station, Miami is very party hearty, celebrating everything from the fact that it's Tuesday night to the debut of a hot new DJ. Within this very bizarre after-dark community, a very colorful assortment of characters emerge, from your (a)typical nine-to-fivers to shady characters who have reinvented themselves as hot shots on the club circuit. While this scene of seeing and being seen may not be your cup of Absolut, it's certainly never boring.

The club music played on Miami's ever-evolving social circuit is good enough to get even the most rhythmically challenged wallflowers dancing. To keep things fresh in Clubland, local promoters throw one-nighters, which are essentially parties with various themes or motifs, from funk to fashion. Because these change so often, we can't possibly list them here. Word of mouth, local advertising, and listings in the free weekly *New Times,* miami.citysearch.com, or the "Weekend" section of the *Miami Herald* are the best ways to find out about these ever-changing events.

Before you get all decked out to hit the town as soon as the sun sets, consider the fact that Miami is a very late town. Things generally don't get started before 11pm. The Catch-22 here is that if you don't arrive on South Beach early enough, you may find yourself driving around aimlessly for parking, as it is very limited outside of absurd $20 valet charges. Municipal lots fill up quickly, so your best bet is to arrive on South Beach somewhat early and kill time by strolling around, having something to eat, or sipping a cocktail in a hotel bar. Another advantage of arriving a bit earlier than the crowds is that some clubs don't charge a cover before 11pm or midnight, which could save you a wad of cash over time. Most clubs are open every night of the week, though some are only open Thursday to Sunday and others are only open Monday though Saturday. Call ahead to get all of this information as up-to-date as possible: Things change very quickly around here. Cover charges are very haphazard, too. If you're not on the ubiquitous guest list (ask your concierge to put you on the list— he or she has the ability to do so, which won't help you with the wait to get in, but will eliminate the cover charge), you may have to fork over a ridiculous $20 to walk past the ropes. Don't fret, though. There are many clubs and bars that have no cover charge—they just make up for it by charging $13 for a martini!

Note: As with anything on Miami's nocturnal circuit, call in advance to make sure that the dance club you're planning to go to hasn't become a video arcade.

Bermuda Bar and Grill   This North Miami Beach spot is a sanctuary for those who'd rather not deal with the hustle, bustle, and hassle of driving and parking in South Beach or Coconut Grove. Bermuda Bar is a mega dance club that is often frequented by young suburban professionals. Good pizzas and grilled foods are available, too. It's usually open until the sun comes up. Wednesday's ladies nights are particularly popular, when women drink free and men are at their mercy. 3509 NE 163rd St., North Miami Beach. ✆ 305/945-0196. Cover $0–$10. No cover before 9pm. Wed–Sat.

Bongo's Cuban Café   Gloria Estefan's latest hit in the restaurant business pays homage to the sites, sounds, and cuisine of pre-Castro Cuba. Bongo's is a mammoth restaurant attached to the American Airlines Arena in downtown Miami. On Friday and Saturday after 11:30pm, it's transformed from a friendly family restaurant into the city's hottest 21-and-over salsa nightclub. Cover charge at that time is a hefty $20, but consider it your ticket to what happens to be an astounding show of some of the best salsa dancers in the city. Prepare yourself for standing room only. At the American Airlines Arena, 601 Biscayne Blvd., Downtown Miami. ✆ 786/777-2100. Cover $20.

Club Space   Clubland hits the mainland with this cavernous downtown warehouse of a club. With over 30,000 square feet of dance space, you can spin around a la Stevie Nicks (albeit to a

⌒ *Tips*   **Ground Rules: Stepping Out in Miami**

- Nightlife on South Beach doesn't really get going until after 11pm. As a result, you may want to consider taking what is known as a disco nap so that you'll be fully charged until the wee hours.
- If you're unsure of what to wear out on South Beach, your safest bet will be anything black.
- Do *not* try to tip the doormen manning the velvet ropes. That will only make you look desperate and you'll find yourself standing outside for what will seem like an ungodly amount of time. Instead, try to land your name on the ever-present guest lists by calling the club early in the day yourself, or, better yet, having the concierge at your hotel do it for you. Concierges have connections. If you don't have connections and you find yourself without a concierge, then act assertive, not surly, at the velvet rope, and your patience will usually be rewarded with admittance. If all else fails—for men, especially— surround yourself with a few leggy model types and you'll be noticed quicker.

techno beat) without having to worry about banging into someone. However, after hours (around 2am), Club Space packs them in. While Saturday caters to a more homogeneous and gay crowd, Friday is a free-for-all. Conveniently, the club often runs shuttles from the beach. Call for more information, as it doesn't have a con- crete schedule. 142 NE 11th St., Miami. ⓒ 305/372-9378. Cover $0–$20.

crobar *(Finds* Still haunted by the ghost of clubs past, the space for- merly known as the Cameo Theatre is now possessed by the mod, millennial, industrial spirit that is crobar. With its intense, dance- heavy sound system, an industrially chic ambience, and crowds big enough to scare away any memories of a sadly abandoned Cameo, this Chicago import has raised the bar on South Beach nightlife with crazy theme nights (the monthly Sex night is particularly, uh, stimulating), top-name DJs, and the occasional celebrity appearance. On Sunday, the club hosts an extremely popular gay night known as Anthem. (See "The Gay & Lesbian Scene," below.) 1445 Washington Ave., South Beach. ⓒ 305/531-8225. www.crobarmiami.com. Cover $25.

Level Overdone and some say overhyped, Level takes the notion of South Beach excess even further with its outlet-mall-size, 40,000-square-foot space featuring four dance floors, three levels, five rooms, and nine bars. Like a video game, your status here is determined by which level you can land on. If you befriend one of the club's owners, you may end up at the top. Leveling out the competition, this club has cornered the market on parties and events, throwing one nearly every night. Because it is the largest club on the beach, the velvet rope scene can be quite harassing, but if you call in advance, the accommodating staff will usually put you on the guest list, which means you don't have to pay the cover, though you will still have to wait in line. Friday night is a very popular gay night, while the rest of the week attracts a mixed crowd of straights, gays, and somewhere-in-betweens. 1235 Washington Ave., South Beach. ✆ **305/532-1525.** www.levelnightclub.com. Cover $20–$30.

Living Room Downtown The downtown satellite of a now defunct South Beach club that was formerly the hautest of the hot (especially amongst European jet-setters), the Living Room Downtown is nearly as velvety chic as its original incarnation, only there's a twist: This one has a 24-hour liquor license. *Note:* This place is not for the weary. 60 NE 11th St., Downtown. ✆ **305/342-7421.** Cover $10–$20.

Nikki Beach Club *Finds* What the Playboy Mansion is to Hollywood, the Nikki Beach Club is to South Beach. This place is the product of local nightlife royalty Tommy Pooch and Eric Omores.

Haute Off the Press

A few nocturnal South Beach haute spots recently opened to pretty impressive reviews. While, once again, we emphasize the fact that you should always check in advance to see if a place is still open, it seems that the new house-music dance club **Spin** (320 Lincoln Rd., South Beach; ✆ **305/532-8899**) and the buzz-worthy lounge **Honey** (645 Washington Ave.; ✆ **305/604-8222**) may outlast the flash-in-the-pan status and actually stick around long enough for you to check them out. Don't be surprised, however, if you find that either space has a new name, new concept, or new management. After just three weeks of its grand opening, Spin lost one of its head honchos to another club. (Sigh.) Just another night in Clubland.

Half-naked ladies and men actually venture into the daylight on Sundays (around 4pm, which is ungodly in this town) to see, be seen, and, at times, be obscene. At night, it's very Brady Bunch–goes-to-Hawaii seeming, with a sexy tiki hut/Polynesian theme/style, albeit rated R. The Sunday afternoon beach party is almost legendary and worth a glimpse—that is, if you can get in. This is not your equal-opportunity beach club. Egos are easily shattered, as surly doormen reject almost everyone who doesn't drive up in a Ferrari. 101 Ocean Dr., South Beach. ✆ 305/538-1111. Cover $10–$20.

Opium Garden Housed in the massive, open-air space formerly known as Amnesia, Opium Garden is a highly addictive nocturnal habit for those looking for a combination of sexy dance music, scantily clad dancers, and, for the masochists out there, an oppressive door policy in which two sets of velvet ropes are set up to keep those deemed unworthy out of this see-and-be-sceney den of inequity. 136 Collins Ave., South Beach. ✆ 305/531-5535. Cover $10–$30.

Rain A very minimalist dance club/lounge, Rain is a great nightspot for many reasons. First and foremost, its location off the beachy path is ideal for those who insist on clubbing and driving. Ample parking in the area definitely makes up for the fact that you'll pay upwards of $9 for a cocktail. Second, the music's great. Local DJ Mark Leventhal's Tuesday night funkfest known as Home Cookin' is particularly fun and comes complete with a free barbecue. 323 23rd St., South Beach. ✆ 786/295-9540. Cover $10–$30.

Rumi Named after a 13th-century Sufi mystic, South Beach's first upscale supper club is command central for hipsters hailing from all coasts. This bi-level space features intimate lounge areas as well as private and public dining rooms, in which haute Floribbean cuisine is served until around 11pm, when the tables disappear and give way to a neo-Zen-like stomping ground for South Beach's chic elite. Make sure to check out the queen-size Murphy bed that snaps down from the wall to make room for late-night lounging. As long as you can get past the velvet ropes (by either looking pretty, being on the guest list, or just getting the doorman on a good day), there is no cover to this bastion of South Beach scene-dom. 330 Lincoln Rd., South Beach. ✆ 305/672-4353. www.rumimiami.com. No cover.

LIVE MUSIC

Unfortunately, Miami's live music scene is not thriving. Instead of local bands garnering devoted fans, local DJs are more admired—thanks to the city's lauded dance-club scene. However, there are still several places that strive to bring Miami up to speed as far as live music is concerned. You just have to look—and listen—for it a bit more carefully. The following is a list of places you can, from time to time, catch some live acts, be it a DJ or an aspiring Nirvana.

Billboard Live Affiliated with the national music industry magazine, this mammoth dance club, bar, recording studio, and live music venue is much cooler than its chain-ish name implies. Although at press time the live acts haven't necessarily been major headliners, the acoustics in this multilevel club are exceptional, as is the Saturday night DJ-ed dance scene and Sunday afternoon, mostly gay Tea Dance Disco parties. The club's first-floor patio restaurant is also a great alternative to the thumping club vibe. 1501 Collins Ave., South Beach. ✆ **305/538-2251.** Cover $0–$20.

Churchill's Hideaway *(Finds* British expatriate Dave Daniels couldn't live in Miami without a true English-style pub, so he opened Churchill's Hideaway, the city's premier space for live rock music. Filthy and located in a rather unsavory neighborhood, Churchill's is committed to promoting and extending the lifeline of the lagging local music scene. A fun no-frills crowd hangs out here. Bring earplugs with you, as it is deafening once the music starts. 5501 NE 2nd Ave., Little Haiti. ✆ **305/757-1807.** Cover $0–$5.

Jazid *(Finds* Smoky, sultry, and illuminated by flickering candelabras, you'll hear live jazz (sometimes on acid), soul, and funk here. Past surprise performers at Jazid include former Smashing Pumpkin's front man Billy Corgan. An eclectic mix of mellow folk convenes here for a much necessary respite from the surrounding Washington Avenue mayhem. 1342 Washington Ave., South Beach. ✆ **305/ 673-9372.** No cover.

Tobacco Road Al Capone used to hang out here when it was a speakeasy. Now, locals flock here to see local bands perform, as well as national acts such as George Clinton and the P-Funk All-Stars, Koko Taylor, and the Radiators. Tobacco Road (the proud owner of Miami's very first liquor license) is small and gritty and meant to be that way. Escape the smoke and sweat in the backyard patio, where air is a welcome commodity. The downright cheap nightly specials, such as the $11 lobster on Tuesday, are quite good and are served until 2am; the bar is open until 5am. 626 S. Miami Ave. (over the Miami Ave. Bridge near Brickell Ave.), Downtown. ✆ **305/374-1198.** Cover $5 Fri–Sat.

Upstairs at the Van Dyke Cafe *(Finds* The cafe's jazz bar, located on the second floor, resembles a classy speakeasy in which local jazz performers play to an intimate, enthusiastic crowd of mostly adults and sophisticated young things, who often huddle at the small tables until the wee hours. 846 Lincoln Rd., South Beach. ☎ 305/534-3600. Cover $3–$6 for a seat; no cover at the bar.

THE GAY & LESBIAN SCENE

Miami and the beaches have long been host to what is called a "first-tier" gay community. Similar to the Big Apple, the Bay Area, or LaLa land, Miami has had a large alternative community since the days when Anita Bryant used her citrus power to boycott the rise in political activism by gays in the early '70s. Well, things have changed and Miami–Dade now has a gay rights ordinance.

Newcomers intending to party in any bar, whether downtown or certainly on the beach, will want to check ahead for the schedule, as all clubs must have a gay or lesbian night to pay their rent. Miami Beach, in fact, is a capital of the gay circuit party scene, rivaling San Francisco, Palm Springs, and even the mighty Sydney, Australia, for tourist dollars.

Academy   Hordes of gay men (and some women) join the Academy at Level every Friday, when the dance floor is packed with wall-to-wall hard bodies. 1235 Washington Ave., South Beach. ☎ 305/532-1525. Cover $20–$30.

Anthem   Sunday nights at crobar sing the gay anthem with this hyperpopular one-nighter featuring Miami's own superstar DJ Abel. 1445 Washington Ave., South Beach. ☎ 877/CRO-SOBE or 305/531-5027. Cover $25.

Cactus Bar & Grill   Somewhere, over the causeway, there is life beyond South Beach—that is, for Miami's gay society. Housed in a large two-story space, Cactus attracts a mix of unpretentious, professional, and very attractive men and women. There's something for everyone here, whether it's the indoor pool tables, the outdoor swimming pool, or drinks that are considerably cheaper than on South Beach. Friday evening happy hours and Sunday afternoon Tea Dances are a virtual cattle call, attracting hordes of folks looking to quench their thirst for fun at Miami's sprawling urban oasis. 2401 Biscayne Blvd., Downtown. ☎ 305/438-0662. No cover.

Loading Zone   A leather and Levi bar known for its cruisability, pool tables, movies, and pitchers of beer. There's also an in-house leather store for the kinky shopper. Open daily 10pm to 5am. 1426 Alton Rd., South Beach. ☎ 305/531-5623. Cover $15–$20.

O-Zone This is the zone of choice for gay men with an aversion to South Beach's cruisy, scene-heavy vibes. It's known for a heavily Latin crowd (mixed with a few college boys from nearby University of Miami) and fantastic, outlandish drag shows on the weekends. 6620 SW 57th Ave. (Red Rd.), South Miami. ℂ **305/667-2888.** No cover for men on Sat; other nights $5–$10.

Score There's a reason this Lincoln Road hotbed of gay social activity is called Score. In addition to the huge pick-up scene, Score offers a multitude of bars, dance floors, lounge-like areas, and outdoor tables in case you need to come up for air. Sunday afternoon Tea Dances are legendary here. 727 Lincoln Rd., South Beach. ℂ **305/535-1111.** No cover.

Twist One of the most popular bars (and hideaways) on South Beach, this recently expanded bar (which is literally right across the street from the police station) has a casual yet lively local atmosphere. 1057 Washington Ave., South Beach. ℂ **305/538-9478.** No cover.

LATIN CLUBS

Considering that Hispanics make up a large part of Miami's population and that there's a huge influx of Spanish-speaking visitors, it's no surprise that there are some great Latin nightclubs in the city. Plus, with the meteoric rise of the international music scene based in Miami, many international stars come through the offices of MTV Latino, SONY International, and a multitude of Latin TV studios based in Miami—and they're all looking for a good club scene on weekends. Most of the Anglo clubs also reserve at least 1 night a week for Latin rhythms.

Añoranzas Taberna You've heard of *son?* Hear it here—along with salsa, cumbia, merengue, vallenato, and house music. This neighborhood Latin disco and nightclub gets going after hours with a wild strobe-lit atmosphere. If you don't know how to do it, just wait. You'll have plenty of willing teachers on hand. Open Friday to Sunday from 8pm to 5am. 241 23rd St. (1 block west of Collins Ave.), South Beach. ℂ **305/538-1196.** No cover.

Casa Panza *(Finds* This *casa* is one of Little Havana's liveliest and most popular nightspots. Every Tuesday, Thursday, and Saturday night, Casa Panza, in the heart of Little Havana, becomes the House of Flamenco, with shows at 8 and 11pm. You can either enjoy a flamenco show or strap on your own dancing shoes and participate in the celebration. Enjoy a fantastic Spanish meal before the show, or just a glass of sangria before you start stomping. Open until 4am, Casa Panza is a hot spot for young Latin club kids, and, occasionally, a few older folks who are so taken by the music and the scene that they've failed to realize that it's well past their bedtime. 1620 SW 8th St. (Calle Ocho), Little Havana. ☎ **305/643-5343**. No cover.

Hoy Como Ayer Formerly known as Cafe Nostalgia, the Little Havana hangout dedicated to reminiscing about Old Cuba, Hoy Como Ayer is like the Brady Bunch of Latin hangouts—while it was extremely popular with old timers in its Cafe Nostalgia incarnation, it is now experiencing a resurgence among the younger generation, seeking their own brand of Nostalgia. Its Thursday night party, Fuacata (slang for "Pow!"), is a magnet for artsy Latin hipsters, featuring classic Cuban music mixed in with modern DJ-spun sound effects. Open Thursday to Sunday from 9pm to 4am. 2212 SW 8th St. (Calle Ocho), Little Havana. ☎ **305/541-2631**. Cover $10 Thurs–Sun.

La Covacha *Finds* This hut, located virtually in the middle of nowhere (West Miami), is the hottest Latin joint in the entire city. Sunday features the best in Latin rock, with local and international acts. But the shack is really jumping on weekend nights when the place is open until 5am. Friday is *the* night here, so much so that the owners had to place a red velvet rope out front to maintain some semblance of order. It's an amusing sight—a velvet rope guarding a shack—but once you get in, you'll understand the need for it. Do not wear silk here, as you *will* sweat. 10730 NW 25th St. (at NW 107th Ave.), West Miami. ☎ **305/594-3717**. Cover $0–$10.

Mango's Tropical Café Claustrophobic types do not want to go near Mango's. Ever. One of the most popular spots on Ocean Drive, this outdoor enclave of Latin liveliness shakes with the intensity of

 The Rhythm Is Gonna Get You

Are you feeling shy about hitting a Latin club because you fear your two left feet will stand out? Then take a few lessons. Thursday and Friday nights at **Bongo's Cuban Café** (American Airlines Arena, 601 Biscayne Blvd., Downtown; ☎ **786/777-2100**) are an amazing showcase of some of the city's best salsa dancers, but amateurs need not be intimidated thanks to the instructors at Latin Groove Dance Studios, who are on hand to help you with your two left feet.

a Richter-busting earthquake. Welcome and *bienvenido,* Mango's is *Cabaret,* Latin style. Nightly live Brazilian and other Latin music, not to mention scantily clad male and female dancers, draw huge gawking crowds in from the sidewalk. But pay attention to the music if you can: Incognito international musicians often lose their anonymity and jam with the house band on stage. Open daily from 11am to 5am. 900 Ocean Dr., South Beach. ℃ 305/673-4422. Cover $5–$15.

3 The Performing Arts

Highbrows and culture vultures complain that there is a dearth of decent cultural offerings in Miami. What do locals tell them? Go back to New York! In all seriousness, however, in recent years, Miami's performing arts scene has improved greatly. The city's Broadway Series features Tony Award–winning shows (the touring versions, of course), which aren't always Broadway caliber, but they are usually pretty good and not nearly as pricey. Local arts groups such as the Miami Light Project, a not-for-profit cultural organization that presents live performances by innovative dance, music, and theater artists, have had huge success in attracting big-name artists such as Nina Simone and Philip Glass to Miami. In addition, a burgeoning bohemian movement in Little Havana has given way to performance spaces that have become nightclubs in their own right.

THEATER

The **Actors' Playhouse,** a musical theater at the newly restored Miracle Theater at 280 Miracle Mile, Coral Gables (℃ **305/444-9293;** www.actorsplayhouse.org), is a grand 1948 Art Deco movie palace with a 600-seat main theater and a smaller theater/rehearsal hall that hosts a number of excellent musicals for children throughout the year. Tickets run from $26 to $50.

The **Coconut Grove Playhouse,** 3500 Main Hwy., Coconut Grove (℃ **305/442-4000;** www.cgplayhouse.com), was also a former movie house, built in 1927 in an ornate Spanish rococo style. Today, this respected venue is known for its original and innovative staging of both international and local dramas and musicals. Tickets run from $37 to $42.

The **Gables Stage** at the Biltmore Hotel, Anastasia Avenue, Coral Gables (℃ **305/445-1119**), stages at least one Shakespearean play, one classic, and one contemporary piece a year. Tickets cost $22 and $28; $10 and $17 for students and seniors.

The **Jerry Herman Ring Theatre** is on the main campus of the University of Miami in Coral Gables (℃ **305/284-3355**). The

University's Department of Theater Arts uses this stage for advanced-student productions of comedies, dramas, and musicals. Faculty and guest actors are regularly featured, as are contemporary works by local playwrights. Tickets sell for $5 to $20.

The **New Theater,** 65 Almeria Ave., Coral Gables (℃ **305/443-5909**), prides itself on showing world-renowned works from America and Europe. As the name implies, you'll find mostly contemporary plays, with a few classics thrown in for variety. Performances are staged Thursday to Sunday year-round. Tickets are $20 on weekdays, $25 weekends. If tickets are available on the day of the performance—and they usually are—students pay half price.

CLASSICAL MUSIC

In addition to a number of local orchestras and operas (see below), which regularly offer quality music and world-renowned guest artists, each year brings a slew of classical music special events and touring artists to Miami. The Concert Association of Florida (CAF), ℃ **305/532-3491,** produces one of the most important and longest-running series. Known for more than a quarter of a century for its high-caliber, star-packed schedules, CAF regularly arranges the best "serious" music concerts for the city. Season after season, the schedules are punctuated by world-renowned dance companies and seasoned virtuosi like Itzhak Perlman, Andre Watts, and Kathleen Battle. Since CAF does not have its own space, performances are usually scheduled in the Miami–Dade County Auditorium or the Jackie Gleason Theater of the Performing Arts (see the "Major Venues" section below). The season lasts from October through April, and ticket prices range from $20 to $70.

Florida Philharmonic Orchestra   South Florida's premier symphony orchestra, under the direction of James Judd, presents a full season of classical and pops programs interspersed with several children's and contemporary popular music performances. The Philharmonic performs downtown in the Gusman Center for the Performing Arts and at the Miami–Dade County Auditorium (see the "Major Venues" section below). 1243 University Dr., Miami. ℃ **800/ 226-1812** or 305/476-1234. Tickets $15–$60. When extra tickets are available, students are admitted free on day of performance.

Miami Chamber Symphony   This professional orchestra is a small, subscription-series orchestra that's not affiliated with any major arts organizations and is therefore an inexpensive alternative to the high-priced classical venues. Renowned international soloists perform regularly. The season runs October to May, and most concerts are held in the Gusman Concert Hall, on the University of Miami campus. 5690 N. Kendall Dr., Kendall. ⓒ **305/858-3500.** Tickets $12–$30.

New World Symphony   This organization, led by artistic director Michael Tilson Thomas, is a stepping stone for gifted young musicians seeking professional careers. The orchestra specializes in ambitious, innovative, energetic performances and often features renowned guest soloists and conductors. The symphony's season lasts from October to May, during which time there are many free concerts. 541 Lincoln Rd., South Beach. ⓒ **305/673-3331.** www.nws.org. Tickets free–$58. Rush tickets (remaining tickets sold 1 hr. before performance) $20. Students $10 (1 hr. before concerts; limited seating).

DANCE

Several local dance companies train and perform in the Greater Miami area. In addition, top traveling troupes regularly stop at the venues listed below.

Ballet Flamenco La Rosa   For a taste of local Latin flavor, see this lively troupe perform impressive flamenco and other styles of Latin dance on Miami stages. 13126 W. Dixie Hwy., North Miami, ⓒ **305/ 899-7729.** Tickets $25 at door, $20 in advance, $18 for students and seniors.

Miami City Ballet   This artistically acclaimed and innovative company features a repertoire of more than 60 ballets, many by George Balanchine, and has had more than 20 world premieres. The company moved into a new $7.5 million headquarters in January 2000—the Ophelia and Juan Jr. Roca Center at the Collins Park Cultural Center in Miami Beach. The City Ballet season runs from September to April. Ophelia and Juan Jr. Roca Center, Collins Ave. and 22nd St., South Beach. ⓒ **305/532-4880** or 305/532-7713 for box office. Tickets $17–$50.

MAJOR VENUES

The **Colony Theater,** on Lincoln Road in South Beach (ⓒ **305/ 674-1026**), has become an architectural showpiece of the Art Deco District. This multipurpose 465-seat theater stages performances by the Miami City Ballet and the Ballet Flamenco La Rosa as well as off-Broadway shows and other special events. The Colony closed in July 2002 for 16 months for a $4.3 million renovation that will add wing and fly space, improve handicapped access, and restore the lobby to its original art deco look.

At the **Miami–Dade County Auditorium,** West Flagler Street at 29th Avenue, Southwest Miami (ⓒ **305/547-5414**), performers gripe about the lack of space, but for patrons, this 2,430-seat auditorium is the only Miami space in which you can hear the opera—for now. For now, though, the Miami–Dade County Auditorium is home to the city's Florida Grand Opera, and it also stages productions by the Concert Association of Florida, many programs in Spanish, and a variety of other shows.

At the 1,700-seat **Gusman Center for the Performing Arts,** 174 E. Flagler St., Downtown (© **305/372-0925**), seating is tight, and so is funding, but the sound is superb. In addition to hosting the Florida Philharmonic Orchestra and the Miami Film Festival, the elegant Gusman Center features pop concerts, plays, film screenings, and special events. The auditorium was built as the Olympia Theater in 1926, and its ornate palace interior is typical of that era, complete with fancy columns, a huge pipe organ, and twinkling "stars" on the ceiling.

Not to be confused with the Gusman Center (above), the **Gusman Concert Hall,** 1314 Miller Dr., at 14th Street, Coral Gables (© **305/284-6477**), is a roomy 600-seat hall that gives a stage to the Miami Chamber Symphony and varied university recitals.

The elegant **Jackie Gleason Theater of the Performing Arts (TOPA),** located in South Beach at Washington Avenue and 17th Street (© **305/673-7300**), is the home of the Miami Beach Broadway Series. This 2,705-seat hall also hosts other big-budget Broadway shows, classical music concerts, and dance performances.

At press time, the city granted a budget in excess of $200 million for its official Performing Arts Center. Planned are a 2,400-seat ballet/opera house and a 2,000-seat concert hall for the Florida Philharmonic Orchestra, Florida Grand Opera, New World Symphony, Miami City Ballet, and a major concert series. Designed by world-renowned architect Cesar Pelli, it will be the focal point of a planned Arts, Media, and Entertainment District in mid-Miami. The complex will be wrapped in limestone, slate, decorative stone, stainless steel, glass curtain walls, and tropical landscaping, and is slated to be complete in mid-2004. For more information, check out the center's website at www.pacfmiami.org.

4 Cinemas, the Literary Scene & Spectator Sports
CINEMAS
In addition to the annual Miami Film Festival in February and other, smaller film events (See "Miami Calendar of Events," in chapter 2, "Planning Your Trip to Miami"), Miami has nearly as many multiplex cinemas as it does palm trees. But if 40 screens of *Jurassic Park III* isn't

your idea of a day at the movies, consider the following arty theaters, known for playing lots of subtitled, foreign films as well as those that get bumped off the big screen by the Jurassic Parks of the celluloid world.

Absinthe Cinemateque, 235 Alcazar Ave., Coral Gables (② **305/ 446-7144**), is a small one-screen theater that shows good movies, often Spanish-language films, without the hustle and bustle of the crowded multiplexes. The Alcazar shows the more artsy of the major films as well as some obscure independents. Tickets are $6.

Astor Art Cinema, 4120 Laguna St. (② **305/443-6777**), is an oasis in the midst of a desert of multiplexes in Coral Gables. This quaint double theater hosts foreign, classic, independent, and art films and serves decent popcorn, too. Tickets are $5.

The **Bill Cosford Cinema,** at the University of Miami, is located on the second floor of the memorial building off Campo Sano Avenue (② **305/284-4861**). This well-endowed little theater was recently revamped and boasts high-tech projectors, new air-conditioning, and a new decor. It sponsors independent films as well as lectures by visiting filmmakers and movie stars. Admission is $5.

The **Mercury Theatre,** Biscayne Boulevard at 55th Street, Miami (② **305/759-8809**), is the city's newest art house cinema, showing classic and contemporary films from all over the world. Tickets are $8 or $6 for seniors and matinees.

THE LITERARY SCENE

Books & Books, in Coral Gables at 265 Aragon Ave. and on South Beach at 933 Lincoln Rd., hosts readings almost every night and is known for attracting such top authors as Colleen McCullough, Jamaica Kincaid, and Martin Amis. For details on their free readings, call ② **305/442-4408.** (Also see p. 148.)

To hear more about what's happening on Miami's literary scene, tune into the "Cover to Cover" radio show, broadcast at 8pm on Mondays on public radio station WLRN (91.3 FM).

SPECTATOR SPORTS

For information on watching baseball, basketball, football, horse racing, ice hockey, and jai alai (many of these games are at night), please see the "Spectator Sports" section of chapter 6, "What to See & Do in Miami," beginning on p. 140.

Index

See also Accommodations and Restaurant indexes below.

ACCOMMODATIONS

Wickedly honest guides for sophisticated travelers—and those who want to be.

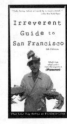

Irreverent Guide to Amsterdam
Irreverent Guide to Boston
Irreverent Guide to Chicago
Irreverent Guide to Las Vegas
Irreverent Guide to London
Irreverent Guide to Los Angeles
Irreverent Guide to Manhattan
Irreverent Guide to New Orleans
Irreverent Guide to Paris
Irreverent Guide to Rome
Irreverent Guide to San Francisco
Irreverent Guide to Seattle & Portland
Irreverent Guide to Vancouver
Irreverent Guide to Walt Disney World®
Irreverent Guide to Washington, D.C.

Available at bookstores everywhere.

FROMMER'S® COMPLETE TRAVEL GUIDES

Alaska
Alaska Cruises & Ports of Call
Amsterdam
Argentina & Chile
Arizona
Atlanta
Australia
Austria
Bahamas
Barcelona, Madrid & Seville
Beijing
Belgium, Holland & Luxembourg
Bermuda
Boston
Brazil
British Columbia & the Canadian
  Rockies
Budapest & the Best of Hungary
California
Canada
Cancún, Cozumel & the Yucatán
Cape Cod, Nantucket & Martha's
  Vineyard
Caribbean
Caribbean Cruises & Ports of Call
Caribbean Ports of Call
Carolinas & Georgia
Chicago
China
Colorado
Costa Rica
Denmark
Denver, Boulder & Colorado
  Springs
England
Europe
European Cruises & Ports of Call
Florida

France
Germany
Great Britain
Greece
Greek Islands
Hawaii
Hong Kong
Honolulu, Waikiki & Oahu
Ireland
Israel
Italy
Jamaica
Japan
Las Vegas
London
Los Angeles
Maryland & Delaware
Maui
Mexico
Montana & Wyoming
Montréal & Québec City
Munich & the Bavarian Alps
Nashville & Memphis
Nepal
New England
New Mexico
New Orleans
New York City
New Zealand
Northern Italy
Nova Scotia, New Brunswick &
  Prince Edward Island
Oregon
Paris
Philadelphia & the Amish Country
Portugal
Prague & the Best of the Czech
  Republic

Provence & the Riviera
Puerto Rico
Rome
San Antonio & Austin
San Diego
San Francisco
Santa Fe, Taos & Albuquerque
Scandinavia
Scotland
Seattle & Portland
Shanghai
Singapore & Malaysia
South Africa
South America
South Florida
South Pacific
Southeast Asia
Spain
Sweden
Switzerland
Texas
Thailand
Tokyo
Toronto
Tuscany & Umbria
USA
Utah
Vancouver & Victoria
Vermont, New Hampshire &
  Maine
Vienna & the Danube Valley
Virgin Islands
Virginia
Walt Disney World® & Orlando
Washington, D.C.
Washington State

FROMMER'S® DOLLAR-A-DAY GUIDES

Australia from $50 a Day
California from $70 a Day
Caribbean from $70 a Day
England from $75 a Day
Europe from $70 a Day

Florida from $70 a Day
Hawaii from $80 a Day
Ireland from $60 a Day
Italy from $70 a Day
London from $85 a Day

New York from $90 a Day
Paris from $80 a Day
San Francisco from $70 a Day
Washington, D.C. from $80 a Day

FROMMER'S® PORTABLE GUIDES

Acapulco, Ixtapa & Zihuatanejo
Amsterdam
Aruba
Australia's Great Barrier Reef
Bahamas
Berlin
Big Island of Hawaii
Boston
California Wine Country
Cancún
Charleston & Savannah
Chicago
Disneyland®
Dublin
Florence

Frankfurt
Hong Kong
Houston
Las Vegas
London
Los Angeles
Los Cabos & Baja
Maine Coast
Maui
Miami
New Orleans
New York City
Paris
Phoenix & Scottsdale

Portland
Puerto Rico
Puerto Vallarta, Manzanillo &
  Guadalajara
Rio de Janeiro
San Diego
San Francisco
Seattle
Sydney
Tampa & St. Petersburg
Vancouver
Venice
Virgin Islands
Washington, D.C.

FROMMER'S® NATIONAL PARK GUIDES

Banff & Jasper
Family Vacations in the National
  Parks
Grand Canyon

National Parks of the American
  West
Rocky Mountain

Yellowstone & Grand Teton
Yosemite & Sequoia/ Kings Canyon
Zion & Bryce Canyon

FROMMER'S® MEMORABLE WALKS

Chicago
London

New York
Paris

San Francisco
Washington, D.C.

FROMMER'S® GREAT OUTDOOR GUIDES

Arizona & New Mexico
New England

Northern California
Southern New England

Vermont & New Hampshire

SUZY GERSHMAN'S BORN TO SHOP GUIDES

Born to Shop: France
Born to Shop: Hong Kong,
  Shanghai & Beijing

Born to Shop: Italy
Born to Shop: London

Born to Shop: New York
Born to Shop: Paris

FROMMER'S® IRREVERENT GUIDES

Amsterdam
Boston
Chicago
Las Vegas
London

Los Angeles
Manhattan
New Orleans
Paris
Rome

San Francisco
Seattle & Portland
Vancouver
Walt Disney World®
Washington, D.C.

FROMMER'S® BEST-LOVED DRIVING TOURS

Britain
California
Florida
France

Germany
Ireland
Italy
New England

Northern Italy
Scotland
Spain
Tuscany & Umbria

HANGING OUT™ GUIDES

Hanging Out in England
Hanging Out in Europe

Hanging Out in France
Hanging Out in Ireland

Hanging Out in Italy
Hanging Out in Spain

THE UNOFFICIAL GUIDES®

Bed & Breakfasts and Country
  Inns in:
  California
  Great Lakes States
  Mid-Atlantic
  New England
  Northwest
  Rockies
  Southeast
  Southwest
Best RV & Tent Campgrounds in:
  California & the West
  Florida & the Southeast
  Great Lakes States
  Mid-Atlantic
  Northeast
  Northwest & Central Plains

  Southwest & South Central
    Plains
    U.S.A.
Beyond Disney
Branson, Missouri
California with Kids
Chicago
Cruises
Disneyland®
Florida with Kids
Golf Vacations in the Eastern U.S.
Great Smoky & Blue Ridge Region
Inside Disney
Hawaii
Las Vegas
London

Mid-Atlantic with Kids
Mini Las Vegas
Mini-Mickey
New England and New York with
  Kids
New Orleans
New York City
Paris
San Francisco
Skiing in the West
Southeast with Kids
Walt Disney World®
Walt Disney World® for Grown-ups
Walt Disney World® with Kids
Washington, D.C.
World's Best Diving Vacations

SPECIAL-INTEREST TITLES

Frommer's Adventure Guide to Australia &
  New Zealand
Frommer's Adventure Guide to Central America
Frommer's Adventure Guide to India & Pakistan
Frommer's Adventure Guide to South America
Frommer's Adventure Guide to Southeast Asia
Frommer's Adventure Guide to Southern Africa
Frommer's Britain's Best Bed & Breakfasts and
  Country Inns
Frommer's Caribbean Hideaways
Frommer's Exploring America by RV
Frommer's Fly Safe, Fly Smart
Frommer's France's Best Bed & Breakfasts and
  Country Inns
Frommer's Gay & Lesbian Europe

Frommer's Italy's Best Bed & Breakfasts and
  Country Inns
Frommer's New York City with Kids
Frommer's Ottawa with Kids
Frommer's Road Atlas Britain
Frommer's Road Atlas Europe
Frommer's Road Atlas France
Frommer's Toronto with Kids
Frommer's Vancouver with Kids
Frommer's Washington, D.C., with Kids
Israel Past & Present
The New York Times' Guide to Unforgettable
  Weekends
Places Rated Almanac
Retirement Places Rated